Palimpsests: Biographies of 50 City Districts

Paul L. Knox

Palimpsests

Biographies of 50 City Districts

International Case Studies of Urban Change

Birkhäuser
Basel

Contents

Preface

Writing this book has given me a great deal of pleasure. While much of my career has been spent generalizing about cities and synthesizing ideas about urbanization, there is no substitute for the direct experience of wandering through (and, in some cases, driving around) the streets. This book has given me a purpose to my wanderings and has allowed me to attempt to articulate two of the enduring fascinations of cities: the way that human spatial organization results in distinctively different kinds of districts, and the way that each district is given character by the layering, in bricks and mortar, of the individual and collective decisions and behaviours of successive generations.

For practical purposes, I have restricted the selection of city districts to Europe and North America. These are the cities I know best, and their broad commonalities of history and political economy allow for at least a degree of comparability and some reasonable representativeness in terms of the variety of city districts. To have ventured beyond, to African, Asian, Latin American, and Middle Eastern cities, would have stretched both budgets and the socio-historical frames of reference too far. The specific selections, though, are not meant to be definitive: I have sought to include both lesser-known, representative districts as well as seminal and iconic districts of particular kinds.

I have been helped enormously by my colleagues, friends, and students. Their thoughts, comments, and skills have been invaluable. I would especially like to recognize the contributions of Stephanie Frank, Dmitri Galkin, Meredith Drake Reitan, and Lisa Schweitzer, who helped me in Los Angeles; Derek Hyra, who introduced me to Shaw, in Washington, D.C.; Ashley Davidson, who introduced me to Zona Tortona in Milan; Heike Mayer, who was my guide in Bern; Nick Phelps, who provided valuable insights on Tysons Corner, Virginia; Anne-Lise Velez, who helped me in North Carolina and London; and Fang Wei, who assisted with the figure-ground diagrams. I have also been fortunate in receiving financial support for my work from Virginia Tech.

Unless indicated otherwise, the photographs in the book are my own. In a number of cases I am indebted to the contributors of images to the Wikimedia Commons. Finally, I would like to acknowledge the professional expertise and assistance of Werner Handschin and Katharina Kulke at Birkhäuser Verlag.

Blacksburg, Virginia, November 2011

Right: **Milan.** The Centro district (foreground) and the Porta Nuova and Centrale districts (in the distance). Every city district carries a record of its history in built form, each layer of development inscribed on the remnants of previous layers, each with something to tell about the nature of urban change.

Introduction: Cities and Their Districts

pal·imp·sest n

1. **A manuscript written over a partly erased older manuscript in such a way that the old words can be read beneath the new.**

2. **Something having usually diverse layers or aspects apparent beneath the surface.**

Cities reveal themselves in the moods and personalities of their districts. In some cases the mere name of a district is evocative: Montmartre in Paris, Beverly Hills in Los Angeles, Mayfair in London, SoHo in New York, Harajuku in Tokyo, Trastevere in Rome, and so on. But other districts in other cities are equally distinctive to people familiar with them, because city districts are more than just collections of people and buildings. They are both text and context: a palimpsest of economic, social, and architectural history in bricks and mortar.

Each city has its own set of internal geographies – its economic geography, social geography, political geography, and so on – and these are expressed in a mosaic of unique districts with particular attributes. We can recognize rich districts, poor districts, ethnic districts, residential districts, commercial districts, industrial districts, transitional districts, and many other kinds. Some city districts are stereotypical, some are archetypal, and some are singular in their attributes. But each has its own distinct character and story, the product of successive waves and cycles of development and of demographic, social, cultural, political, and administrative change. Each chapter in a district's history leaves its mark, for better or worse, in the layout of its streets, the fabric of its buildings, the nature of its institutions, and the cultural legacies of its residents. The layering and imprint of these is, of course, uneven; some elements are more durable than others, some are more cherished, and some are simply bypassed or left unchanged. Hence the palimpsest metaphor in the title of this book: the notion of 'reading' and understanding city districts as successively overwritten texts of urban development.

Places, in other words, can tell us stories. Urban landscapes are communicative of community values and identities; they symbolize and insinuate political and moral values. They are mute manifestations of ideology and power, of changing ideals in architecture, urban design, and planning, of changing imperatives in real estate development, and of the changing tastes and aspirations of consumers.

City districts draw much of their character from the people who inhabit them. As people live and work in city districts they gradually impose themselves on their environment, modifying and adjusting it as best they can to suit their needs and express their values. Yet at the same time people themselves gradually accommodate both to their physical environment and to the people around them. There is thus a continuous two-way process in which people create and modify urban spaces while at the same time being conditioned in various ways by the spaces in which they live and work.

Urban landscapes not only echo and embody the fortunes of successive generations of a district's inhabitants, they also reflect individual behaviour and the way in which communities collectively think and act. City districts provide people with a sense of place and a group identity. They are the settings for social interaction that, among other things, structure the daily routines of economic and social life; influence people's life paths (providing them with both opportunities and constraints); provide arenas in which everyday, 'commonsense' knowledge and experience are gathered; and provide sites for processes of socialization and social reproduction. People's daily surroundings are thus powerful but stealthy backdrops that can naturalize and reinforce dominant political and economic structures as if they were simply given and inevitable.

Laden with layers of symbolic meaning, everyday landscapes – including the people who inhabit them, their comportment, their clothes, and their possessions – comprise moral geographies that both echo and tend to reproduce a community's core values and perform vital functions of social regulation. It follows that districts are always 'in process', changing size, shape, and character. Some, such as the Trastevere in Rome (page 248) and the Marais in Paris (page 164), reflect a long and chequered history of change. Others, relatively new, such as Cary in greater Raleigh (page 50) and SouthPark in Charlotte (page 224), are relatively straightforward transcripts of recent change. It also follows that many districts have accumulated multiple characteristics that defy simple categorization. Thus, for example, South Beach, Miami (page 218) is simultaneously a destination district, a retirement district, and an historic design district, while the Mission District in San Francisco (page 170) is at once an ethnic district, a gay district, and a neobohemian district.

As a result, it is often difficult to determine where one district ends and another begins. Some districts have relatively clear boundaries. Some, such as the City of London (page 56) and Encino, Los Angeles (page 76), are coincident with administrative boundaries. Some, such as Bournville, Birmingham (page 40), Belgravia, London (page 30), the New Town in Edinburgh (page 174), Kentlands, Maryland (page 132), and Levittown, New York (page 146), are clearly bounded by the sites laid out by developers. Some, such as Hufeisensiedlung, Berlin (page 120), Scharnhauser Park, Stuttgart (page 202), and Quartier Vauban, Freiburg im Breisgau (page 256), have been demarcated by planners; and some, such as New York's Fashion District (page 86) and Milan's Zona Tortona (page 266) have been defined and branded by business associations.

Most city districts, though, are loosely defined, the aggregate products of the perceptions and 'mental maps' of their inhabitants. People generally structure their mental image of a city in terms of different kinds of memorable elements: paths (e.g., streets, transit lines, canals), edges (e.g., lakeshores, walls, steep embankments, cliffs), nodes (e.g., plazas, squares, busy intersections), and landmarks (e.g., prominent buildings, signs, monuments). Districts are structured with nodes, defined by edges, penetrated by paths, and sprinkled with landmarks. They are also framed by the routine use of place names, some formal and some informal. In large cities the number of districts that can be identified in this way can be overwhelming. In London, for example, more than 500 districts can be identified through the everyday informal designations used by Londoners, labels that are mostly adapted from historic parish, borough, or ward boundaries.

Each district has its own particular built environment, economic activities, and sociocultural attributes. This mix of attributes can be understood, in large measure, as the product of the broad sweep of change at national and international scales – the particular mix of attributes depending on the district's role within its wider metropolitan setting. In addition, many districts exhibit a degree of distinctiveness that derives from something unique, some feature that exists nowhere else, the particularity of which can be accounted for by a unique combination of general processes and local responses. Occasionally a district's distinctiveness derives from singular events or influences, such as the impact of influential individuals or the result of a localized disaster, as in the Lower 9th District of New Orleans (page 160).

One of the most persistent shapers of city districts is the tendency for people to segregate and congregate in terms of socioeconomic status and ethnicity. The territorial sorting of different groups into city districts helps to minimize conflict between groups while endowing specific social groups with a more cohesive political voice. Another important reason for the residential clustering of social and ethnic groups is the desire of its members to preserve their own group identity or lifestyle. There are also, of course, negative reasons for the persistence of residential segregation. Beginning with fear of exposure to 'otherness', these extend to personal and institutionalized discrimination on the basis of class, culture, gender, sexual orientation, ethnicity, and race. The Ghetto in Venice (page 94) was an early antecedent of ethnic districts such as Shaw, Washington, D.C. (page 210), and Little Saigon, Los Angeles (page 150), in contemporary cities. Gay districts like Schöneberg in Berlin (page 206) are a more recent phenomenon.

Arguably most important of all in shaping and reshaping city districts are the economic changes that drive urbanization. The sequence and rhythm of economic change will be a recurring theme in tracing the changing fortunes of individual districts. Some districts, such as Bryggen in Bergen (page 46), Zähringerstadt in Bern (page 262), The Kuip in Gent (page 136), and Old Town, Alexandria, Virginia (page 180) are carryovers from preindustrial eras. In many cases it is the evolution of capitalism itself that is the key factor. Thus we can see Ancoats, in Manchester (page 22) as the archetype of the new working-class industrial districts created in the era of competitive capitalism, the heyday of free enterprise, and laissez-faire economic development. Similarly, Levittown, New York, was the archetype of the residential settings of the era of mass production and mass consumption associated with corporate capitalism. Districts like False Creek, Vancouver (page 80), and La Défense, Paris (page 140), will likely be seen as the archetypes of city districts reshaped by transnational capitalism.

Cities' fundamental role as engines of economic development has resulted in all manner of specialized economic districts: central business districts like the City in London and the Loop in Chicago (page 154); former factory districts like New York's Fashion District; market districts like Pike Place, Seattle (page 186): entertainment districts like Theatreland in London (page 240); media districts like Hollywood (page 110); and shopping districts like the Grands Boulevards in Paris (page 100), Tysons Corner, Virginia (page 252), and the Quadrilatero della moda, Milan (page 194). Changing building and transportation technologies, meanwhile, have shaped other kinds of districts: railway exurbs like Riverside, Chicago (page 198), streetcar suburbs like Dorchester, Boston (page 64), and automobile suburbs like Encino, Los Angeles, and Cary, near Raleigh.

The reform movements prompted by various phases and stages of capitalism have also resulted in some important archetypes and exemplars. These include London's Boundary Street Estate (page 34), Bournville, Birmingham, Forest Hills Gardens, New York (page 90), Greenbelt, Maryland (page 106), Hufeisensiedlung, Berlin, Scharnhauser Park, Stuttgart, and Vauban, Freiburg im Breisgau. Some of these archetypes and exemplars are now protected through historic preservation legislation, as are some of the most striking preindustrial cityscapes, such as Bern's Zähringerstadt and Bergen's Bryggen.

Districts of many kinds now bear the imprint of the most recent structural economic shifts and sociocultural trends. In numerous cities in Europe and North America the old economy, based on manufacturing industries, is being displaced by a 'new economy' based on digital technologies, biotechnology, cultural industries and design, and advanced business services. It is an economy that is increasingly dominated by large transnational corporations and intimately tied in to complex flows of information and commercial networks that are global in scope. It has had a pronounced impact on the nodal districts of global cities, such as the City of London, where the real estate effects often spill over into neighbouring districts. Spitalfields, for example (page 228), just to the north of the City, is now deep in the process of being reconstructed both physically and socially. The emergence of the new economy has also produced new specializations in some city districts: weapons technologies and Internet industries in Tysons Corner; science and technology in Berlin's Adlershof district (page 18), and design services in Milan's Zona Tortona, for example.

Meanwhile, former industrial districts like Abandoibarra in Bilbao (page 12), Ancoats in Manchester, the Isle of Dogs in London (page 126), and False Creek in Vancouver have experienced the urban decay, unemployment, and out-migration associated with deindustrialization. This has, in turn, made space for another characteristic feature of urban change: the gentrification of certain inner-city districts. Gentrification typically involves an influx of more affluent households seeking the character and convenience of less-expensive but well-located residences, as in Hoxton, London (page 114) and Prenzlauer Berg, Berlin (page 190).

In some cases developers have assisted the process by renovating old industrial spaces (as in Ancoats, Manchester, for example) or demolishing older housing stock and replacing it with 'new-build gentrification' in the form of upscale condominiums (as in False Creek). The incoming households are typically dominated by young professionals involved in the new economy. Their arrival, meanwhile, tends to displace lower-income households as a result of escalating rents and house prices and consequent increases in property taxes.

As economic and occupational structures have changed, new cultural and political sensibilities have emerged and been transcribed into cityscapes. Of particular importance has been the trend toward neoliberalism: the return to free-market ideas as championed by Margaret Thatcher and Ronald Reagan in the 1980s. Public funds for almost everything except security have decreased dramatically as a consequence of grass-roots resistance to taxation. Municipalities, no longer having the capacity to provide or maintain a full range of physical infrastructure or to effectively manage economic development and social well-being, have either abrogated many of their traditional responsibilities or become dependent on public-private partnerships to meet them. Neoliberal strategies for urban regeneration through public-private real estate projects have resulted in dramatic changes to the urban landscapes of many districts, including deindustrialized districts like Abandoibarra, Ancoats, the Isle of Dogs, and False Creek, and of abandoned waterfront districts like Amsterdam's Eastern Harbour (page 70).

Closely associated with the rise of neoliberalism has been a shift in cultural sensibilities in which the emphasis has been on materialism, spectacle, and competitive consumption. Even 'community' and 'neighbourhood' have become commodified, with ready-made settings furnished by the real estate industry in New Urbanist subdivisions like Kentlands, Maryland. Consumerism is also writ large in residential districts like SouthPark, Charlotte, in retail districts like Milan's Quadrilatero della moda, and Washington, D.C.'s Tysons Corner, and in districts such as Temple Bar in Dublin (page 234) that have become 'cultural quarters'. On the other hand, countercultural movements have left their mark on other districts: neobohemias like Hoxton, London and 'green' districts like Vauban, for example.

Abandoibarra
Bilbao

Abandoibarra is widely regarded as an archetypal property-led urban regeneration district. Formerly a prosperous shipbuilding, engineering, and metallurgical district, it experienced a classic phase of deindustrialization in the 1970s and 1980s that resulted in high levels of unemployment and left it with extensive tracts of derelict sites. It then became a central component of Bilbao's aggressive gamble: investing more than a billion euros in infrastructure, high-end urban design, and cover-shot architecture in the hope of fostering a postindustrial economy and so halting the depreciation of the city's real estate while repositioning the city within the new context of a global economy.

Abandoibarra was once at the heart of a heavy industrial complex that stretched for 12 km or so along the valley of the River Nervión from Bilbao to the sea. By the end of the nineteenth century the region was producing 20 per cent of the world's steel. Eventually, however, Spain's entry into the newly configured European Union in 1986 forced Bilbao's antiquated and uncompetitive metallurgical complex to shut down, leaving deserted streets and scores of silent ruins awaiting demolition. Without its economic base, the city promptly fell into a downward spiral of unemployment, disinvestment, falling property values, and increasing social problems. In keeping with urban planning practice at the time, the city sought to respond with a programme of urban regeneration. The planners' emphasis was on high-quality architecture and urban design. The scale and scope of their plan was unprecedented and it has made Abandoibarra world-famous.

Bilbao has a tradition of aspiring to a global role and the discourse surrounding the city's regeneration strategy was dominated by the ambition of repositioning the city within the context of a global 'informational economy', to be achieved by attracting foreign direct investment in advanced business services. In practice, the plan relied heavily on strategic beautification. It was implemented through a distinctively neoliberal mode of urban governance, concerned less with the distribution of goods and services within the city and more with investment in image-building processes in order to attract new economy jobs.

A Master Plan developed by the city in the late 1980s identified Abandoibarra as a key strategic 'opportunity location'. The detailed proposal for the district was defined only after

Figure-ground diagram of the Andoibarra district. Extensive open space surrounds large structures and provides a threshold between the city centre and the river.

an international competition, won by César Pelli, Diana Balmori, and Eugenio Aguinaga. In accordance with the Master Plan's emphasis on the informational economy, their proposal included the designation of more than 200,000 m^2 of 'high-level' office space as well as key infrastructure improvements. Responsibility for the implementation of the Plan was given to a specially created development agency, Bilbao Ría 2000. However, it quickly emerged that the centrepiece of the district's regeneration was not to be international office space, but a museum.

Against all odds and in absolute secrecy, an unlikely alliance between the city and the Solomon R. Guggenheim Foundation resulted in an agreement for the city and the Basque regional authorities to fund a franchise of the famous New York museum. The Guggenheim wanted to develop a global market, while the city and the region wanted the global branding that was anticipated as a result of having a world-class museum in an iconic building designed by a star architect. With this key development, the regeneration of Abandoibarra – and of the city as a whole – shifted from a production-oriented strategy to a consumption-based development featuring signature structures as symbols of modernity and economic revitalization. In addition to the Guggenheim, these investments in the symbolic capital and brand equity of postindustrial Bilbao include the Euskalduna Juaregia conference centre and concert hall (architects Federico Soriano and Dolores Palacios); a new metro system with striking fan-shaped entrances (Foster + Partners); the Campo Volantin footbridge (Santiago

The Guggenheim Museum Bilbao, the flagship of the city's regeneration scheme, designed by Frank Gehry. It opened in 1997, attracting more than a million visitors in its first year. The cost – €144 million – was covered entirely with public-sector funding, shared by the provincial and regional governments. Photo: John Harper/Corbis.

The Pedro Arrupe footbridge gives access to the Paseo de la Memoria and the Guggenheim Museum Bilbao from the right bank of the River Nervión. Photo: Romain Cintract/Hemis/Corbis.

Calatrava), and the Pedro Arrupe footbridge (Lorenzo Fernández-Ordóñez) spanning the River Nervión; a forty-storey office tower for the Iberdrola electric utility company (César Pelli); and the Gateway project, a mixed-use quayside development containing luxury flats, cinemas, and restaurants and featuring twin twenty-two-storey glass towers (Arata Isozaki).

All this has been financed with support from the European Union, the Spanish and Basque governments, and public-private partnerships. The Guggenheim itself cost 144 million euros. It opened in 1997 and drew 1.36 million visitors in its first year. The numbers began to decline somewhat after three years but by then Bilbao had already become one of the leading weekend tourist destinations in Europe and the building itself had been featured in countless books, magazine articles, photo shoots, and movie scenes, including the opening sequence of the James Bond film *The World Is Not Enough*. Bilbao has become a national and international tourist destination, something that was unimaginable even for the most optimistic planners and consultants in the 1990s. Although only 1,000 or so jobs have been directly created as a result of the expansion of cultural/architectural tourism, the increased number of visitors has generated many new and upgraded restaurants, bars, cafés, shops, small hotels, and service outlets in Abandoibarra. The magnetic effect of the Guggenheim has also resulted in a spatial clustering of galleries, antique shops, and auction houses in the district, as well as prompting a dramatic increase in residential real estate prices.

This success has made Abandoibarra the standard case study of urban regeneration in urban studies. Indeed, with the increasing aestheticization of consumer sensibilities and the

The Gateway project, designed by Arata Isozaki, on a 42,000-m² quayside area just up-river from the Guggenheim Museum Bilbao. The footbridge, the Puente del Campo Volantin, was designed by Santiago Calatrava. Photo: Atlantide Phototravel/Corbis.

increasing sensitivity of city governments to the ways in which their cities are perceived by businesses and tourists, new 'signature' buildings have become a common aspect of urban development. In the celebrity-oriented global culture that is now pervasive, about all it takes for signature status is for a building to be the product of a brand-name architect.

When the building is also spectacular and/or radical in design, it can rebrand an entire city and elevate its perceived status within the global economy. The success of the Guggenheim Museum in Bilbao has prompted many other cities to engage brand-name architects in attempts to replicate the 'Bilbao Effect' (or, alternatively, 'the Guggenheim Effect'). As Dejan Sudjic observes:

Sometimes it seems as if there are just thirty architects in the world. … Taken together they make up the group that provides the names that come up again and again when another sadly deluded city finds itself labouring under the mistaken impression that it is going to trump the Bilbao Guggenheim with an art gallery that looks like a train crash, or a flying saucer, or a hotel in the form of a twenty-storey high meteorite.

The Edifice Complex, London: Allen Lane, 2005, p. 296

More generally, the Bilbao Effect has given credibility not only to the idea that urban regeneration can successfully be anchored by iconic buildings by star architects, but also that postindustrial economies can thrive on strategic beautification and the creation of 'museum quarters' or 'cultural quarters'. As a result, scores of cities have embarked on the creation of 'designscapes': distinctive ensembles of new buildings, cultural amenities, renovated spaces,

The Guggenheim and the Paseo de la Memoria. Photo by Georges Jansoone, used under a creative commons Attribution-Share Alike License at Wikimedia Commons.

The Pedro Arrupe footbridge from the right bank of the River Nervión. Photo courtesy of Bilbao Ría 2000.

The Paseo de la Memoria, the riverside gardens of the Abandoibarra. Photo courtesy of Bilbao Ría 2000.

The Puente del Campo Volantin footbridge and the right bank of the River Nervión. Photo: Arcaid/Corbis.

landscaping, and designer street furniture, often incorporating new or renovated museums.

But even in the paradigmatic example of Abandoibarra the success of the strategy is not unqualified. Physical revitalization has failed to attract a significant amount of international capital and advanced business services to the city. It also ignores and even compounds social polarisation. The emphasis on iconic structures and aestheticized urban design masks structural problems of poverty and inequality, of affordable housing, and of inadequate educational and health care facilities. Meanwhile, the adjacent downtown residential area, the Abando, always inhabited by the city's more affluent households, has had its socially exclusive nature reinforced. Finally, the strategy has prompted a secondary Guggenheim Effect, inducing a certain amount of gentrification, driving up land and housing prices and restricting the housing opportunities of younger and less affluent households not only in Abandoibarra but also in nearby riverside districts such as Bilbao la Vieja and San Francisco.

Further reading on Abandoibarra

Rodríguez, Arantxa, et al., 'Uneven Redevelopment. New Urban Policies and Socio-Spatial Fragmentation in Metropolitan Bilbao', *European Urban and Regional Studies* 8.2 (2001), 161–78. *Provides a detailed analysis of changes in urban policy making in relation to Bilbao's regeneration strategy.*

Santamaria, Gerardo del Cerro, *Bilbao: Basque Pathways to Globalization*, Bingley: Emerald Group, 2007. *A detailed and well-documented study of the Basque response to globalization and the city of Bilbao's response.*

Adlershof Berlin

Adlershof Science and Technology Park is one of the largest districts of its kind in the world. Located on an old airbase that subsequently became the site of Berlin's film studios before being occupied by the East German Academy of Science in the German Democratic Republic (GDR), it is situated in an emerging corridor of development between central Berlin and the new Berlin-Brandenburg International Airport, to the southeast of the city.

The site was originally developed in 1912 as Johannisthal airbase, the headquarters of the German Experimental Institute for Aviation (*Deutsche Versuchsanstalt für Luftfahrt*). Germany's first motorized aircraft took off from there. Some of the laboratories, test beds, wind tunnels, and hangars used by pioneer manufacturers Albatros-Flugzeugwerke, Fokker Aeroplanbau, Rumpler Flugzeugwerke, and Flugmaschine Wright have been preserved as historical landmarks. After World War I the Treaty of Versailles restricted aircraft development in Germany, allowing several of the hangars to be converted into film studios. Then, after World War II, the studios became the headquarters of East Germany's national television service, while other parts of the old airfield were used to house a Guard Regiment, along with the nine institutes of the GDR Academy of Sciences in the fields of physics and chemistry. By 1989, on the eve of the reunification of Germany, more than 5,600 people were working in Adlershof.

After reunification the GDR scientific institutes were disbanded but their workers provided an important initial advantage for the current Science and Technology Park financed by the city of Berlin and the Federal Republic of Germany. Eight of the twelve research institutes now located in Adlershof, in fact, are directly descended from the former GDR institutes. Ambitions for the new science and technology park ran high in the years directly following reunification: a complete urban transformation was envisioned which would generate 30,000 jobs and a 'city within a city', an 'integrated scientific and business landscape' of 15,000 inhabitants, envisaged as a modern version of the preindustrial European town. The original plans zoned some 130 hectares for residential use, while about 70 hectares were reserved for mixed-use development and 70 more for green space (including the old airport).

The reasons for this scope of ambition were twofold. First, the Berlin government expected a large population increase due to reunification and therefore a strong demand for residential housing. Forecasts projected a population growth in Berlin from 3.3 million inhabitants in the early 1990s to 5–6 million by 2010. Second, it was expected that reunification would significantly boost Berlin's role as a global city, bringing transnational firms to the city and, in particular, to settings like those envisaged for Adlershof, with a strong infrastructure and plenty of inexpensive space. These forecasts turned out to be too optimistic. Berlin's population remained stable, while Adlershof was not

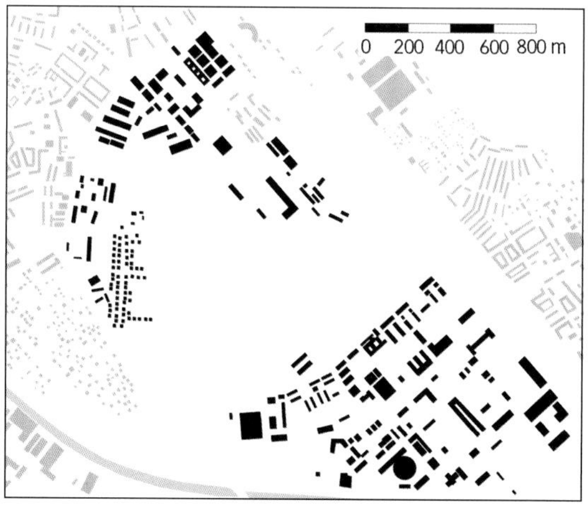

Figure-ground diagram of Adlershof. The district is strictly zoned, with the Business Park, Media City, Science Park, and Humboldt University facilities to the southeast, a residential area to the west, commercial and industrial land uses to the north, and a large nature park in the centre.

given priority in subsequent national urban and regional policies. The new park has struggled to get international firms to move in.

Adlershof's planners have nevertheless persisted in extending the project to residential, commercial, and recreational land use. Meanwhile, they have sought to facilitate growth by exploiting the agglomeration economies resulting from the clustering of high-tech industry and allied research and higher-education functions. At the heart of the district are four major technology clusters, each with its own research and development centre in a flagship building: the Innovation and Business Incubation Centre, the Centre for Photonics and Optical Technologies, the Centre for Information and Media Technology, and the Centre for Materials and Microsystems Technology. Photonics and Optical Technologies is the largest technology cluster in Adlershof, with more than 50 companies and research institutions and about 900 employees. The technology cluster with the highest growth rate, however, is Environmental, Bio and Energy Technology, with a special focus on the field of solar energy and photovoltaics.

The Humboldt University of Berlin has moved six of its scientific institutes – Computer Science, Mathematics, Chemistry, Physics, Geography, and Psychology – into Adlershof and has built a new Information and Communication Centre with a library, conference facilities, a cafeteria, and a computing centre that can be used jointly by both the university and the research and development centres. The old film and television studios, meanwhile, have been

Centre for IT and Media Technology. This, the first of three new buildings for the centre, was completed in 1996. With more than 100 companies in the area of information and media technologies, Adlershof is Berlin's most important media location.

Humboldt University campus. The university has established six of its scientific institutes in Adlershof. Photo © Adlershof Projekt GmbH.

redeveloped into a high-tech media centre, with more than 120 companies involved in producing television series, films, digital media, and media-related events.

Part of the old airfield has been transformed into a 68-hectare park that includes a nature park, a landscaped park, and a recreational area with tennis courts, a football pitch, skater paths, and outdoor basketball courts. A small residential development of 360 single-family homes has been built on the edge of the park, while part of Humboldt University's allocation of land has been set aside for townhouses and multistorey apartment buildings.

The entire district is run by a management company that is responsible for fostering the nexus of university-industry-government relations; developing a portfolio of technology-oriented investments that maximize the agglomeration economies of clustering; attracting key personnel; organizing conferences and exchanges of researchers and professionals; and providing guest offices for visitors from foreign science and technology parks and for companies interested in locating to Adlershof. The management company is also responsible for fostering certain aspects of the 'urbanity' of the district: the provision of neighbourhood services, kindergartens and schools, as well as leisure facilities such as access to parks, for example.

Adlershof is still some way from maturing into the kind of integrated urban setting originally envisaged. The lack of housing – especially affordable housing – in the district means that almost all of its 14,000 workforce and 6,700 students are commuters. They stream in by bus and from the S-Bahn stop at the northern perimeter of the district in the mornings, departing at the end of the work day and leaving the district empty and lifeless on evenings and weekends. Even on a weekday the overall atmosphere in Adlershof is bleak and uninviting. There is a nascent commercial centre and a small shopping centre with a supermarket, a pharmacy, and some shops, but few 'third places' that draw people together to socialize, relax, and dwell in the district for a while.

Corporate research facilities. Photo © Adlershof Projekt GmbH.

Further reading on Adlershof

Bachman, Marie, 'Berlin-Adlershof: Local Steps into Global Networks', *Framing Strategic Urban Projects*, ed. W. Salet and E. Gualini, London: Routledge, 2006, 115–45. *A systematic review and analysis of Adlershof as a case study of a large-scale urban project.*

Neumann, Helge, 'Redevelopment of a Former East Berlin Military Site into a Site of Science and Technology', ed. A. Inzelt and J. Hilton, *Technology Transfer: From Invention to Innovation*, New York: Springer, 2011, 121–34. *A detailed account of the development of the district.*

Mixed-use development with street-level commercial space.

Humboldt University campus, established in Adlershof between 1993 and 2003. Photo © Adlershof Projekt GmbH.

Media City, where film and television studios and offices employ almost 1,500 people in more than 100 different firms.

Ancoats Manchester

Ancoats was the world's first industrial suburb, a direct product of the Industrial Revolution. Linked to the rest of the city's economy through an innovative system of industrial canals and to the emergent global economy through the Salford docks on the other side of the city, Ancoats acquired notoriety not only for its revolutionary economic base but also for its new industrial architecture. Ancoats also became famous as a site of class struggle and an exemplar of the social deprivation consequent to unregulated industrial urbanism. Having gone full cycle through processes of deindustrialization, it is now the focus of urban regeneration efforts, with a conservation area at its core.

Manchester in the early 1800s was the archetypal form of an entirely new kind of city – the industrial city – whose fundamental reason for existence was not, as in earlier generations of cities, to fulfill military, political, ecclesiastical, or trading functions. Rather, it existed simply to assemble raw materials and to fabricate, assemble, and distribute manufactured goods. Over the course of the nineteenth century the city, with its cotton textile mills, was the principal engine of economic growth in the United Kingdom; what Manchester was to the United Kingdom, so Ancoats was to the city itself: its first industrial suburb and the hearth of the city's economy.

The development of Ancoats began in the late 1700s as entrepreneurs sought new sites for textile mills that could exploit the dramatic new combination of James Watt's steam engines and Samuel Crompton's innovative spinning mule. The district grew up around the Murray Mill, which opened in 1789. Piecemeal speculative building then drove the further expansion of the district in expectation of the opening of new industrial canals and the thousands of migrants from the countryside and from Ireland and Italy who had begun to flock to Manchester in search of factory work.

The Rochdale Canal opened in 1804 and linked Ancoats through (and under) the city centre to the well-established and thriving district of Castlefield, where it joined the Bridgewater Canal, the city's link to the Lancashire coalfields. As the canals ran through the city they sprouted branches with wharves for the cotton mills that were steadily added to the productive capacity of the city. In Ancoats these included the Decker Mill (1799), the New Mill (1802), Sedgwick Mill (1818), Beehive Mill (1824), Fire Proof Mill (1842), Little Mill (1908), Paragon Mill (1912), and Royal Mill (1912).

The mills were enormous brick structures from four to eight storeys high, with each floor devoted to a particular part of the manufacturing process. They were distinctive for their many windows (to maximize the daylight for the workforce) and for the tall, tapering chimneys attached to their engine houses. Some of them used the revolutionary new structural building material – iron – in combination with brick or tile flooring (instead of traditional timber construction with wooden floors that were vulnerable to fire, especially after being saturated with the oil that inevitably dripped from the machinery). After the introduction of power looms in the 1820s, another innovative element of industrial

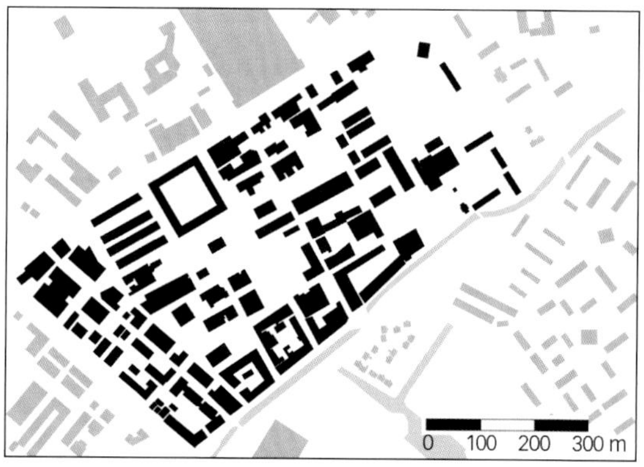

Figure-ground diagram of Ancoats Conservation Area.

Anita Street. Part of a small development of model housing, built by Manchester Corporation in the 1890s. Originally called Sanitary Street, a few letters were dropped from the name in the 1960s. At the end of the street is the western block of Victoria Square.

architecture was added to the landscape. Power looms generated significant vibrations, so they were housed in long, ground-floor sheds with characteristic sawtooth-shaped glazed roofs to admit the maximum amount of daylight.

Around the mills, the district developed into a dense grid of back-to-back two-storey houses around small courts or, more commonly, along terraces. At the peak of the Industrial Revolution, in the mid-nineteenth century, Ancoats was a full-blown industrial suburb, an almost self-contained community with public houses and shops (installed by speculative developers), churches, and schools (funded by religious groups). In addition to the cotton mills, the district also attracted several other industries, including hat making, clothing manufacture, furniture making, and a glassworks. Immigrant workers from across Europe came to the district, the size of the Italian community prompting Ancoats to be labelled as Manchester's Little Italy.

Working and living conditions in the district, however, were harsh. With little regulation, factory owners were free to exploit their workforces and speculative developers and landlords were similarly free to exploit their tenants. Inevitably, it led not only to impoverishment, deprivation, and squalour but also to political unrest. Radical meetings in Ancoats in 1812, during which thirty-eight workers were arrested on charges of sedition, were a precursor to the notorious 'Peterloo massacre', when cavalry charged into a crowd of more than 60,000 that had gathered in central Manchester to demand the reform of parliamentary representation. It was the conditions in the back-to-back slum dwellings of Ancoats textile workers that Friedrich Engels famously described in the mid-nineteenth century and that so influenced the theoretical writings of Karl Marx. Ancoats, observed Engels,

... contains a vast number of ruinous houses, most of them being, in fact, in the last stages of

inhabitableness. … I have to deal here with the state of the houses and their inhabitants, and it must be admitted that no more injurious and demoralising method of housing the workers has yet been discovered than precisely this. The working-man is constrained to occupy such ruinous dwellings because he cannot pay for others, and because there are no others in the vicinity of his mill; perhaps, too, because they belong to the employer, who engages him only on condition of his taking such a cottage.

F. Engels, *The Condition of the Working Class in England*, London: Lawrence & Shoot, 1973, p. 89

Later in the nineteenth century, after the Public Health Act of 1875, some of the worst back-to-back housing in Ancoats was replaced by bylaw housing that set minimum standards for layout and construction. The district also saw the first municipal housing development in Manchester: Victoria Square, a block of flats with internal bathrooms and shared laundries with drying facilities. As Manchester grew in size and extent, Ancoats became an inner-tier suburb but still retained its physical and social make-up as a stereotypical working-class industrial district.

During World War II many of the mills were converted to the manufacture of military uniforms and parachutes, but after the war they all suffered acutely from competition from new producers in India and the Far East. The mill complexes were gradually sold off or rented out for low-grade uses such as machinery repairs and the storage of imported clothing. The national programme of slum clearance and urban renewal in the 1960s saw much of the housing in Ancoats demolished as being unfit. Residents were moved to new public housing estates, many of them on the northern and eastern fringes of the city, a few of them in tower blocks of public housing on the edges of Ancoats itself. With the loss of population, many of the shops, churches, schools, and public houses closed and Ancoats fell into a spiral of decline. The mills,

Victoria Square. Built in 1889 to provide homes for more than 800 mill workers, Victoria Square was the first example of municipal housing in Manchester. The corner sites were originally occupied by shops. The building is still owned by the local authority and currently provides accommodation for elderly residents.

Royal Mills complex and the Rochdale Canal. Now part of the Ancoats Urban Village regeneration project, the complex consists of Royal Mill (1797; rebuilt 1912), Murray's Mills (1789–1840), Sedgwick Mill (1818), Sedgwick New Mill (1912), and Paragon Mill (1912). All are now being remodeled to provide apartments, shops, and office space.

Albion Mills (foreground) and Vulcan Mills. Both of these industrial buildings have been converted to residential and office space.

seemingly unattractive at any rent, fell into disrepair. Some small businesses carved out new roles in the district: car maintenance and repair under railway arches, and scrap yards and daily parking on cleared sites.

In the 1970s a broad section of the district between the Rochdale Canal and the Ashton Canal was redeveloped as the Cardroom estate, replacing the remaining nineteenth-century terraced housing with low-rise, 'suburban-style' public housing. It quickly proved to be unpopular and unworkable. The low density of population meant that there were not enough people to make the area function properly: not enough people to support the shops or a pub; not enough children to warrant a primary school. There were no through roads and there was little definition between public and private space. Over time, the culs-de-sac turned into no-go areas, havens for drug dealing, for dumping stolen cars, for breaking and entering. In the 1980s the frontage of the district's bounding arterial road, Great Ancoats Street, was redeveloped as Central Retail Park, a row of big-box stores fronted by sterile parking space. Behind it, the Cardroom area became a 'sink estate' where the police wouldn't go, where mail-order vans wouldn't deliver, and where taxis wouldn't drop off. For two decades or more Ancoats came to represent the stereotypical inner-city industrial district, characterized by physical decay, unemployment, poverty, and social malaise. The district had gone from being the birthplace of the Industrial Revolution to its graveyard.

In 1989 part of Ancoats was designated a Conservation Area with thirteen buildings listed, seven of them at Grade II*, putting them in the top 8 per cent of listed buildings in the country. (English Heritage Grade I buildings are considered to be 'of exceptional interest, sometimes considered to be internationally important'; Grade II* buildings 'are particularly important buildings of more than special interest'; and Grade II buildings – 92 per cent of all listed buildings – 'are nationally important and of special interest'.) Then, during the 1990s, Manchester itself experienced something of a renaissance. The city designated the district immediately to the southwest of Ancoats – also shabby and depressed throughout the 1970s and 1980s – as a 'creative quarter' and branded it as the Northern Quarter. Carried along by the city's overall economic resurgence, the Northern Quarter began to prosper, at which point developers started to show interest in the potential of the old textile mills of neighbouring Ancoats. 'Trader developers' began to buy properties in Ancoats with the idea of securing planning consent for conversion to new uses and then selling on the buildings for others to convert.

But the huge 'conservation deficit' between the costs to repair and convert them and the

New Islington. In the foreground, next to the Ashton Canal, is Islington Wharf Tower, an 18-storey tower with ground floor office space and 142 apartments. Beyond are two other new-build developments, Chips and Milliners Wharf.

Clockwise from top left: **Chips**, a New Islington apartment building that also offers studio and commercial space; **derelict loom building**, New Islington; **Central Retail Park**, Ancoats; **Quantum Waterside** apartments, on Ashton Canal; **Bargemaster's house** on Ashton Canal; **Ancoats Hospita**l, under renovation and conversion to 178 apartments.

Islington Square. The first scheme to be built in New Islington, Islington Square provided twenty-three new homes for former residents of the demolished Cardroom estate.

subsequent end-value of the buildings under new uses meant that redevelopment was not commercially viable. Little activity took place until several regeneration agencies combined to facilitate redevelopment. The Ancoats Buildings Preservation Trust was established in 1995 as a registered charity with the aim of regenerating historic buildings in the district whose cost of repair is uneconomic for the private sector. It is supported by the central government's Architectural Heritage Fund. The Ancoats Urban Village Company was subsequently established as an interagency partnership in order to promote the district and facilitate its development as a mixed-use neighbourhood for up to 5,000 people.

In 2002 the North West Regional Development Agency acquired wide-ranging powers to acquire private property to facilitate regeneration in the Conservation Area. Property owners who did not have the will or the ability to participate received compensation at market price, and the agency worked with the Ancoats Building Preservation Trust to secure Lottery Fund money to repair and convert the district's most important listed buildings. The Cardroom development, only thirty years old, was demolished to make way for New Islington, a public-private development based on a Master Plan by architect Will Alsop. The result is that Ancoats has begun to be repopulated and now stands on the threshold of economic regeneration and, inevitably, gentrification.

Almost nothing remains of the housing that Engels wrote about, but the surviving mill buildings, warehouses, and canals are sufficient to lend character to the district. New apartment buildings and canalside condominiums have appeared, while the district's old infrastructure is being refurbished and the canals cleared and relinked with a new marina in anticipation of further new-build gentrification.

Further reading on Ancoats

Miller, Ian, and Wild, Chris, *A & G Murray and the Cotton Mills of Ancoats*, Oxford: Oxford Archaeology, 2007. *Presents the findings of a survey of the eighteenth-century steam-powered cotton spinning mills of Adam and George Murray.*

Parkinson-Bailey, John, *Manchester – An Architectural History*, Manchester: Manchester University Press, 2000. *A comprehensive and critical examination of the city's architecture in context of the city's overall growth.*

Peck, Jamie, and Ward, Kevin, *City of Revolution: Restructuring Manchester*, Manchester: Manchester University Press, 2002. *A comprehensive and critical analysis of the processes of urban transformation in Manchester.*

Belgravia
London

Having been transformed from marshy farmland to a speculative housing development in the 1820s, Belgravia has consistently stood as a super-élite residential district over an unbroken span of more than 180 years. As such, it is an exception: a city district where the palimpsest metaphor is barely relevant. It has remained largely unchanged in physical appearance for more than 100 years and broadly unchanged in terms of the socio-economic status of its residents. Its proximity to Westminster has seen some of its residences converted into consulates and embassies, while its proximity to the exclusive retailers, restaurants, and clubs of Knightsbridge have precluded any significant invasion of commercial activity.

The district had come into the possession of the Grosvenor family in 1656, when the daughter and sole heiress of Alexander Davies, of Ebury Farm, married Sir Thomas Grosvenor. For a long time the boggy farm, located on the site of an old lagoon of the Thames to the west of London, had seemed an unlikely asset. The Grosvenor family's wealth was based on mining interests in the north of England, but as London grew in the boom years of the Regency after victory at Waterloo (1815) the land suddenly took on real potential for development. The conversion of the old Buckingham House, just to the east of the farm, into Buckingham Palace made the land even more valuable. Richard Grosvenor (who had inherited the family fortune) saw the potential and secured an Act of Parliament to permit the site to be drained and its level raised in order to allow development. Thomas Cubitt, one of London's great entrepreneurial developers, also saw the potential and took on the project. Cubitt spent considerable sums of money draining and preparing the ground, and installing sewers, road surfaces, and pavements. His workers dug out the district's clay (turning it into bricks) and replaced it with enough soil and gravel from excavations at St Katharine Docks, farther down the Thames, to raise the site above flood level. Belgravia, as it was called, was then laid out in the classic Regency style of squares, streets, and crescents aligned to overlook private gardens.

The centrepiece of the entire development, designed by young architect George Basevi, was Belgrave Square. Cubitt realised that the Square had to succeed as a unified element, with no risk of individual parcels being let out just when the speculative market permitted. He therefore refinanced the building of the square with a group of City bankers whose credit would guarantee that the entire project was completed as planned. As a result, the unity of the whole scheme was maintained over the ten years of its development. This was in contrast with other speculative landed-estate developments in London, where building styles typically changed considerably in a desperate effort to maintain sales during the cyclical downturns of the real estate market. The other key element in the overall design of Belgravia was Eaton Square (named after Eaton Hall in Cheshire, the principal residence of the Grosvenor family).

Belgravia is situated in the fashionable West End of London, close to the institutional core of the city.

Between and around these principal squares were grand terraces of white stucco houses of uniform mass, height (mainly four- and five-storey) and architectural treatment (Italianate). To the rear of the terraces, accessed by narrow paved lanes, were mews – rows of stables and carriage houses, with living quarters above, each associated with one of the grand residences on the principal streets.

The Earl of Essex was the first to buy one of the houses in Belgrave Square, after which other wealthy and aristocratic families moved in, making the square immediately fashionable. Belgravia quickly became a synonym for snooty respectability, so much so that endless small-time developers have subsequently named avenues, drives, suburban estates, and condominium towers after it. From the start, Belgravia attracted the rich, famous, and powerful, and has been home – or townhome – to a succession of aristocratic families, prime ministers, cabinet members, wealthy industrialists, and celebrities. After World War II some of the larger houses ceased to be used as residences and were taken over as embassies, charity headquarters, and professional institutes, while most of the mews cottages and carriage houses were converted into apartments. But further change was precluded by the Grosvenor Estate's strict leases and by the district's designation as a Conservation Area in 1968.

From the mid-1980s London's prominence as a hub of the global economy began to draw increasing numbers of the élite international

Belgrave Square. Built in the 1820s by Thomas Cubitt and designed by George Basevi for Sir Robert Grosvenor, each side of the square consisted of a terrace of eleven or twelve large white stuccoed residences in Italianate neoclassical style. It is one of the grandest of London's speculatively built residential squares. Today Belgrave Square boasts more than a dozen embassies, high commissions, ambassadorial residences, and international cultural institutes. This photograph shows the northwestern side of the square.

Sir Robert Grosvenor, the First Marquess of Westminster (1767–1845) and the developer of Belgravia, is commemorated by a statue in northern corner of Belgrave Square. On the plinth is a quotation by John Ruskin that reads 'When we build let us think we build for ever'.

Belgravia in 1843. This map, produced by the Society for the Diffusion of Useful Knowledge, shows the morphology of the crescents and garden squares, along with the proximity of Buckingham Palace. Map extract from the David Rumsey Map Collection, <www.davidrumsey.com>.

super-rich to Belgravia and nearby Chelsea and Mayfair. The embassies remained and were joined by five-star hotels – The Berkeley, The Halkin, and the Sheraton Belgravia – but the offices of many of the charities and institutes that had moved into Belgravia in the 1950s and 1960s moved out to the newly gentrifying districts of inner London, leaving their premises to be reconverted to residential space.

Today Belgravia is one of the world's quintessential élite residential districts, accessible only to the very affluent who are able to afford its remodelled contemporary studio apartments, its elegantly proportioned flats with high ceilings, and its mews cottages; and to the seriously wealthy who are able to afford its larger townhomes. There is little activity on the streets and few visitors to the district's private gardens except for maids exercising residents' pet dogs. The restrained neoclassical facades of the buildings mask extravagance and luxury that is only

Eaton Square Garden. One of the six private gardens for the exclusive use of residents. Few people, other than infants with their nannies or housekeepers with owners' dogs, actually use the gardens. Photo courtesy of Anne-Lise Velez.

Wilton Crescent. Built in 1925, Wilton Crescent has been home to many prominent figures, including Earl Louis Mountbatten of Burma (1900–1979). George Bernard Shaw's play, *Major Barbara*, is partly set in (fictional) Lady Britomart's house in Wilton Crescent.

Belgrave Mews North. One of the few streets in the district to have retained its original cobbled surface. As in other mews, the stables have long ago been converted to garages or to front rooms.

hinted at by the expensive automobiles that occupy the limited on-street parking. Number 11 Eaton Square, for example, with a relatively modest frontage like all its neighbours, has 1,138 m² of living space, including six bedrooms, six bathrooms, and large entertaining rooms. There are three kitchens, a colonnaded indoor swimming pool, three staircases, and an orangery. At the rear the mews house has three bedrooms and two bathrooms, plus a two-bedroom staff flat and separate chauffeur's bedroom and bathroom.

Within Belgravia there is very little commercial activity, except for the discreet collection of designer shops, hair and beauty salons, dry cleaners, estate agents, and a patisserie in Motcomb Street (referred to by local residents and property professionals as 'Belgravia Village'). But just to the south of the district are Elizabeth Street and Pimlico Road, with their Michelin-starred restaurants, pubs, bars, and small, exclusive boutiques. Harrods department store, meanwhile, is located at the northwest corner of the district, with the upscale stores and galleries of Knightsbridge and Brompton Road just a few hundred metres to the west.

Further reading on Belgravia

Anon., 'The Western Suburbs: Belgravia', British History Online. *A richly detailed history of the development of the district.*

Hebbert, Michael, *London*, Chichester: Wiley, 1998. *Hebbert's second chapter, 'The First Six Miles', provides a fine account of the overall context for the development of Belgravia.*

Boundary Street Estate London

The Boundary Street Estate in Shoreditch is a landmark district in terms of both urban policy and urban design. It was one of the earliest social housing schemes and the world's first local authority housing, revolutionary in its provision of facilities for residents.

The original Boundary Street ran along the eastern boundary of an old priory. Unplanned and uncontrolled building on the land to the east of the street in the eighteenth and nineteenth centuries turned what had been a rural hamlet on the fringe of London into the Old Nichol Rookery: a district whose name became a byword for poverty, crime, and disease. The slum took its nickname from land leased from John Nichol in 1680. Originally the site was used for brick making but the area steadily developed in piecemeal fashion to accommodate workers in the silk-weaving trade that spread eastward from Spitalfields early in the eighteenth century. When the weaving industry collapsed under pressure from cheaper Continental imports in the latter half of the eighteenth century, the tenements of the Old Nichol were subdivided and intermixed with backroom workshops and 'manufactories' where residents eked out a living making matches, matchboxes, clothes pegs, shoes, and cheap clothes.

By the mid-nineteenth century the district had become notorious as one of London's worst. In 1848 Hector Gavin, medical officer of health whose responsibilities included the Old Nichol, wrote that it surpassed the rest of the East End:

> *... in filth, disease, mortality, and wretchedness ... it abounds with the most foul courts, and is characterized by the presence of the greatest nuisances, and perennial foulness.*
>
> *Sanitary Ramblings, being Sketches and Illustrations, of Bethnal Green*, London, 1848, p. 42

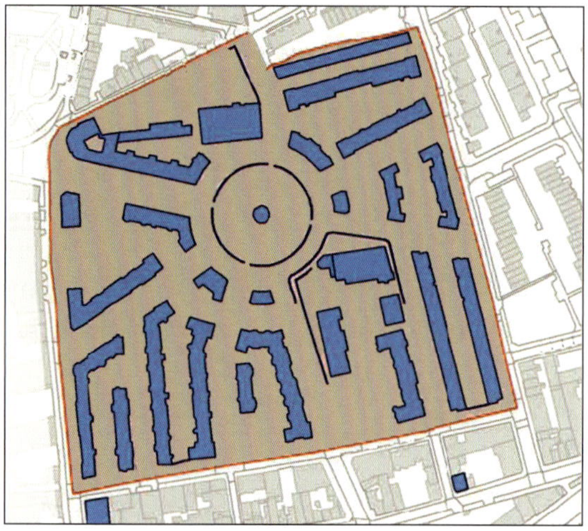

Boundary Street Conservation Area. The district contains twenty Grade-II Buildings of Special Architectural or Historic Interest (in blue). Map extract after London Borough of Tower Hamlets, *Boundary Estate Conservation Area* (2007), p. 3.

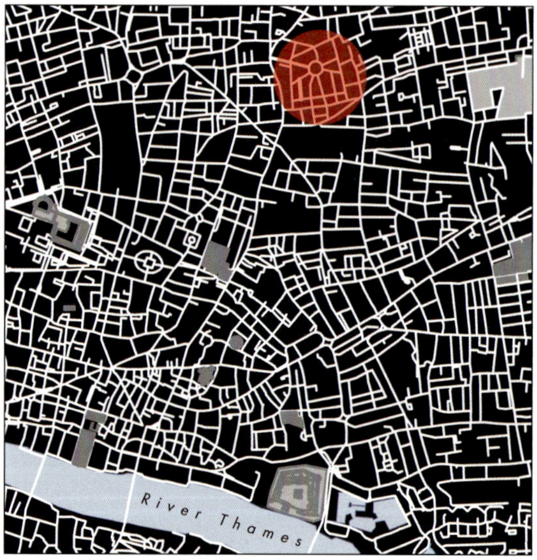

The Boundary Street Estate is situated in London's East End, just 1.5 km due north of the Tower of London.

An article in the *Illustrated London News* on 24 October 1863 described the district as:

... one painful and monotonous round of vice, filth and poverty, huddled in dark cellars, ruined garrets, bare and blackened rooms, reeking with disease and death, and without the means, even if there were

the inclination, for the most ordinary observations of decency and cleanliness.

After a great deal of campaigning by reformers like Edwin Chadwick, Henry Mayhew, and the district's local vicar, Osborne Jay, the Old Nichol was officially declared a slum under the auspices of a landmark piece of parliamentary legislation, the Housing of the Working Classes Act, 1890. This allowed the London County Council (LCC) to announce a clearance scheme for the district on the grounds of public health. It prompted fierce opposition from the district's major landlords, including Baroness Kinloss and the Ecclesiastical Commission, who supported the scheme in principle but wanted their own property excluded.

Another obstacle was that the LCC could not find private developers who would pay a reasonable market price for the land and take on redevelopment of the cleared site. Reluctantly the LCC decided to accept responsibility for providing workers housing by building it themselves. Under the terms of the 1890 Act, this paid landlords handsomely for their property and relieved them of any responsibility for re-housing tenants.

The dilemma for the LCC, though, was how to redevelop the cleared site: the Council was constrained by its own standing order not to subsidize housing from local taxes and to charge rents that were comparable to the going rate in the borough. The Old Nichol was home to 5,719 people in 1890 and this provided the target number to be re-housed in the new LCC estate following the slum clearance. There were, however, no precedents as to how to go about it.

The Master Plan presented to the LCC's Public Health and Housing Committee in 1893 by Owen Fleming, the architect-in-charge, was a significant departure from the barrack-like dwellings on grid layouts that were typical of the philanthropic housing in London provided by charitable trusts like the East End Dwellings

Pioneering social housing. The interior courtyard between Abingdon House and Benson House. Built in 1899, the structures are now statutorily protected as Grade-II listed buildings.

Pre-automobile urban design featured several narrow streets within an estate layout that has proven remarkably adaptable to many aspects of contemporary urban life.

Rochelle Street School. The original school opened in 1879, predating the residential buildings of the Estate. The completion of the Estate required additions that were completed in 1899.

Co., the Guinness Trust, and the Peabody Trust. Fleming's plan envisaged a picturesque urban village, featuring a central open space that was laid out as an ornamental garden with seven tree-lined streets radiating from it. Each block was named after a Thames beauty spot. With a layout based on a new road pattern, the buildings were able to be conceived as street architecture, relating to each other as well as to the larger conception of the estate. The architectural language of the Arts and Crafts movement was adopted as the common theme, with decorative brick- and tile-work and a variety of roof styles, including dormer, pitched, mansard, and 'Dutch' gabling.

Part of the original concept of the estate was that 'if a line is drawn from the sill of any window at an angle of 45 degrees, it is clear of all obstruction from adjacent buildings'. This provided residents with a variety of spatial experiences and vistas. Open areas between the housing blocks were designed to ensure 'every living room received sunlight at some point of the day' and provided sequestered play areas for children. The central garden – allegedly the site of a plague pit – was raised on a mound of rubble from the cleared slums, landscaped with terraced flower beds and walks, with a playground and bandstand at the top.

The estate also accommodated a live/work community, with small workshops included in the design in the hope of promoting local business and employment. Calvert Street, the original main road leading from Shoreditch High Street, was widened and extended to provide a grander entrance to the estate. It was lined with trees and remodelled with shops facing onto the road and workshops to the rear. A new

Arnold Circus. Reputedly built from the rubble of former slums, Arnold Circus forms a mound around which the streets of the district radiate. To the left of Chertsey House, in the centre of the photograph, is Palissey Street; to the right, Rochelle Street.

school was located in the heart of the estate, on Rochelle Street. Altogether, the Boundary Street Improvement Scheme consisted of 1,069 tenements housing 4,566 residents. They had the use of a central laundry with twelve baths, and most of the tenements had their own toilet facilities. The cost of improvement, combined with the LCC's constraints on subsidizing rents, meant that the new tenants were the 'quiet poor', as Charles Booth called them: cigar makers, clerks, cabinet makers, tailors, shoemakers, nurses, and post office sorters who could afford the rents that the LCC had to charge. The labourers, matchbox makers, hawkers, and dealers who had occupied the Old Nichol before clearance were meanwhile displaced further east into Dalston or Bethnal Green.

The Boundary Street estate escaped direct hits during the blitzkrieg of World War II, and in the 1970s the tenements were restored and consolidated to create contemporary bed-sit apartments and one-, two-, and three-bedroom flats, with a reduced overall capacity of 1,500 tenants. The entire estate was designated a Conservation Area under the Planning (Listed Buildings and Conservation Areas) Act, 1990, and the buildings themselves designated as Grade II Listed. There are also more than fifty tree preservation orders within the Estate. As a result, the physical integrity of the district is assured: listed buildings may not be demolished, extended, or altered without special permission, and consent is required even for minor work such as replacing railings or felling trees.

Meanwhile, the sociocultural composition of the district continues to change. At the time of the construction of the estate the district's population was predominantly Jewish; today it

Old Nichol Street, named after the slum that stood on the site of the Boundary Street Estate in the mid-1800s. The built environment has changed little since the construction of the estate in the 1890s, while the demography of the estate has changed continually with London's changing population.

is predominantly Bangladeshi. It is still predominantly working-class and still an area with its share of street crime and nuisance behaviour. But there is an increasing degree of cosmopolitanism to the demographic profile of the district, and in the evenings its restaurants and bars are increasingly frequented by the designer-clad media set who live and work nearby. On Sunday mornings the estate is traversed by affluent young singles doing the 'walk of shame' home, still wearing their Saturday-night party gear.

In short, this district is becoming emblematic of the socioeconomic polarisation characteristic of contemporary global cities. The low rents of commercial space in the district, combined with proximity to the offices of the City and nearby gentrifying neighbourhoods, have brought a degree of retail gentrification to streets where,

Boundary Street. The Albion Cafe, located in an old Victorian warehouse, the café signals the gentrification that is taking place around the western and southern edges of the district. The café and its shop leverage the working class history of the district, specializing in traditional classics like pie and mash and cauliflower cheese.

until recently, many of the storefronts were boarded up. In 2009 Sir Terence Conran opened The Boundary, an upscale restaurant, hotel, food store, and café, in a converted Victorian warehouse on the fringe of the estate. Other arrivals along the streets surrounding the estate include a private members' club, a Mexican restaurant and tequila bar, a French brasserie, and a series of designer furniture stores. In the heart of the estate itself an organic café has opened on Calvert Avenue, while the Rochelle Street School is now an arts centre.

Further reading on the Boundary Street Estate

Anon., 'Bethnal Green: Building and Social Conditions from 1876 to 1914', British History Online. *A detailed account of the conditions in the district at the time of its development.*

Steffel, R. V., 'The Boundary Street Estate: An Example of Urban Redevelopment by the London County Council, 1889-1914', *Town Planning Review* 47.2 (1976), 161–73. *A comprehensive account of the development of the district, focusing on design and policy issues.*

Tarn, John, *Five Percent Philanthropy*, Cambridge: Cambridge University Press, 1973. *An architectural history of working-class housing in Britain between 1840 and 1914.*

Community Launderette, Calvert Avenue. The launderette operates as a cooperative and serves as an informal community centre for residents of the estate.

A remnant of the rag trade, a local tailor on Calvert Avenue is one of the few reminders one of the district's staple occupations in the nineteenth century. Photo courtesy of Anne-Lise Velez.

Bournville
Birmingham

A landmark district in the context of city planning, Bournville is widely acknowledged to have been the first attempt to demonstrate to speculative builders that the construction of low-density workers' housing could be a profitable activity. It is also credited with having played an important part in the development of the Garden City movement. The layering of its development, however, reflects a more nuanced and much more pragmatic story. It was founded in response to exclusionary impulses, established as an arcadian middle-class subdivision, and then transformed – rather opportunistically – as an embryonic model community that has matured into a garden suburb.

From the very start, Bournville was closely associated with the firm of Cadbury Brothers Cocoa Manufacturers and, in particular, with the firm's principal, George Cadbury. Unlike other model communities with nineteenth-century roots, Bournville was never a company town; Cadbury workers were always a minority of the district's residents. The initial development of the site was for a new factory. By the last quarter of the nineteenth century, the firm had outgrown its city centre site, while living and working conditions in central Birmingham had become increasingly difficult as well as unsuitable for food production.

In 1878, Cadbury purchased a 6-hectare greenfield site 6.5 km to the southwest of the city centre. It had plenty of space for the factory, and the surrounding countryside allowed Cadbury Brothers to promote the firm's image of a manufacturer of pure products, produced in a wholesome environment. The new factory, opened in 1879, had many progressive facilities: heated dressing rooms, kitchens where workers could prepare their own food, sports fields, and separate swimming pools for women and men. Progressivism was accompanied by a strong sense of paternalism: works outings to the country were organized, together with summer camps for young boys, and all workers were expected to attend morning prayers and daily Bible readings. The one practical disadvantage was that Cadbury's employees – all except a few foremen – had to commute to the new factory from central Birmingham. Fifteen houses for senior foremen were built adjacent to the factory, while for the rest of the workforce the firm negotiated cheap fares with the Birmingham West Suburban Railway.

Within ten years the original floorspace of the factory buildings had doubled and the number of employees had risen from 230 to 1,200. Meanwhile, speculative suburban development had begun to encroach on nearby villages, prompting George Cadbury and his

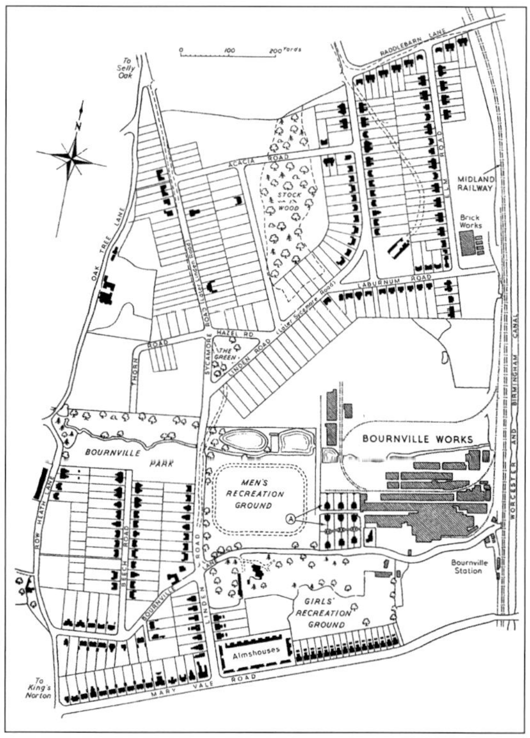

Bournville in 1898. This plan shows the nucleus of the original settlement, around the factory. Subsequent development of the community took place on land purchased to the west of this nucleus. Courtesy of Bournville Village Trust.

Village Shops. The parade of shops facing the village green on Sycamore Road. The everyday routines associated with this small commercial element provide the district with an important sense of identity and belonging.

brother Richard to become concerned that one of their factory's greatest marketing assets, its arcadian surroundings, would be devalued by small-scale property speculators. In 1893, George Cadbury purchased 49 hectares adjoining the factory and established the Bournville Building Estate, with A. P. Walker as the estate architect.

The estate was never intended as a model community; it consisted solely of houses. According to an 1895 sales leaflet, the objective of the estate was 'to make it easy for working men to own houses with large gardens secure from the danger of being spoilt either by the building of factories or by interference with the enjoyment of sun, light, and air' (cited in Bryson and Lowe, 2002, p. 29). The estate was intended to keep speculative builders away while showing them that high-quality, low-density housing could be built at a profit. But unlike some of its

Rest House. The centrepiece of the village green, built to celebrate the silver wedding anniversary of George and Elizabeth Cadbury. The design was based on a seventeenth-century yarn market in Dunster, Somerset. It now functions as a visitor centre for the Bournville Village Trust.

contemporary projects, it was not geared to the incomes of the 'deserving poor'. Rather, it was aimed at the emerging middle class of 'honest, sober, thrifty' families. Thus, the first 134 dwellings were semi-detached houses of picturesque character.

The area of the estate was doubled in 1898. By then Cadbury had realized that 'honest, sober, thrifty' families were unable to purchase property or did not wish to do so, and so the next phase consisted of 227 smaller houses in groups of two, three, or four, for weekly rent rather than purchase. Tenants had to pay a fair economic rent, sufficient to meet interest charges on capital invested plus a return of 4 per cent. The only community facilities provided on the estate were the Bournville Almshouses, provided and endowed by Richard Cadbury: thirty-three cottage-like homes set in a quadrangle around a central garden on the southern edge of the estate. Rents from thirty-eight adjacent houses were designated toward maintaining the almshouse foundation.

A. P. Walker, like many other architects of the time, drew heavily on the Arts and Crafts movement for the estate's buildings. Prompted by a reaction to the dehumanizing effects of industrialization and inspired by a romantic idealization of the craftsman taking pride in his personal handiwork, the Arts and Crafts movement flourished between 1880 and 1910, led by William Morris and deeply influenced by the writings of John Ruskin and Augustus Pugin and their advocacy of Gothic Revival styles. Natural materials were preferred and the dominant design motifs were stylized flowers, allegories from the Bible and literature, upside-down hearts, Celtic patterns, and Japanese art.

Walker's first houses were built in straight rows with no more than four houses in a terrace, but this soon gave way to more interesting layouts, with groups of houses set back from tree-lined roads, each house with its own front garden and vegetable garden with fruit trees at the back.

With Birmingham expanding and local land prices rising, George Cadbury felt that he had to act fast to buy more land – otherwise the opportunity for more facilities and housing might be lost, together with the estate's green spaces and rural charm. He also feared that on his death the estate itself would succumb to speculative builders. To prevent this he transferred ownership of the estate in 1900 to a charitable trust to be known as the Bournville Village Trust (BVT). The Deed of Foundation made allowance for land and buildings devoted to community purposes, covering physical, spiritual, and educational needs.

It was no coincidence that Ebenezer Howard's influential book, *Tomorrow: A Peaceful Path to Real Reform*, had been published just two years before (later reissued as *Garden Cities of Tomorrow*). Howard's concept was for model communities that would cater not only to the middle classes but to the full spectrum of society, with jobs and civic amenities as well as homes: 'restorative utopias' amid the maelstrom of industrialization. Howard's rationale and plans drew heavily on philanthropic ideas of the time, together with the aesthetic principles of William Morris and John Ruskin, the communitarianism of Charles Fourier, the socialist anarchism of Peter Kropotkin, and the socialist ideals of William Morris. Howard portrayed the garden city ideal as providing the possibility of combining the best of city life (jobs, higher wages, civic amenities, social interaction, etc.) with the best of life in the countryside (clean air, natural beauty, open space) while avoiding the downside of both (the congestion and pollution of cities, the limited employment opportunities and poor infrastructure of rural areas).

In September 1901, Cadbury hosted the first Garden City Association conference at Bournville. More than 300 delegates from

Maple Road. Close to the factory and part of the original development, this street was not developed until the 1900s.

municipal councils, religious denominations, trades unions, and friendly societies attended, and the proceedings received extensive media publicity. As Bryson and Lowe observe:

The transformation of the Bournville Building Estate into the BVT model village provided the Garden City Association with a successful example of a fully functioning planned garden village. ... Cadbury repackaged the building estate by appropriating the garden city movement, in return the garden city movement also appropriated Bournville by using it as a working example of a model garden village.

2002, p. 37

Selly Manor, a Tudor building moved to Bournville in 1914 by George Cadbury from its original site almost 2 km away.

Bournville Sports and Crown Green Bowls Club building, located adjacent to the factory site. Photo by Benkid77, used under a creative commons Attribution-Share Alike License at Wikimedia Commons.

New building in Bournville subsequently focused less on middle-income housing and more on small working-class terraced properties. All profits over the anticipated 4 per cent return were to be put toward further development of the model community. But many of Bournville's 'model' features evolved from bottom-up community pressures rather than from top-down planning: it was only after the formation of the Trust that schools, places of worship, and shopping facilities were provided. It took eight years for the Trust to get around to providing a park, a few shops, and an elementary school, another six years before a church hall was built, and a further thirteen years before the community had its own church.

Meanwhile, the Trust extended the paternalistic atmosphere that the Cadburys had established in their factory. George Cadbury, as chairman of the Trust, sought to propagate a wholesome family life constructed around the garden, with the man's role as both breadwinner (in the chocolate factory or elsewhere) and provider of vegetables grown in the garden. Tenants with neglected gardens would get a letter of reproof from the Trust. The woman's role, meanwhile, was that of housewife. By 1911 Bournville had become enveloped within the boundary of the city of Birmingham. Sensing further suburban encroachment, the Trustees turned their attention to establishing a greenbelt, purchasing an additional 1,200 hectares of surrounding agricultural land. Today the Bournville Estate itself covers more than 400 hectares, with about 7,600 properties housing 19,000 people. Overall, about 60 per cent of the properties are privately owned. Among the rental units there are twelve different types of socially oriented schemes, from bungalows for the elderly to a hostel for people with learning difficulties. Several properties have been included on the United Kingdom's Statutory List

Village extension. Part of the eastern extension of the estate, along Hay Green Lane. The houses here – mostly semi-detached homes and short terraces – were built in the 1920s and feature open frontages with generous sidewalks.

of Buildings of Special Architectural or Historic Interest, while the Birmingham City Council has designated two parts of the district – including the earliest part of the Bournville Estate – as Conservation Areas.

Today Bournville presents itself as a stereotype of Middle England: tree-lined avenues of semi-detached and detached homes in rustic styles, each with well-tended gardens. Most of the houses have been adapted in some way or another with extensions – some well-executed, others not – that provide extra living space. Many have also been altered to provide off-street parking but, even so, the district's rustic affect is undermined by the parked vehicles that line every street. The parade of shops at the heart of the district contains a tea room as well as a grocery store, a bakery, a newsagent, and a bank. Together, they generate a steady rhythm of domesticity that is in sharp contrast to the looming adjacent chocolate factory, where production has given way to an 'experience' tourist attraction, Cadbury World.

Further reading on Bournville

Bryson, John R., and Lowe, Philippa A., 'Story-Telling and History Construction: Rereading George Cadbury's Bournville Model Village', *Journal of Historical Geography* 28.1 (2002), 21–41. *This paper shows how and why the initial housing estate at Bournville was transformed into the model community of the 'accepted' narrative of planning history.*

Cherry, Gordon, 'Bournville, England, 1895–1995', *Journal of Urban History* 22 (1996), 493–508. *An appreciation of the district by a leading scholar of city planning and former chairman of the Bournville Village Trust.*

Harrison, Michael, *Bournville: Model Village to Garden Suburb*, Chichester: Phillimore, 2000. *The best extended study of the history and development of the district.*

Bryggen
Bergen

The late medieval waterfront district in Bergen is well known because of its picturesque buildings. Its significance, however, goes well beyond its charm for tourists. It is the best remaining example of the trading districts that were pivotal to the Hanseatic League, the intercity trading system that brought prosperity to northern Europe after the introverted and impoverished local economies of the Dark Ages. Rebuilt several times after catastrophic fires, the Bryggen district has become emblematic of the city itself (a stylized wharfside frontage is used as a logo of the city) and a key element of Norway's maritime heritage. The international significance of the district was recognized by UNESCO in 1979, when Bryggen was added to the World Heritage List.

The city of Bergen was founded in the eleventh century, and for 200 years or so was controlled by patrician merchants who had acquired a monopoly on fish trading. The *bryggen* (wharf) area became their neighbourhood as well as the seat of their operations. In the mid-fourteenth century the powerful Hanseatic League gained control of the district, drawn by Bergen's strategic situation along both north-south and east-west trading routes, and by its sheltered anchorage, open year-round as a result of the moderating influence of the northerly currents of the Gulf Stream. Bergen itself was not a member of the Hanseatic League; rather, it was one of four cities (along with Bruges, London, and Novgorod) in which the League established *kontors*: trading enclaves that were set apart from other parts of the towns. These districts were almost entirely populated by German merchant colonists and their staff. They were communities for men only.

The *kontor* in Bergen grew to between 200 and 300 principals, whose trade employed around 2,000 men during the busy summer months. The merchants – mostly from Lübeck, the linchpin of the League – enjoyed a monopoly-like role but had to stick to particular rules, the *kontor* statutes, in order to preserve their trading privileges in the district (known in Bergen as the *Tyskbryggen*, or 'German Wharf').

The League's North Sea and Baltic Sea trading network shipped raw materials such as timber, furs, resin, flax, honey, wheat, and rye from the East Baltic region and the northwestern parts of present-day Russia; metal ores (principally copper and iron) from Sweden; fish from North Sea and Baltic ports; flour, malt and beer from north-central Europe; cloth and manufactured goods from England; and wine and spices from southern Europe. The main export from Bergen was dried cod, which was produced in northern Norway on the Lofoten and Vesterålen Islands and shipped to Bergen in August each year. The fish was sorted and packed in Bryggen during the winter months and exported in the spring in exchange for flour, malt, and beer. But what made Bergen especially profitable for the German merchants was the extra income gained from east-west trade. Dried fish from Bergen was shipped to England's east coast port of Boston, a subsidiary of the Hanseatic League and the principal exporter of the luxury woollen

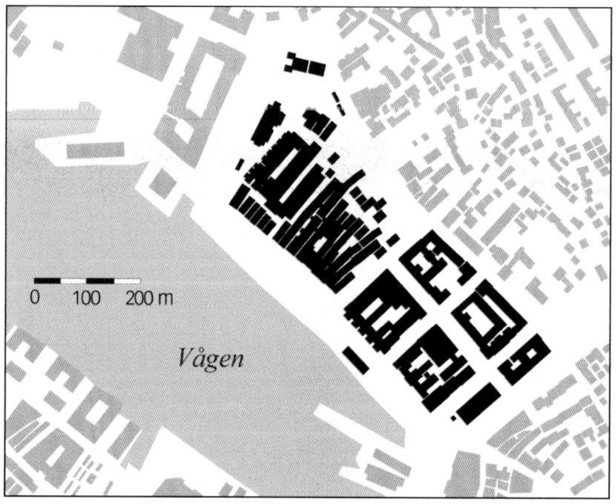

Figure-ground diagram. Bryggen is located on the northern shore of Bergen's narrow harbour, formed by Vågen Bay.

cloths produced in the area around Lincoln and Stamford. By 1600 Bergen had become the largest city in Scandinavia. After the Hansa merchants left in 1754, trade and industry continued and eventually the *Tyskbryggen* designation of the wharf district was shortened to Bryggen.

The buildings and morphology of Bryggen reflect the medieval roots of the district. The wooden buildings are arranged in long double rows, with a narrow common passageway between the buildings and their gable ends facing the harbour. The long buildings provided space for living quarters, as well as offices, storehouses, and other commercial activities. Behind the inland end of the buildings it was common to have a shared courtyard (*gård*), beyond which was a small warehouse or storeroom (*kjellere*) of stone, to protect the area against fire. Nevertheless, Bryggen has always been vulnerable to fire, with major recorded fires in 1170, 1198, 1248, 1332, 1339, 1413, 1476, and 1702. The worst was the conflagration of 1702, when almost 90 per cent of the entire city was burned to ashes. Bryggen, though, was always repaired and reconstructed in accordance with the original plan, and using traditional techniques – until 1901, when the southern half of wooden rows was demolished and replaced by slightly bigger buildings constructed in brick. The new buildings repeated the gable pattern of the former buildings and were a conscious attempt to harmonize with the historic context. The remaining wooden tenements were listed as protected by statute in 1927.

In 1955 a devastating fire destroyed about half of these surviving buildings, leaving the remainder under threat of demolition and urban renewal. There were even noisy public demonstrations calling for the wooden buildings to be torn down. Several renewal proposals were developed, all based on boxlike concrete structures, several of which were already taking shape across the harbour on the Nordnes peninsula. The proposals for Bryggen were eventually thwarted by a combination of two of the dominant themes of the 1970s: global economic recession and the emergence of the historic preservation movement. The preservation movement in Bergen was led by Asbjørn Herteig, curator of the Historical Museum at the

Bryggen townscape, viewed across Vågen (Bergen's central harbour) from the Nordnes peninsula.

Bryggen
Bergen

Restored Hansa buildings in the heart of Bryggen.

Left: **Bryggen**. The picturesque unevenness of the buildings is a result of subsidence of the infill on which the district was built, aggravated by the explosion of a munitions ship in the harbour in 1944, which caused the buildings to sink and lean heavily.

University of Bergen, who orchestrated a coalition of government and business interests that established Foundation Bryggen in order to protect the buildings at Bryggen in accordance with Norway's Cultural Heritage Act. The surviving ensemble of sixty-one wooden buildings, covering 13,000 m², was preserved and eventually recognized by UNESCO as a World Heritage site in 1979. When a key site at the southern end of the district was redeveloped to accommodate a new hotel and a Hanseatic Museum, the designs (by architect Øivind Maurseth) sought to harmonize with the medieval morphology and townscape. Six shortened rows face the harbour, built with a concrete frame but clad with painted wooden boards to replicate the Hansa buildings. Behind them and partly hidden, the hotel consists of seven double-pitched rows built of bricks and slightly taller than the wooden ones.

Bryggen today is one of the most visited attractions in Norway. The impact of tourists on the district is both seasonal and tied to the rhythm of the cruise ships that bring more than 150,000 passengers to the city every year. Almost all of them find their way to Bryggen, and during the summer the district's narrow passages are full of tourists, the cruise ship passengers coming through, one wave after another.

Although picturesque, there is nothing left of the original character and function of the district. The upper lofts of the restored buildings are let as studios and offices to artists, architects, and business services, while ground-floor premises are occupied by tourist shops, handicraft stores, galleries, cafés, restaurants, and pubs. Roof windows have been added, entrance doors have been given glass openings to permit light into the stores, and flowerpots have been hung on the fences of the outdoor balconies. The tourist shops have their share of troll dolls and junk, but many of them sell high-quality handicraft, knitwear, silverware, glassware, and leatherwork. Meanwhile, the latest threat to the district is the fact that it is sinking, a result of its original construction on infill, compounded by decades of heavy vehicular traffic on the quayside.

Further reading on Bryggen

Burkhardt, Mike, 'The German Hanse and Bergen – New Perspectives on an Old Subject', *Scandinavian Economic History Review* 58.1 (2010), 60–79. *Provides a detailed account of Bryggen's role in the Hanseatic League and of the social and economic organization of the district at the time.*

Cary
Raleigh

Cary is a stereotypical 'boomburb', a new and distinctive kind of district that is stealthily eclipsing traditional city districts in terms of economic and demographic vitality. Like other boomburbs, Cary has maintained double-digit rates of population growth for several decades, growing from just 7,600 in 1970 to 138,000 in 2010.

Boomburbs typically develop along the interstate beltways that ring large U.S. metropolitan areas. They are the hubs of America's 'exit ramp economy', focused on office parks and could-be-anywhere retail strips and malls – all surrounded by affluent, wooded suburban subdivisions with condominiums and single-family homes. While boomburbs possess most urban elements – housing, retailing, entertainment, and offices – they are not typically patterned in a traditional urban form. Boomburbs almost always lack, for example, a dense or identifiable business core. Boomburbs can thus be seen as distinct from traditional urban centres, not so much in their function as in their low density and loosely configured spatial structure. As Robert Lang and Jennifer LeFurgy put it (p. 28), 'Boomburbs are urban in fact, but not in feel'.

Cary is one of fifty-four boomburbs identified by Lang and LeFurgy: suburban jurisdictions with more than 100,000 residents that have maintained double-digit rates of population growth between 1970 and 2000. Other examples include Arlington, Texas; Chandler, Arizona; Coral Springs, Florida; and Mesa, Arizona.

Cary is situated amid one of America's fastest-growing metropolitan regions and close to the centre of the 'Research Triangle' that is anchored by the University of North Carolina (Chapel Hill), Duke University (Durham), and North Carolina State University (Raleigh). This location has made Cary very attractive to the industries associated with the so-called new

Edgeless city. Office employment is scattered throughout the wooded terrain of Cary's metroburban landscape. Shown here is the campus of the SAS Institute. Copyright © 2010. SAS Institute Inc. All rights reserved. Reproduced with permission of SAS Institute Inc., Cary, NC, USA.

economy that is based on digital technologies, biotechnology, and advanced business services. These industries have tended to seek out new settings – like Cary – well away from congested central city areas. Modern just-in-time production systems and flexible specialization strategies require easily accessible factories; biotechnology firms require specialized new laboratories; and almost every back-office facility and business service requires buildings that are flexible in layout and prewired or easily wired for access to digital communications networks.

New-economy industries require business and industrial parks with single-storey structures and designer frontages, loading docks at the rear, and interior spaces that can be used for offices, research and development (R&D) labs, storage, or manufacture, in any ratio. To be competitive they must also be packaged as 'planned corporate environments' with built-in daycare facilities, fitness centres, jogging trails, restaurants and convenience stores, lavish interior décor, and lush exterior landscaping and signage.

Cary now has a total office space market of more than 511,000 m^2, a retail space market of almost 557,000 m^2, and a flex-space market approaching 93,000 m^2. It is home to many new-economy corporations, scattered throughout the district in small office parks and commercial corridors. They include the SAS Institute (the largest privately held software company in the world and Cary's largest single employer), Geotek Mapping, 3D Learning Solutions (simulation software for the military), Deutsche Bank Global Technologies, R. R. Donnelley (publisher), Infineon Technologies, Research in Motion (smartphone manufacturer), and Epic Games (video game developer).

Cary's new-economy corporations have brought residents from across the country. A much-recited witticism is that the district's

McMansions. The district's affluence is manifest in its many high-end subdivisions and gated communities.

Demographic diversity. Cary's 'new economy' employers have attracted a diverse population. The Hindu community has built the Sri Venkateswara Temple, one of the largest facilities of its kind in the United States.

name is an acronym, standing for Containment Area for Relocated Yankees. Not all Yankees, perhaps, but the great majority are 'relos': affluent middle-class households that have had to relocate as a result of the increasing fluidity and flexibility of corporate location strategies within the new economy.

The first real growth in Cary's population took place in the early 1970s with the success of Research Triangle Park, the first (and arguably the most successful) science and technology district in the United States, located a few kilometres to the northwest on Interstate 40. Kildaire Farms, a 400-hectare private master-planned development, was the first, in 1971, of what has become a sprawling patchwork of sequestered residential settings. As Cary's economy expanded, so its population grew not only in size but also in educational attainment and diversity. More than 60 per cent of adult residents in Cary hold a baccalaureate degree or higher. The diversity stems mainly from the large fraction (about one-sixth) of the population born outside the United States, the largest single group coming from South Asia. But despite Cary's sizeable international population and specialized shops that serve its ethnic populations, the influx of people from outside the United States seems to have done little to diversify everyday life in Cary. The district boasts one of the most frequently visited Hindu temples in the country, but it is tucked away out of sight and many Cary residents remain unaware of its existence.

On paper, Cary's affluence and sustained growth have resulted in its appearance on lists of the Best Places to Live in national journals like *Money Magazine*. On the ground there is plenty of evidence of money but little evidence of conviviality, community, or culture. Cary's affluent

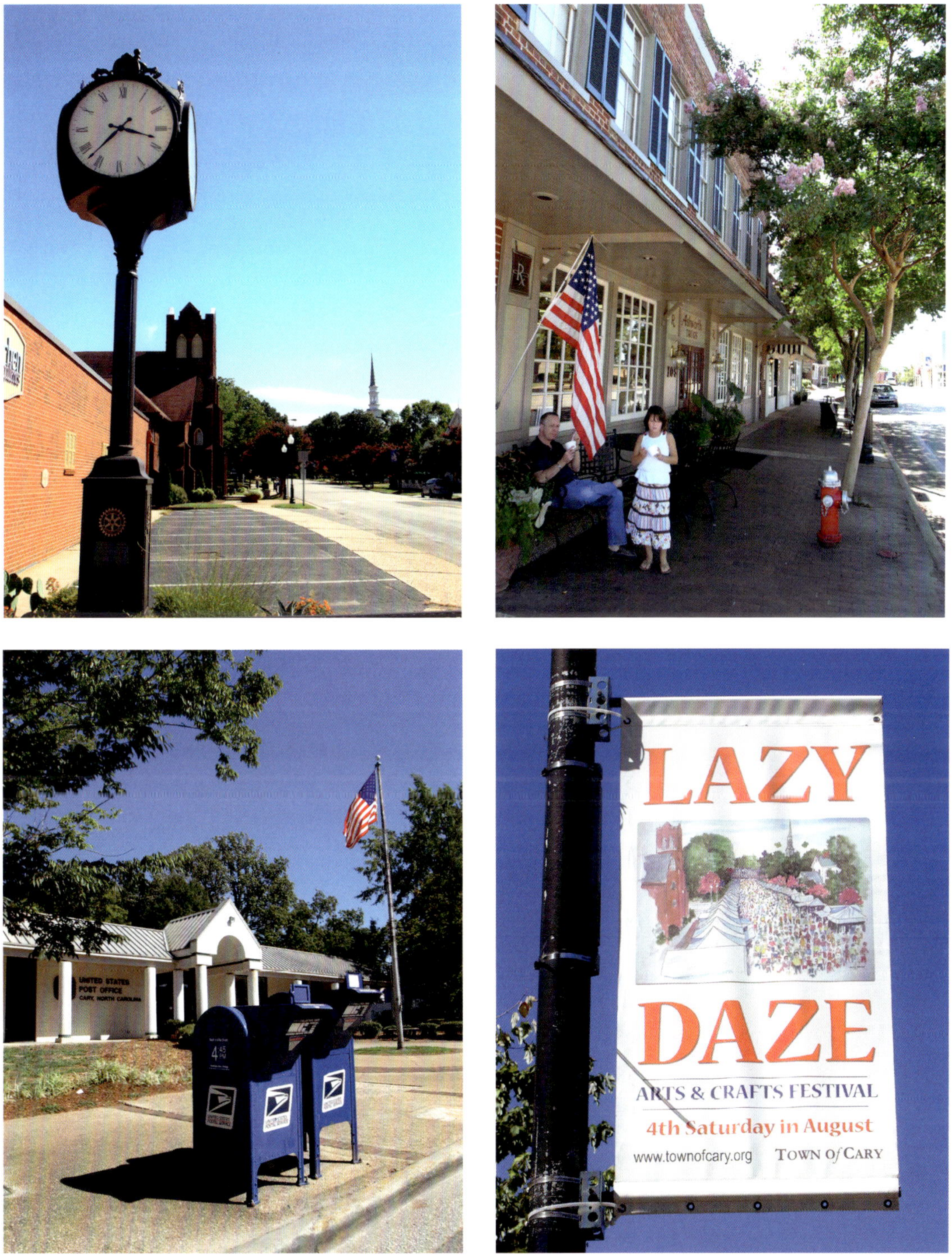

Clockwise, from top left: **Cary town centre**: South Academy Street, at the town's central crossroads; **Cary's 'Main Street'**: Ashworth drug store, on West Chatham Street, also at the town's central crossroads; **community branding**, emphasizing arts and crafts; **Cary's 'downtown' post office**, striving for a small-town rather than a suburban image.

Retirement community: the Manor Village at Preston.

Single-family housing in a gated community.

population is accommodated in a collection of subdivisions with no focal point and with only the signature facades of retail stores and restaurants – Circuit City, OfficeMax, Lowe's, Wal-Mart, Gap, Trader Joe's, PetSmart, Olive Garden, Red Lobster, Food Lion, Rite Aid, Starbucks, Target, and the rest – to serve as landmarks in a generic and placeless suburban landscape.

There is a residual core to the district adjacent to the tiny railway station that was the nucleus of the district before it took off as a boomburb. It is, though, largely devoid of life and activity. Town festivals like Lazy Daze are marketed as being typical of the safe, neighbourly environment that comes with living in Cary. A downtown pharmacy does boast a still-functional old-fashioned soda fountain, and the blocks surrounding downtown do contain stately Victorian houses and well-maintained churches.

Cary Town Hall, the size of which is commensurate with the district's wealth.

Suburban shopping mall, 'The Shoppes' of Kildaire.

Condominium housing: 'The Marquis' at Preston.

But the same downtown blocks also have vacant lots and struggling businesses with decaying buildings. The wealthy tax base of the district has provided a large new civic building and a lot of expensive sculpture (some of it evocative of Norman Rockwell's kitschy and nostalgic illustrations of small-town America) and neotraditional street furniture, but the net effect is more of a void than a focal point.

The district's residential subdivisions are also rather inert. Neatly landscaped and self-consciously expensive homes are packaged with the full array of features and amenities, but whatever the time of day or night there are few signs of life save the landscape crews, watering and weeding plantings that the residents will glimpse from their driveway as they arrive home. Gates – real or implied – suggest a sense of security and exclusivity to many subdivisions, though in fact the district as a whole has very little reported crime and the exclusivity is all relative. The gates, like the landscaping and fancy street furniture, are mainly for show.

Further reading on Cary

Lang, Robert, and LeFurgy, Jennifer, *Boomburbs: The Rise of America's Accidental Cities*, Washington, D.C.: Brookings Institution Press, 2007. *An economic and demographic analysis of the 'boomburb' phenomenon in the United States.*

The City
London

In the heart of London, on the site of the capital of Roman Britain, the City has become the specialized office district that anchors London's status as a truly global city. Its built environment reflects its long history as the commercial heart of the British Empire as well as its current role as a hub of international business, its dense fabric and narrow streets containing an eclectic mixture of architecture.

'The City' is traditionally equated with the jurisdiction of the City of London, the municipal nucleus of London and its historic commercial core (London's institutional core, of palaces and national government buildings, developed around Westminster, 4 km upstream on the same northern bank of the River Thames). The contemporary office district is often referred to simply as the City (or the Square Mile, as it is just over 2.90 km^2 [1 mi^2] in area). The dominance of office employment in the City grew out of London's role as a centre of world shipping. The insurance industry was established in the seventeenth century as merchants and shipowners gathered to exchange information and spread their risks; financial markets originated in London's sea trade, while commodities and futures markets were a byproduct of London's entrepôt function.

With the expansion of the British empire, trade boomed, and so did the associated finance and advanced business services. In the nineteenth century, City banks and finance houses provided capital for the development of manufacturing around the world, together with credit to finance the import of primary products from the colonial world. London's emergence as a dominant world city meant that office development gradually displaced other activities in the Square Mile; in parallel, the resident population of the City decreased from 208,000 in 1700 to 27,000 in 1900 and to less than 10,000 in 2010. The daytime working population of the City, however, is now more than 300,000, the great majority of whom are office workers.

The cornerstones of the City economy are the London Stock Exchange, Lloyd's of London, and the Bank of England. In general, the City specializes in the wholesale side of financial services, that is, services to other financial business or corporate customers, together with international lending, bond trading, foreign exchange trading, and investment management. There are about 500 banks with offices in the City, many of them specializing in areas such as foreign exchange markets, eurobonds, and energy futures. The City also accounts for a quarter of the world market for marine insurance and more than a third of the market in aviation risks; it has meanwhile emerged as an important Alternative Investment Market (AIM), providing equity for smaller firms from around the world.

The City's location in the heart of the metropolis is at once one of its biggest advantages and one of its greatest challenges. Its centrality gives it both access and accessibility within

The City is situated at the heart of the metropolis and occupies the site of the Roman and medieval city of London.

the broader context of the metropolis while simultaneously contributing to an atmosphere of centrality. Its 1,000-year history contributes an affect of gravitas and permanence. But it is hemmed in by the commercial districts of the West End and by the residential and workshop communities of the East End and has a legacy of outdated infrastructure.

The City suffered extensive damage during World War II. Although St Paul's Cathedral famously survived, large swathes of the City did not. A significant amount of rebuilding took place in the decades following the war, including the 1960s redevelopment of the bomb-damaged Barbican area on the City's northern edge. The Barbican incorporated all the latest thinking about Modernist urban design: pedestrian walkways, underground car parks, and Brutalist-style concrete buildings. Postwar redevelopment was constrained, however, by historic preservation orders on more than 500 buildings and 23 streets as well as by building height limits designed to protect views of St Paul's Cathedral. Since 1938 the City of London Corporation has operated a unique policy known as the St Paul's Heights to protect and enhance important local views of the cathedral from the South Bank, from the Thames bridges, and from certain points to the north, west, and east. In addition, local views of St Paul's Cathedral along Fleet Street, Ludgate Hill, Watling Street, and Cannon Street are protected by setback limitations. Upon redevelopment, the upper stories are required to be set back from the building frontage in order to respect pedestrians' views of St Paul's.

The globalization of the economy that began in the mid-1970s has provided the impetus to overcome these challenges and constraints.

City workers are predominantly commuters from elsewhere in the capital. The medieval street pattern and high density of development make for high levels of congestion during the district's extended rush hours. Photo courtesy of Anne-Lise Velez.

Lloyd's of London building, designed by Richard Rogers and built between 1978 and 1986. The building was innovative in having its infrastructure on the outside, leaving an uncluttered space inside. Photo courtesy of Anne-Lise Velez.

Global business. Lloyds of London provides insurance and reinsurance for a global market. Lloyd's syndicates write a diverse range of policies, including policies for fine art, aviation, marine, and other insurances. Photo courtesy of Anne-Lise Velez.

Global symbol. The headquarters of the Swiss Reinsurance Company at 30 St Mary Axe, designed by Foster + Partners, dwarfs pedestrians and has become a landmark London skyscraper, part of the City's brand image.

Britain's first skyscraper, the 183-m, 42-storey Natwest Tower (now re-labelled as Tower 42), was opened in 1980. Competition from the two other global financial centres – New York and Tokyo – was met with legislation in 1986 that lifted restrictions on entry to the London Stock Market and replaced face-to-face dealing on the floor of the Stock Exchange with an electronic share-price display system, allowing screen-based trading. The result was the Big Bang: a restructuring, realignment, and resurgence of firms in stock and bond markets, and an overall recasting of the City's office employment profile.

The compactness of the old urban core turned out to be well suited to the operation of a global financial service centre. Electronic trading has not reduced the need for face-to-face meetings at all. For many advanced business services and specialized financial services, a tightly bound geographical location is essential in fostering localized networks, both formal and informal, which are an important vector for knowledge accumulation and transfer. Proximity allows meetings to be called at short notice and takes advantage of clients, suppliers, customers, and others being able to walk to the meeting place. The compactness of the City allows a greater density of interaction and produces social and cultural spillover effects in terms of the personal relationships among firms, clients, suppliers, professional bodies, the state, and financial regulators that help to sustain the primacy of London's financial cluster. As a result, the City has an unusually strong

Lunch break at Broadgate, an office and retail development built above the approaches to Liverpool Street railway station. The public space at the heart of the development has been heavily used since it was upgraded in 2002 to designs of the architectural firm SOM.

City skyline includes the Heron Tower, left; Lloyd's building (right foreground); and 30 St Mary Axe, popularly known as The Gherkin.

pedestrian character for an office district, with people walking to one another's offices, to lunches, and to after-hours bars, private members' clubs, and fitness centres.

These social settings are also important in binding together the business of the City. In the pubs, bars, cafés, restaurants, gyms, and clubs of the City, banking, insurance, and accountancy professionals mix with lawyers, traders, editors, business journalists, consultants, recruiters, and market researchers. People talk, they compare notes, and they exchange tips, rumours, and opinions. The informal exchange of knowledge often ends up translating into tacit insider knowledge and into people's business practices.

The agglomeration economies of the district and its overall dominance as a global financial centre mean that a credible address in the City of London is highly desirable for banks, legal firms, and management consulting businesses. A City of London location turns a law firm into a City law firm, a form of branding that projects image, trust, and reputation and so helps gain market share. A City location also helps in recruiting skilled individuals from the local labour pool, something that is particularly important for banking. Highly qualified professionals, meanwhile, are attracted into the district because of the prestige of developing a career path in London, and the City in particular, and because the size of the labour market allows for mobility between firms and sectors.

The tight-knit networks and interdependencies among firms has resulted in a pronounced spatial clustering, with law firms and associated businesses dominating the western end of the City around the Inns of Court, and financial services (accountancy, banking, insurance, auxiliary finance, and recruitment) in the east. The growth of advanced business services employment in the City since the Big Bang has extended office development into a northern fringe featuring design-related and business support firms. It has also been displaced across the river, notably to the More London Riverside development around City Hall, between Tooley

Concrete brutalism. The Barbican Estate, a residential complex built in the 1960s on a site devastated by World War II bombings. At the centre of the estate is the City of London School for Girls, a public library, and the Barbican Centre, a large multi-arts and conference venue.

The City of London's coat of arms marks the boundary of the district.

Street and The Queen's Walk on the South Bank, and the nearby Shard London Bridge, a 310-m tower. New office development within the core of the City, meanwhile, has occupied space over the tracks and platforms of railway stations (Liverpool Street, Cannon Street, and Fenchurch Street), in former newspaper buildings along Fleet Street, and in several iconic office towers, including 30 St Mary Axe (known fondly as The Gherkin, 180 m), Broadgate Tower (164 m), Heron Tower (202 m), and Bishopsgate Tower (The Pinnacle, 288 m).

The Big Bang also encouraged both the government and private investors in the development of a major new office district, Canary Wharf, 2 km to the east of the City on the site of the derelict quays of the Isle of Dogs. While this initially resulted in an oversupply of office space, it also had the effect of a marked improvement in the cost of office space in the City and made room for an eventual improvement in quality of available space in the City. After several business cycles, Canary Wharf is now viewed as an adjunct of the City rather than a separate, rival office cluster.

Further reading on the City

Hebbert, Michael, *London*, Chichester: Wiley, 1998. *An excellent survey of the development of Greater London that provides an important context for understanding the changing role of the City.*

Kenyon, Nicholas (editor), *The City of London*, London: Thames and Hudson, 2011. *An historical overview of the City's development and illustrated analysis of the architecture and of the district.*

Sassen, Saskia, *The Global City: New York, London, Tokyo*, New York: Princeton University Press, 2001. *This classic work chronicles how New York, London, and Tokyo became command centres for the global economy and in the process underwent a series of massive and parallel changes.*

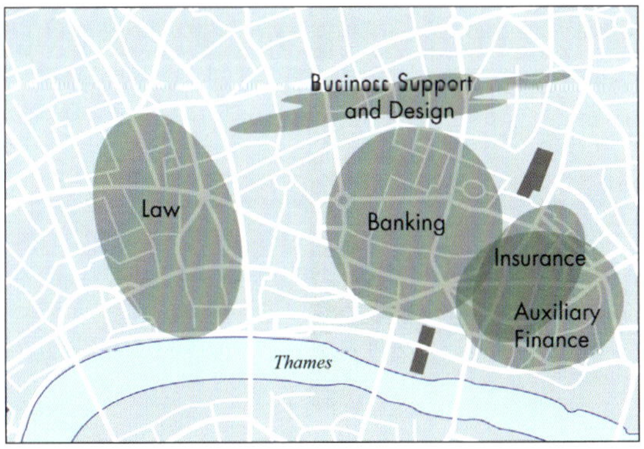

Functional specialization. Above left: The City is large enough to have developed its own internal spatial clustering of different kinds of advanced business services. The long history and complex economy of the City has left a rich legacy of specialized settings and services. Right, top: **Ede and Ravenscroft**, London's oldest tailor and robe maker, specializing in custom tailoring, classic and contemporary menswear, academic robes, legal wigs and regalia; middle: the **Counting House**, a pub that caters to City workers, located in a former banking hall; bottom: **Leadenhall Market**, a covered market originally specializing in meat, game and poultry but now diversified with pubs and commercial retailing as well as fresh food.

Dorchester Boston

The new transportation technologies of the nineteenth century – railways and streetcars – turned cities inside out, allowing the growing population of middle-class households to escape from crowded and unhealthy downtown districts. Dorchester is a typical example of the 'streetcar suburbs' that came to surround most major cities. Built on farmland between 3 and 6 km from central Boston, Dorchester was a product of an intensive fifty years of speculative development that produced a novel suburban landscape that became home to successive generations of upwardly mobile immigrants.

In the mid-seventeenth century the rolling uplands to the south and west of the emergent town of Boston attracted immigrant farmers. Villages grew up around rural crossroads at Roxbury, Quincy, Hyde Park, Dedham, and at Meeting House Hill in what is now Dorchester. Many of the settlers around Meeting House Hill came originally from southwestern England, and some from Dorchester in Dorset, birthplace of many of the Pilgrims who emigrated from England to the Massachusetts Bay Colony. Each village was connected with Boston by rugged country roads that accommodated themselves to the contours of the land, and for a long time the small farming community served Boston's growing market.

By the beginning of the nineteenth century, however, the city was beginning to grow rapidly in size as industrialization took off. The appearance of all kinds of noxious industrial land uses, together with the arrival of thousands of immigrants and their transformation into a restless and occasionally threatening proletariat, repelled many of the city's new class of white-collar workers. In addition, there were the hazards of epidemic disease and the intensifying stresses and conflicts of city life. A few families, wealthy enough to afford private carriages or hire hackney carriages, had moved out to exclusive exurban settings at the first signs of industrial squalor. But it was not possible for others to join them until the development of short-haul passenger railway routes, horsedrawn omnibuses, and horsecar systems.

First to come, in the 1840s and 1850s, were the railways. The New York and New England Railway Company ran a line through Dorchester in 1855, crossing the level farmlands and building stations at such rural clusters as existed. In this way railway construction reinforced the existing settlement pattern. During the 1850s and 1860s railway commuters began to move to the area and their houses dotted the hills and clustered along the main village roads. They were soon joined by commuters using the mid-century innovation of horse-drawn cars on

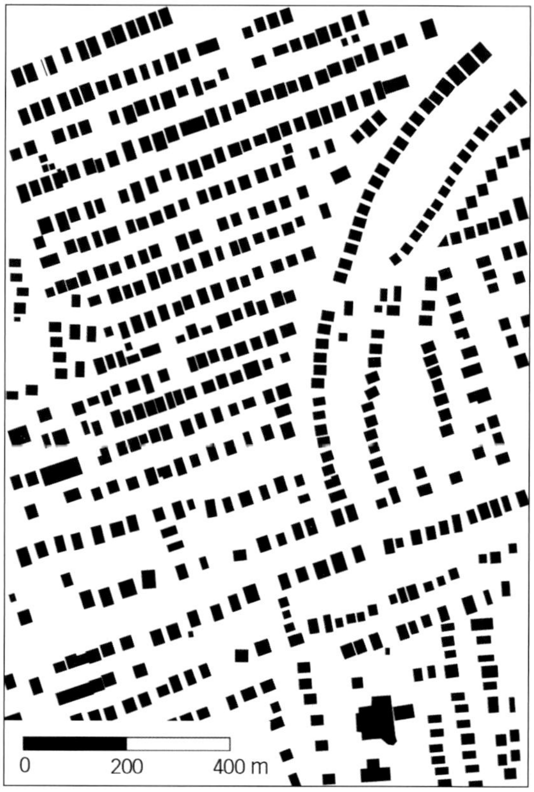

Figure-ground diagram of part of Dorchester, between Fields Corner and Shawmut.

rail lines that were embedded in existing roadways. In Boston, Henry Whitney established an integrated horsecar system that covered the entire city and drew settlement out to village centres up to 4 km from City Hall. As Sam Bass Warner Jr. noted in his landmark study of Boston's streetcar suburbs:

> *To real estate men the simple procedure of placing a coach on iron rails seemed a miraculous device for the promotion of out-of-town property.*
>
> 1962, p. 23

This brought speculative suburban development to the northern fringes of Dorchester, where the villages of Meeting House Hill, Town Meeting Square, and Upham's Corner experienced a suburban building boom that created a kilometre-deep belt of one- and two-family homes within walking distance on either side of the horsecar lines. This first suburban boom was halted by the national economic depression of 1873, but it was already reaching its limits because of the relatively slow speed of the horsecars (few commuters were prepared to spend more than 45 minutes each way, the time it took from Meeting House Hill to downtown Boston) and their cost (affordable only to limited numbers of better-off white-collar families).

It was the innovation of the electric streetcar that unleashed the growing demand for suburban living. By the time Frank Sprague had perfected an electrically driven version of the horsecar, powered by overhead cables, that opened for business in Richmond, Virginia, in the spring of 1888, Boston's population had exceeded half a million. The following year Whitney began to extend the radial lines of his horsecar system and convert it to electric

Tightly packed three-deckers. The distinctive form of the three-decker is vital to the sense of place of Dorchester and other Boston streetcar suburbs.

Dorchester
Boston

Two-family homes in southeastern Dorchester. Common front porches and single front doors give the appearance of single-family homes.

Left: **Triple-decker apartment houses** on St Marks Road.

streetcars. The total length of track in 1887 had been just over 320 km; by 1904 it was almost 725 km. By making it feasible to travel up to 15 km from Boston's downtown office district in 30 minutes or so, the streetcar greatly increased the territory available for the development of extensive tracts of suburban homes.

Dorchester had been isolated from Boston by the then-unfilled South Bay inlet, but with the establishment of the electric streetcar system the district's land was suddenly thrown open to mass development. So much land became accessible at once that the price of land was kept down. Combined with the cheaper operating costs per passenger-kilometre of the streetcars (because of their larger carrying capacity and the efficiency of electric power), this ensured that developers of streetcar suburbs instantly found an eager market among Boston's solid middle-income groups, and there was a rush of speculative suburban sprawl as developers and streetcar operators worked together. Dorchester's farm fields made easy sites for the developers, who sought to meet the demand for what historian Robert Fishman memorably described as Bourgeois Utopias.

The dominant form of building in Dorchester was the triple-decker: a three-storey building of light-framed wood construction, each floor usually consisting of a single apartment. Unlike the three-storey row houses common in many other American cities in the late nineteenth century, Boston's triple-deckers had no common walls, so they could have windows on each side as well as front and back. This allowed for significantly larger floor plans and an abundance of natural light and air. They were also an efficient means of accommodating Boston's rapidly expanding middle class. The cost of the land, basement, and roof were spread amongst three (sometimes six) apartments. Buyers could live in one unit and rent out the others, ensuring that they could afford payments and upkeep for years to come.

Built by a multitude of different independent contractors, there was no set footprint or

Speculatively built triple-decker apartment houses on South Munroe Terrace. Note the relatively generous spacing between buildings.

design for the triple-decker. Most had a horizontal cornice line hiding a gently sloping roof to the back of the house. Most also had tiers of porches front and rear, and many had a vertical column of bay windows on the front corner of the building. The variations of triple-decker plan configuration and facade treatment provided a versatile building type that could be constructed for wealthy families as well as families of more modest means. While typically lacking the ornamentation found on other homes of the Victorian period, their versatility allowed builders to keep pace with prevailing architectural fashions, including Greek Revival, Shingle, and Queen Anne styling.

Builders in Dorchester also constructed a lot of two-family buildings as well as a few custom-built single-family homes. The two-family homes came in a great variety of styles, though they were generally in the form of two apartments stacked one on top of another, rather than as semi-detached two-storey homes.

The impact of the streetcar suburbs on the city and urban life cannot be overestimated. The great housebuilding boom of the 1890s and 1900s was accompanied by an enormous public effort that produced scores of schools, libraries, and minor public buildings. Meanwhile, the sudden departure of thousands of middle-income households gave much-needed scope for the reassignment of space to nonresidential uses in downtown Boston. The ease and inexpensiveness of travel on streetcars led suburban housewives to use them on weekday downtown shopping trips outside rush hours, helping to sustain the more specialized shops of the central business district. To counter the lack of commuters on weekends and holidays, streetcar companies promoted the idea of outings to amusement parks, picnic grounds, and even cemeteries that were located near streetcar terminus stops, and they soon attracted a variety of ancillary services such as restaurants and convenience stores.

The families that moved in to Dorchester were headed by commuters whose jobs remained in the old districts of central Boston: small manufacturers, professionals, tradesmen,

Social and architectural variety. Left: single-family home; centre: two-family home; right: six-family triple-decker.

salesmen, and artisans. Most of them were descendants of the first-wave Canadian, English, and Scottish immigrants, but about a quarter of them were Irish or of Irish descent and, by the mid-1900s, Italians and Russian and German Jews were beginning to make their presence felt.

As the district became established, so its character changed. Initially, the arterial streets were the most popular and the most expensive. They were also the most convenient and the easiest to develop. Before long, though, the noise of streetcars and other traffic began to repel residences while their accessibility attracted commercial development, usually in the form of rows of stores in tall, narrow three-deckers with apartments above. Meanwhile, cheaper housing in pockets of the least desirable land were developed for lower-income households.

As the housing stock aged over the next century, the district gradually filtered down the socioeconomic ladder. In the 1950s and 1960s the ethnic composition of the district changed as some sections were colonized by African American households migrating from the South. This prompted a certain amount of 'white flight', which led in turn to the arrival of immigrants from the Caribbean, Vietnam, and parts of Latin America, Asia, and Africa. In recent years the cosmopolitanism of the district has attracted some gentrification and a certain amount of reinvestment. Much of the fabric of Dorchester, meanwhile, has maintained a good deal of its character and appearance, a direct consequence of the quality of the original housing stock.

Further reading on Dorchester

Sammarco, Anthony Mitchell, *Dorchester: A Compendium*, Charleston, SC: The History Press, 2011. *A social history of the district, compiled from the author's column in the Dorchester Community News.*

Warner, Sam Bass, Jr., *Streetcar Suburbs: The Process of Growth in Boston, 1870–1900*, Cambridge, MA: Harvard University Press, 1962. *The landmark study of streetcar suburbs. Includes rich detail on the development of Dorchester as well as other Boston streetcar suburbs such as Roxbury and Tremont Street.*

Eastern Harbour Amsterdam

Amsterdam's eastern docklands were built in the last quarter of the nineteenth century to handle the city's transoceanic trade and passenger traffic. They were constructed as artificial peninsulas, with quays, warehouses, railway sidings, and a passenger hotel. A hundred years later they had all become obsolete and the district was promptly occupied by an alternative community of squatters and houseboat dwellers. In the past quarter-century, the docklands have become a paradigmatic case of urban waterfront redevelopment and an important component of Amsterdam's 'compact city' strategy.

The sequence of redevelopment across the docklands reflects changing architectural and urban design concepts as well as the changing priorities of the city. The net result is a broad spectrum of housing at high densities and an array of architecture and urban design that has made the Eastern Harbour District a popular destination on the twenty-first-century equivalent of the architectural Grand Tour.

The Eastern Harbour was built to accommodate the deepwater steamships that dominated world trade from the late nineteenth century to the mid-twentieth century. The golden era of the district was the period between the two World Wars, when the docklands developed an extensive infrastructure of cargo handling, warehousing, and light industry. Merchant shipping brought imports from the former Dutch East and West Indies and Africa. The harbour's new peninsulas were given names reflecting these trading connections, while some of the warehouses were named after the continents. The Eastern Harbour was also an important passenger terminal, handling big passenger liners bound for the Americas.

The decline of the docklands began in the 1960s as passengers opted to travel by air rather

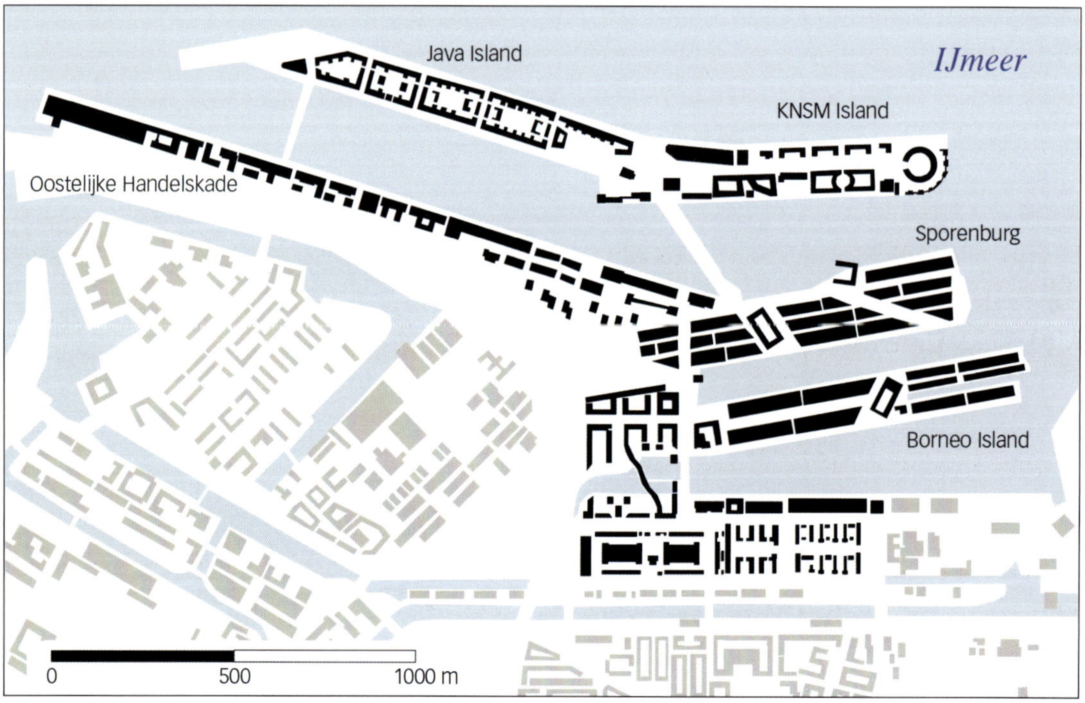

Figure-ground diagram of the Eastern Harbour. Much of the adjacent docklands has also been redeveloped into residential blocks.

than by sea and as general mixed-cargo ships were replaced by specialized container ships and bulk transport vessels. A new container port was installed to the west, and by the early 1970s the Eastern Harbour had lost all of its commercial functions and had been taken over by squatters and an alternative community of artists and hippies living in old buses, caravans, huts, and houseboats.

Meanwhile, the city of Amsterdam had targeted the Eastern Harbour for redevelopment, primarily as a residential district. Building in the docklands at high densities – about 100 dwellings per hectare – was seen as an opportunity to counter suburban sprawl. High-density development was also necessary because of the huge investment required in remediating the land and installing an infrastructure of bridges, roads, and public transport. Although the overall strategy was for a residential district, it was also the intention to develop several small-scale industrial and commercial estates in order to provide a local employment base. The first plan was drawn up in 1980 and in 1987 the first phase of redevelopment took place close to the landward side of the district in the south, on the site of the old cattle market, slaughterhouse, and customs depot. This first phase was unexceptional: 600 dwellings, 85 per cent of which were for rent in the public sector, built in the conventional three- and four-storey blocks of the period.

Planning strategies changed significantly in the late 1980s, however, as Amsterdam's city council and its planners were drawn, like their counterparts in many other cities, into neoliberal policies and urban entrepreneurialism. This meant that the Eastern Harbour

Sporenburg peninsula. Low-rise private housing on the southern bank of the peninsula (Panamakade). Photo by Martin van Dalen, used under a creative commons Attribution-Share Alike License at Wikimedia Commons.

was reconceptualised as a potential setting for higher-income households wanting an urban lifestyle with proximity to the jobs, shops, restaurants, and the public transport network of the city centre. In 1990 the plans for the district were redrawn, giving priority to private housing and luxury rented houses and allowing for a mix of residential and commercial uses along with some social housing.

The idea was to develop small-scale business spaces for offices, workshops, and studios on the ground floor of apartment blocks in order to increase the area's vitality and diversity. The scheme included approximately 8,500 dwellings, 100,000 m^2 of commercial spaces, and 20,000 m^2 of educational and service facilities. Architectural distinction and urban affect became important criteria. The existing harbour basins were to be preserved and existing marine buildings reused. It was to be, basically, new-build gentrification.

An independent urban designer was selected for each island. Reflecting the shift in Dutch housing policy during the 1990s, Adriaan Geuze developed a scheme for private sector housing on the twin peninsulas of Borneo-Sporenburg featuring low-rise dwellings for families with children. In an attempt to create an urban context, many of the dwellings have individual front doors on the street and the ground floors of some low-rise dwellings have been designed to accommodate small businesses. The basic framework of low-rise housing has been deliberately interrupted on each peninsula by a large apartment building sited at an angle to the grid. The most distinctive feature of Borneo-Sporenburg, however, is the strip of housing along the north bank of the canal-like inlet at the eastern end of the Borneo peninsula. Here, sixty narrow parcels of land were allotted to buyers, who were required to select an architect from an approved list and build, within specified

Borneo peninsula. 'Dockland chic' in the form of individually designed luxury waterfront homes on freehold parcels.

KNSM Island. The circular apartment complex ('Emerald Empire') and attendant waterside satellite blocks, designed by Jo Coenen.

Java Island. Mid-rise apartment buildings along the Javakade, the southern waterfront of the peninsula.

dimensions, their 'dream home'. The result is a classic ensemble of 'dockland chic'.

On KNSM Island (the outermost island, named after the shipping company, Koninklijke Nederlandsche Stoomboot Maatschappij, which used to be based there), the architect Jo Coenen went for monumentalism, with 'superblocks' along a central avenue, mimicking the organization of the island's former warehouses and storage buildings. Among the superblocks on KNSM are a 300-apartment building in dark brick by German architects Hans Kollhoff and Christian Rapp; a 321-apartment building in postmodern style by Belgian architect Bruno Albert; and, dominating the eastern tip of the island, a 224-apartment building by Jo Coenen, with a circular shape that optimizes views of the water while providing a sheltered central area.

Mimesis was also the inspiration for the scheme developed by Sjoerd Soeters for Java Island, but here it was based on the city's old canal district. The central idea was therefore to foster a unified waterfront facade consisting of multiple dwellings that are individually differentiated through their building materials and detailing. Soeters also reframed the morphology of the island to mimic Amsterdam's old canal district, dividing it into four by cutting narrow channels and joining the four sections with small arched bridges for pedestrians and cyclists. Numerous architects contributed to the design of individual townhouses and apartments, and the net result was widely acclaimed and very popular.

Overall, the district has a creative and innovative atmosphere. Although the bulk of

Sporenburg. Houseboat living along the Panamakade. The few remaining houseboats lend a certain character to the district.

the district's redevelopment has involved new construction, some old maritime buildings have been preserved and reused, and these have contributed significantly to the character and appeal of the district. In the first phase of development, around the old cattle market, some warehouses were converted into dwellings. A warehouse formerly used for cocoa storage is now the Brasilia shopping centre, while an old warehouse on KNSM is now an artists' workshop and design centre. The historic Lloyd Hotel, used by emigrants from central and Eastern Europe to the Americas in the early twentieth century, has been renovated and is now an hotel and cultural centre, while the Lloyd Quarantine Building is now a restaurant and a centre for young artists. Drawn by the fashionable atmosphere, many small businesses, mainly in cultural industries and the arts, have moved in, along with restaurants, cafés, and clubs. It has become one of the most sought-after places to live in Amsterdam and is occupied by people of all types, ranging from young professionals to families. With its palpable sense of high design it is especially attractive to affluent young professionals and designers. And although not originally intended

Java Island. Canal houses along the Brantasgracht, one of the lateral canals that cut through the peninsula. Most of the houses have a back garden and a roof terrace.

for families with young children, the Eastern Harbour has actually turned out to be quite an attractive place for them to live: traffic-free and with parks and public spaces interspersed throughout the neighbourhoods.

Further reading on the Eastern Harbour

Abrahamse, Jaap, et al., *Eastern Harbour District Amsterdam. Urbanism and Architecture*, Rotterdam: NAi Publishers, 2006. *Provides a complete overview of the district, with extensive documentation on every project and detailed background on the planning process and principles, and the cultural and social impact of the redevelopment of the district.*

Hoppenbrouwer, Eric, and Louw, Erik, 'Mixed-Use Development: Theory and Practice in Amsterdam's Eastern Docklands', *European Planning Studies* 13:7 (2005), 967–83. *A detailed analysis of the rationale and strategy of mixed-use redevelopment in the district.*

Above, top **Sporenburg**, block of dwellings on Ertskade with living areas above garages, designed by Neutelings Riedijk Architects; bottom: **Borneo Island**, owner-occupied dwellings on Stokerkade, architects Van Herk and De Kleijn.

Left, top: **KNSM Island**, superblock by Bruno Albert; bottom: **Java Island**, bicycle path along the central spine of the peninsula.

Encino
Los Angeles

Encino is emblematic of American suburbanization. A product of the post-World War II economic boom, it is part of an enormous swathe of more than 500 km^2 of development, mostly suburban in character, that has spilled over into the San Fernando Valley north of Los Angeles. In many ways its landscapes are symbolic of the United States itself, while in detail it incorporates elements of several of the classic architectural ecologies of Los Angeles.

The San Fernando Valley was originally settled as ranchlands and farmed as citrus groves. Sequestered from the early growth of Los Angeles by distance (more than 35 km) and the Santa Monica Mountains, it did not begin to be developed until the early twentieth century. Even then development was patchy, with small depot towns and exurban communities separated by extensive tracts of agricultural land. Encino, like most of the communities in the Valley, did not really grow much until the 1950s when, along with the rest of the Valley's settlements, it was transformed dramatically. A prolonged building boom created an archetypal suburbia of single-family homes in one Valley settlement after another, eventually creating a vast region of suburban sprawl. Encino, like other Valley districts such as Northridge, Tarzana, and Van Nuys, developed a commercial core of retailing and personal and professional services to cater to its suburban households. As land became scarce, developers began to add condominiums and high-density 'garden' apartments to house the district's resident service workers and retirees.

Encino owed its postwar growth to several factors: the backlog of unfulfilled demand for housing from the Depression and war years, the postwar baby boom, high rates of migration into southern California from the rest of the country, and a dramatic increase in prosperity and a consequent rise of consumerism. Between 1948 and 1973 the U.S. economy grew at unprecedented rates. Median income more than doubled (in constant dollars). These factors were reinforced by several aspects of federal policy. In 1944 the Servicemen's Readjustment Act (the 'GI Bill') had created the Veterans Administration, one of the major goals of which was to facilitate home ownership for returning veterans. It did so through a programme of mortgage insurance. Soon afterwards the lending powers of the Federal Housing Administration were massively increased under the terms of the 1949 Housing Act. There was also a significant phase of road building as a result of the Federal Aid Highway Act (1956), which authorized 66,000 km of limited-access highway.

Historian Lizabeth Cohen has traced the emergence of a 'consumers' republic' in the United States in this era: a society based on mass consumption of automobiles, houses, and manufactured household goods, all celebrated by the new medium of television. This was the era of the 'sitcom suburb', a democratic utopia of ranch and split-level homes, where:

Encino is situated in the San Fernando Valley, separated from central Los Angeles by the Santa Monica Mountains.

Encino's 'Miracle Mile'. Encino Commons is a Business Improvement District (BID) involving 75 property owners and more than 300 businesses. It was established in 2000 in the hope of revitalizing the commercial strip along Ventura Boulevard and providing the district with a stronger sense of place. Photo: J. G. Klein, released to public domain on Wikimedia Commons.

> *... model houses on suburban streets held families similar in age, race, and income and whose lifestyles were reflected in the nationally popular sitcoms of the 1950s and 1960s, including* Leave It to Beaver, Ozzie and Harriet, *and* Father Knows Best.
>
> Dolores Hayden, *Building Suburbia*, New York: Pantheon, 2003, p. 128

Encino was, in fact, the setting for ABC television's *Leave It to Beaver*.

Thanks to the U.S. Supreme Court's decision in the landmark *Euclid v. Ambler* case (1926), sitcom suburbs like Encino were founded on local government zoning regulations that prohibited apartments, duplexes, small houses, or small lots as well as stores and offices. Federal intervention also contributed significantly to the creation of standardized suburban settings dominated by detached single-family homes occupied by white families. It was not until the civil rights legislation of the 1960s and the Community Reinvestment Act of 1977 that the built environment and demographics of America's sitcom suburbs began to change. By then Americans had developed a distinctive way of life and a new social and spatial order – suburbia – that had become the cradle of national personality. Indeed, California Suburbia, along with the stereotypical New England townscape and the typical Main Street of Middle America, has been identified by the distinguished geographer Donald Meinig as powerfully symbolic of the United States as a whole. California suburbia's commonplace landscape of single-family dwellings fronted by open green lawns is widely associated with a particular lifestyle for middle-class nuclear families: individualistic, private, informal, and recreation- and consumption-oriented. It is the American Dream made manifest, a moral landscape that embodies a distinctive ideology.

The sitcom suburbs' centrality to American identity was reinforced during the Cold War as the United States showcased its suburban

Ventura Boulevard features a mix of mid-rise office buildings and retail developments.

'Dingbat' apartment complexes are clustered around the higher-density corridors that cross the district.

Foothills neighbourhoods feature large single-family homes on relatively small lots.

McMansion on a 'scrape-off' site. Note how far out of scale the pink building is, compared with the surrounding homes.

lifestyles and consumer culture by way of contrast with the Soviet Union's regimented lifestyles and modest levels of living. This new narrative also enabled Americans to distinguish themselves from the Old-World culture associated with European cities, simultaneously adding another dimension to the notion of American exceptionalism.

In detail, Encino echoes the major morphological regions, or architectural ecologies, identified by architectural historian Rayner Banham. The classic 'Foothills' setting is to be found along the southern fringe of the district. Reflecting the marked correlation in Los Angeles between altitude and socioeconomic status, it is characterized by upscale single-family homes on narrow, tortuous residential roads serving precipitous house plots that often back up directly on unimproved wilderness. Sitcom suburbia, in contrast, dominates the flatlands in the Valley proper. It is characterized by much more modest single-family homes on small lots: single-storey ranch, Craftsman bungalow, or split-level homes of 100 m^2 or so. Most are well kept up but some show visible signs of age, and on some streets there is the odd oversized new single-family home, evidence of a 'scrapeoff' project and the beginning of a singular form of gentrification. Banham called the flatlands of Los Angeles 'The Plains of Id':

Sitcom suburbia, the classic postwar fabric of California Suburbia.

> *... an endless plain endlessly gridded with endless streets, peppered endlessly with ticky-tacky houses clustered in indistinguishable neighbourhoods, slashed across by endless freeways that have destroyed any community spirit that may once have existed, and so on ... endlessly.*
>
> 2009, p. 201

The flatlands of the sitcom suburbs are bisected by the district's principal commercial strip, Ventura Boulevard. Typical of the Los Angeles metropolitan area, land use along the strip intensified during the 1980s and 1990s as land prices in the metropolis escalated and a substantial amount of office employment and retailing decentralized. But development along Ventura Boulevard was typically just one parcel deep. The result was that it was almost impossible to build a multistorey structure along the strip without casting shadows or otherwise interfering with the life of the adjacent residential neighbourhoods. A notorious early example was the Fujita Building, where a sheer six-storey wall abutted against lawns and swimming pools in the backyards of a single-family neighbourhood. The inexorable logic of real estate development has meant that, as development along the strip has intensified, some of the adjacent single-family housing has been replaced by big condominium buildings and high-density gated complexes of apartments. Running parallel with the strip is the Ventura Freeway, a product of the heyday of highway construction in the 1950s and an overlay of another of Banham's architectural ecologies: 'Autopia' – dominant enough in the landscape of the metropolis to amount to 'a single comprehensible place, a coherent state of mind, a complete way of life' (Banham, 1973, p. 213).

Further reading on Encino

Banham, Reyner *Los Angeles: The Architecture of Four Ecologies*, Berkeley: University of California Press, 2nd ed., 2009. *A broad overview that relates the social geography of the city to its built environment in an innovative and interesting way.*

Barraclough, Laura R., *Making the San Fernando Valley: Rural Landscapes, Urban Development, and White Privilege*, Athens, GA: University of Georgia Press, 2011. *Puts Encino in broader context as part of the San Fernando Valley. The author's blend of social history and cultural critique includes urban planning decisions that have shaped the Valley and an analysis of contemporary life in California suburbia.*

False Creek Vancouver

False Creek is a landmark example of inner-city conversion: from an industrial district with some working-class housing to a primarily upper-middle-class residential district with some recreational infrastructure. Its transition has been central to the city's politics, often reflecting broader economic and sociopolitical changes, including globalization, structural economic change, and a shift in social sensibilities toward quality of life and sustainability. The transition, however, has taken a strikingly different course – with correspondingly different outcomes – on either side of the creek that gives the district its name. The southern shore of the creek was transformed in the image of progressive, liberal planning ideals, whereas the northern shore has been the product of market forces.

In premodern, preindustrial times, the creek itself was much larger. Filled with fish and wildlife, it was the winter home of people of the Squamish Nation. The first Europeans arrived in the mid-nineteenth century. As Vancouver grew as an entrepôt and resource processing centre, the creeksides were developed as sites for warehouses, sawmills, metalworking, and marine engineering. Early in the twentieth century the easternmost part of False Creek was filled in to create new land for the yards and terminals of the Great Northern Railway and the Canadian Northern Pacific Railway. By the 1960s, however, the district had become run down, forming an extensive belt of obsolescent industrial land uses. Outdated production technologies generated high levels of negative externalities in the form of air and water pollution, contaminated sites, and excessive noise. Situated immediately to the south of the city's expanded business district, False Creek represented both an eyesore and an opportunity for redevelopment.

In keeping with the professional planning ideology of the time, city bureaucrats and the ruling city government had developed a plan for a spoke-and-hub freeway network that would have thrust through Vancouver's inner districts into the downtown core. But in keeping with popular sentiment at the time, many

Figure-ground diagram of False Creek. It was named by a disappointed English sea captain who had ventured into the inlet hoping it would be a shortcut to the eastern reaches of Burrard Inlet, to the north of False Creek.

citizens were opposed to the federal bulldozer. The issue prompted a group of influential citizens to form The Electors Action Movement (TEAM) to oppose the freeways and to take a radically different approach to urban planning. Elected to office in 1972, TEAM councillors gave priority to diversity, an emphasis on social and environmental values, the provision of public housing, and a postindustrial economy. Central to their new vision was the comprehensive redevelopment of city-owned lands on the south shore of False Creek as a residential area, with an emphasis on quality of life. The urban design featured a continuous system of parks and open spaces along the seawall, with an uninterrupted pedestrian, jogging, and bicycle route. Vehicles were relegated to peripheral and underground locations, while the curving interior streets were given names like Forge Walk and Sawcut, meant to evoke False Creek's industrial heritage.

The most significant element of False Creek South was the purposeful mixing of lifestyles, income groups, and tenure types. About one-third of the housing was for low-income households, one-third for middle-income, and one-third for high-income households. Tenure types included a mix of subsidized rentals, cooperatives, and owner-occupier condominiums, while dwelling types included low-rise, high-rise, and townhouses as well as houseboats. Overall, as geographer David Ley observed, the development was:

> *... the most dramatic landscape metaphor of liberal ideology, of the land use implication of the transition from industrial to post-industrial society, from an ethic of growth and the production of goods to an ethic of amenity and the consumption of services.*
>
> 1980, p. 252

The popularity of False Creek South was enhanced by the redevelopment of Granville Island, a peninsula near the western end of the creek that had been the site of dozens of small

Contrasting cityscapes on either shore of the creek: the Sea Village boathouse community on the southern shore, and condominium towers on the northern shore.

Condominium towers on False Creek's north shore, a product of global capital and neoliberal planning policies.

factories associated with marine engineering, construction, forestry, and mining. By the 1960s many of them had become vacant and in the 1970s the entire site was redeveloped by the federal government. Under the management of the federal government's Canada Mortgage and Housing Corporation, Granville Island has flourished; most of its industrial spaces having been replaced with a marina, a thriving public market, craft studios and art galleries, a community centre, several performing arts theatres, a design school, and a boutique hotel. The island's industrial heritage is still very visible, however, both in a large cement works that lends a muscular authenticity to the entire island and in the many vestiges of the past such as tin and stucco siding, industrial-style doorways, cranes, and relict rail tracks. The Project for Public Spaces, a New York-based nonprofit organization, has named Granville Island to its list of sixty 'Great Public Spaces' in the world, and number one among the twenty best neighbourhoods in North America.

Highly successful in themselves, both Granville Island and False Creek South have, however, contributed to an unintended élitism, their popularity helping to inflate housing demand in the centre of the city. The 1970s and 1980s had seen a significant expansion of the downtown office sector and the emergence of incipient clusters of creative and design-based services in Vancouver's inner city. Land prices in and around False Creek skyrocketed, pushing out lower-income households from nearby districts and accelerating the process of gentrification and the 'embourgeoisement' of the inner city.

Meanwhile, the provincial government had identified the north shore of False Creek as the site of the 1986 international exposition, Expo '86, which led to the displacement of many of the district's remaining rail yards, warehouses, freight forwarding operations, and workshops. This coincided with Vancouver's integration with the economies of the Pacific Rim and an increasing flow of global capital into the city. It

Low-density apartment homes on False Creek's south shore, a product of liberal reform and social planning.

was perhaps not surprising, therefore, that following Expo '86 the site was bought by a Hong Kong property tycoon, Li Ka-shing, who brought proposals for a higher-density waterfront residential community to the north shore of the district. By this time the TEAM administration had long lost control of the city council. The shift in both local politics and in the more widespread shift toward neoliberalism was reflected in the city's Central Area Plan of 1991, which supported megaprojects such as the one proposed for False Creek's northern shore by Ka-shing's real estate investment company, Concord Pacific. The Plan's emphasis on upscale residential development and mixed-use projects has had a dramatic effect in reshaping the city's built environment. It has made the inner city:

> *... increasingly an economic, social, political and ideological space dominated by the new middle class, and by planning policies that favour the new middle class.*
>
> Olds, 2001, p. 97

The manifestation of this on False Creek's north shore is a series of developments dominated by high-rise towers. These include Granville Slopes (at the western end) and CityGate (at the eastern end) as well as Concord Pacific's International Village and Pacific Place projects, which occupy the central section of the north shore.

By the 1990s, when most of False Creek had been redeveloped, a new element – sustainability – entered the discourse on city planning and development. Calls for greater attention to the promotion of sustainable forms of development were focused on the southeastern corner of the creek, still undeveloped. Initial proposals, while seeking to exploit the broad appeal of the concept of sustainability, nevertheless bore a strong resemblance to the glassy towers of the north shore developments. They were rejected in response to widespread opposition by an electorate that was increasingly preoccupied with issues of housing affordability and neighbourhood quality as well as sustainability.

The north shore from Granville Street bridge. The green area in the middle ground is George Wainborn Park, one of a string of small parks along the landscaped shore, each connected through walkways and bicycle paths.

Between 1997 and 2004 a protracted campaign of public participation produced a new set of sustainability principles, goals, and practices, only to be brought into question by advocates of economic rather than social or environmental sustainability. The impasse was finally resolved by deciding to use the site as the athletes' village for the 2010 Olympic and Paralympic Winter Games. The theme of sustainability was carried through by featuring many 'green' design elements in the village. Following the games, the land was sold to a development company, Millennium, with an agreement to build out the site to a capacity of 5,000 residential units – again featuring green design – along with a community centre, childcare facilities, an

The central section of the north shore at dusk, emblematic of Vancouver's prosperity and the 1990s real estate boom.

Granville Island (foreground) from the Granville Street bridge. The island's mix of industrial, commercial, educational, hotel, and recreational land uses stands in sharp contrast to the high-density residential settings along the north shore (opposite).

elementary school, restored heritage buildings, a public park, and a redeveloped waterfront with an intertidal fish habitat, a boardwalk, and a seaside bikeway.

Further reading on False Creek

Ley, David, 'Liberal Ideology and the Postindustrial City', *Annals of the Association of American Geographers* 70.2 (1980), 238–58. *Provides a detailed account of the ascendance of liberal planning and policy ideals in Vancouver and their eventual expression in South False Creek.*

Olds, Kris, *Globalization and Urban Change: Capital Culture and Pacific Rim Megaprojects*, Oxford: Oxford University Press, 2001. *The author's chapter on Vancouver places the redevelopment of the north shore of False Creek in context of processes of globalization.*

Fashion District New York

New York's Fashion District occupies a four-by-six-block area bordered to the north by 40th Street, to the south by 34th Street, to the east by Fifth Avenue, and to the west by Ninth Avenue. At one time the city's most notorious vice district, it became a mass-production garment manufacturing centre and an important driver of New York's economy before developing into one of the world's most influential centres of couture and contemporary prêt-à-porter fashion. More recently it has been a catalytic element in the development of the city's expanding clusters of creative arts and design services. In between, the district has been the subject of a landmark land-use zoning law, mobster exploitation, and deindustrialization.

In the late 1800s the district was known as the Tenderloin. A mixture of theatres, hotels, casinos, and bars made for a boisterous atmosphere, and the district's original wealthy households promptly moved away to new residences Uptown and on the Upper West Side of Manhattan. The only residents who were both willing and able to pay rents in the rapidly emptying area were high-class prostitutes, and the new social ecology of the district soon acquired an underworld of bootlegging, betting, and racketeering.

It might have stayed that way for a long time if not for discrimination against the Jewish garment manufacturers of the city's original garment district, who had begun to encroach upon the territory of Fifth Avenue luxury stores from their base on the Lower East Side. The original garment district first emerged in the mid-1800s to meet a surge in consumer demand as the United States was experiencing its first signs of industrialization and urbanization. Its rise and expansion coincided with the invention of the sewing machine in 1846, which allowed for volume production, while a supply of skilled but cheap labour was on hand as a result of a major wave of immigration from southern and Eastern Europe. By 1910, the garment industry accounted for about 45 per cent of the industrial labour force in the city and was producing 70 per cent of the nation's women's clothing.

When the workshops and sweatshops of the garment district began to intrude on Fifth Avenue, the powerful Fifth Avenue Association, a group composed of some of the country's wealthiest and most influential citizens, embarked on a 'Save New York' campaign, pressuring banks to refuse loans for the construction of new workshops and lobbying the city to keep garment lofts from entering the area. The result was the country's prototype land-use zoning ordinance, drafted by lawyer Edward Bassett and passed in 1916. It was based on the premise that restrictions on land use are constitutional because they enable city governments to carry out their duties of protecting the health, safety, morals, and general welfare of their citizens – and it established an important precedent. By

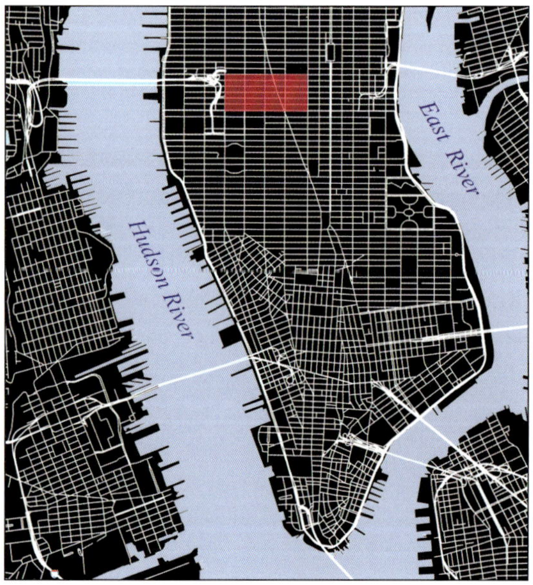

Located in the heart of midtown Manhattan, the Fashion District occupies valuable real estate that is coveted by other industries.

the spring of 1918, New York had become a place of pilgrimage for citizens and officials wanting to find out how zoning worked.

Pushed out of the Fifth Avenue area, the garment industry moved into the Tenderloin, where it was subsequently effectively quarantined by further zoning legislation. The district was rebuilt in the image of its new function, with massive loft buildings to house the garment district's manufacturers, wholesalers, and specialist retailers. A construction boom in the 1920s resulted in 7th Avenue, running north-south through the middle of the district, becoming the main axis – 'Fashion Avenue' – with surrounding blocks being developed in a new vocabulary of architectural form. Architects such as A. E. Lefcourt, Louis Adler, and Ely Jacques Kahn transformed the district, bringing high-rise buildings with an austere aesthetic based on the interplay of light and dark, void and solid.

With the closure of Paris as a centre of couture as a result of Nazi occupation in 1940, the district's women's wear industry gained a certain amount of prestige. Then, in the postwar economic boom, there was a surge in domestic demand for ready-to-wear clothing, including the huge new markets for leisure wear and designer sportswear. Brand-name designers like Bill Blass, Ralph Lauren, Donna Karan, and Calvin Klein were closely associated with New York, but the garment district itself remained rather unglamorous, a tight-knit agglomeration of fashion-related enterprises in now-aging workshops, offices, and showrooms.

But while the district's reputation for design grew, its manufacturing base fell into decline as a result of overseas competition. Undercapitalized firms, facing financial ruin in the 1960s and 1970s, turned increasingly to racketeers for loans. The notorious Gambino family took control of the garment district, manipulating the unions and taking over the hauling companies that served the industry. By the 1980s, the Gambinos controlled more than 90 per cent of the trucks that worked with firms in the district, while extorting a significant percentage of the profits of business owners. In 1981, the garment industry honoured Thomas Gambino as its Man of the Year. But the mobsters were siphoning off the profitability of the district, and more and more owners found that they could no longer afford to do business there. Between 1958 and 1977, the number of garment manufacturing firms in Manhattan was cut in half, from 10,329 to 5,096, and tens of thousands of jobs were lost. The trend continued after the mobsters' influence on the district had been purged; by 1996, the city had only 72,000 workers in the apparel industry overall, less than half the workforce of the 1950s.

Sidewalk Catwalk, a public art event held in 2010 featuring thirty mannequins, creatively interpreted by American designers; this one by Norma Kamali. Branding the Fashion District has become increasingly important to the city's identity as a centre of creative industries. Photo: Richard Devine/Alamy.

Meanwhile, New York City has become increasingly aware of the importance of the fashion industry to the city's image. The catwalk shows and associated events of Fashion Weeks have become critical to reinforcing the city's claims to cosmopolitan 'world city' status. They bring together a diverse range of interests and specializations – event organizers, fashion designers, fashion retailers and wholesalers, clothing manufacturers, textile makers and designers, the fashion media, as well as cosmetics, personal care and hospitality services, and other specialized fashion intermediaries. In doing so, they add momentum to the creation and capture of value through circuits of capital that pivot not only around the garment industry but also luxury consumables, media products, design services and real estate. Retaining a manufacturing base for the industry has also been recognized as important: without production in the garment district, there would be no reason for designers and suppliers to cluster there, where they can walk to sample rooms, visit pattern makers, and drop in on factories to oversee production quality.

Since 1987 the city has protected the district through special zoning that restricts landlords from converting factory space to offices and budget hotels, both of which command higher rents than garment workshops. In 1993 a Business Improvement District (BID) was established as a nonprofit public-private partnership to promote the positive development of the district. The garment district was rebranded as the Fashion District, replete with a Fashion Center Information Kiosk and a Fashion Walk of Fame on 7th Avenue. The district is still home to the majority of New York's major fashion labels and their showrooms and still caters to all aspects of the fashion process – from design and production to wholesale selling. In addition to apparel manufacturers and contractors, several thousand fashion-related businesses operate

The district's distinctive architecture combines heavy massing, elaborate detail, and functional street-level loading bays.

Garment worker statue on 7th Avenue, commissioned from the sculptor Judith Weller by the International Ladies Garment Workers Union in 1984. Photo: Ambient Images/Alamy.

Garment manufacturing lofts on West 35th Street, in the heart of the garment district, now rebranded as the Fashion District.

Economic stress. Workers in the garment industry and their supporters rally in October 2009 to prevent the rezoning of the district. Photo: Frances Roberts/Alamy.

there, including textile suppliers, purchasing offices, forecasting services, trade publications, and fashion design schools, as well as a variety of legal, financial, and supply services. Much of the distinctiveness of the district derives from the clustering of specialty retailers and wholesalers. There is one shop that only sells feathers; others specialize in thread, zippers, tools, shoulder pads, lace cloth, sequins, appliqués, artificial flowers, specialty bridal headpieces, Czech beads, Chinese silk brocades, or French silk ribbons.

Nevertheless, manufacturing has continued to decline at the same pace as before the special zoning legislation of 1987. Where there used to be scores of small factories specializing in decorative stitching, there are now only four. Factories that used to do all the work for a designer now produce a single sample, to be shipped to China where the apparel can be produced cheaply. As production has moved abroad, the district has evolved into a more of a design centre than it had ever been. Architects, artists, graphic designers, small theatre companies, technology firms, and not-for-profit arts organizations have moved in, drawn by the district's prime location and the relatively cheap rents of its large, loftlike spaces. They, in turn, have attracted new restaurants and retail tenants; overall, the district is now divided equally between fashion and nonfashion tenants.

Further reading on the Fashion District

Montero, Gabriel, 'A Stitch in Time. A History of New York's Fashion District', New York: Fashion Center Business Improvement District. Online at fashioncenter.com. *A good summary of the history of the district, commissioned by the Fashion Center Business Improvement District.*

Rantisi, Norma, 'How New York Stole Modern Fashion', *Fashion's World Cities*, ed. C. Breward and D. Gilbert, Oxford: Berg, 2006, 109–22. *The author astutely explores the intricate network of diverse suppliers and firms that collaborate within the tightly knit economy of the Fashion District.*

Forest Hills Gardens
New York

Forest Hills Gardens is a pioneering commuter suburb in Queens, twenty minutes from downtown Manhattan by rail. The district was designed in 1909 by landscape architect Frederick Law Olmsted Jr. and architect Grosvenor Atterbury, inspired by English garden cities and conducted as an experiment in applying the new 'science' of city planning to a suburban setting. The suburb still exists today, relatively unchanged and distinguished by an arcadian ambience, striking architectural detail, and a durable sense of place.

At the turn of the twentieth century, America's expanding middle class began to have an increasing influence on the country's cities. In addition to the suburbanization of the middle classes that had been unleashed by railways and streetcar systems, the politics and ideals of the middle classes made their presence felt on the city as a whole in a number of ways. These included scientific reform, professionalism, voluntarism, and private philanthropy, but above all it was the politics of the Progressive Era (1895–1920) that framed and channelled the middle-class vision of urban America. Progressive Era politics pivoted around reform movements aimed at reducing corruption, ridding urban governance of machine politics, and creating healthier and more efficient places for all. The intellectuals of the period emphasized the moral superiority of domesticity and the virtues of sanitary reform.

This led to the widespread acceptance of a vision of 'restorative utopias' – ideal suburban settings that combined the morality attributed to Nature with the enriching and refining influences of cultural, political, and social institutions. The Arts and Crafts movement, at its peak between 1880 and 1910 and based on a romantic idealization of preindustrial crafts, was an important aspect of the arts during the Progressive Era. Progressive intellectuals advocated a programme of 'popular refinement' involving the creation of a whole series of institutions and settings such as public libraries, galleries, museums, and parks, in order to bring out the best in 'ordinary' people.

Meanwhile, the ideals of America's architectural *avant-garde* fused with the reformist ideology of the Progressive Era, giving rise to the City Beautiful movement, an explicit and rather authoritarian attempt to create moral and social order in the face of urbanization processes that seemed to threaten disorder and instability. The thrust of the movement was decisively toward the role of the built environment as an uplifting and civilizing influence. The preferred architectural styles and motifs were drawn from the classic and vernacular palette of northwestern European cities, thus helping to legitimize America's Anglo-Saxon ruling classes and institutions at a time of massive immigration and profound socioeconomic change.

Forest Hills Gardens was a product of all of these elements. Its financiers and designers hoped to demonstrate both the practicality and the profitability of good design and comprehensive planning. They believed that the primary

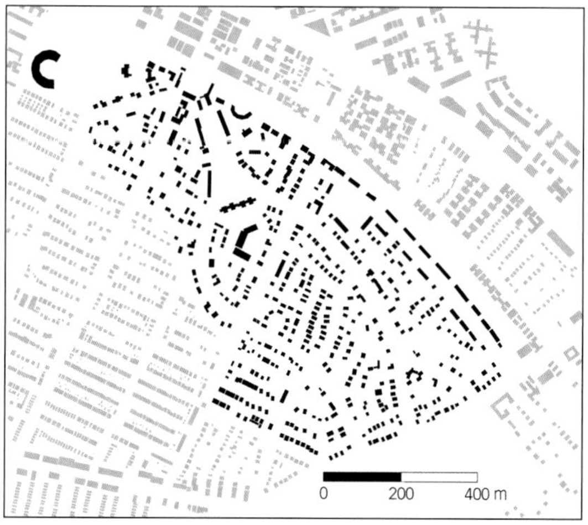

Figure-ground diagram of Forest Hills Gardens. Note the contrast with the gridded street pattern on either side of the district.

Mock-Tudor residence. The Anglo-Saxon architectural styling of Forest Hills Gardens was an important dimension of its commercial success at a time of unprecedented demographic change in America.

importance of the project was educational, as a demonstration that would set a new national standard for design and development for suburban subdivisions. The sponsor of the project was the New York-based Russell Sage Foundation, established in 1907 with a $10 million endowment from the widow of financier Russell Sage. The foundation's lawyer, Robert de Forest, was an important influence on its philanthropic focus: social betterment through improved living conditions.

Within two years of the creation of the foundation, de Forest had purchased a 57-hectare parcel of land from developer Cord Meyer. Meyer had acquired a large tract in Queens adjacent to the route of the newly electrified Long Island Rail Road. His own development was a conventional gridded residential tract of upper-middle-class residences, which he named Forest Hills in reference to Forest Park, a 216-hectare public park nearby.

The Sage Foundation's goal for its planned development, Forest Hills Gardens, was to show that it was possible to make money on an attractive suburb, intelligently designed according to the most modern town planning principles, and so spur private developers like Meyer to imitate and extend the experiment. In fact, the foundation was to lose $360,800 on its investment. Nevertheless, the design of Forest Hills Gardens was to prove highly influential. On behalf of the foundation, de Forest acquired the services of landscape architect Frederick Law Olmsted Jr. and architect Grosvenor Atterbury, both of whom fervently believed that design could be a tool for solving social problems.

Olmsted designed Forest Hills Gardens to a pedestrian scale, assuming that residents

Teutonic massing and mock-Tudor styling in the central apartment block (formerly an hotel, designed by Grosvenor Atterbury) that faces the railway station. The building and its immediate neighbours are connected to the station by enclosed passages at the second-storey level.

would use the railway in order to commute to Manhattan and to access its amenities. The corollary of this was the design of Station Square – a brick plaza below the railway platform embankment – as the grand entrance to the district. The rest of the district was laid out to a modified grid plan that followed the natural contours of the land. In keeping with the sensibilities of the time, Atterbury's architecture was a rather kitschy mix of styles and features, evoking associations with medieval European university and cathedral towns. Atterbury aspired to an Arts and Crafts flavour, deploying preindustrial features such as arched entryways, Tudor half-timbering, complex rooflines, prominent chimneys, and second-storey overhangs. The unifying signature element of the district was a reddish-brown terra cotta roof tile. The overall effect was a heavy Teutonic appearance, softened a generation later by the mature landscaping that had been designed by Olmsted.

One of the first to move in to Forest Hills Gardens in 1912 was Clarence Perry, a planning theorist and community activist. Inspired by the feel of the district and by the distinctive neighbourhood structure designed by Olmsted, Perry developed a conviction that the layout of a project could, if handled correctly, foster 'neighbourhood spirit'. All very well, perhaps, in an exclusive district like Forest Hills Gardens.

Perry subsequently developed the widely influential concept of the 'neighbourhood unit', defined by the catchment area of an elementary school, focused on a central community space, and bounded by arterial streets wide enough to handle through-traffic. Somewhat of a reactionary, Perry saw the neighbourhood unit as an opportunity for social engineering that would assist in nation building and the assimilation

Clockwise, from top left: **Forest Hills Station**, still an important commuter stop; **apartment buildings** with bizarre half-timbered upper storey; **single-family residences**: perhaps not quite what might have been expected as a result of a philanthropic Trust's attempt at 'social betterment through improved living conditions'.

of immigrants: the idea of 'neighbourhood spirit' also went down well with communitarians, while the idea of handling traffic went down well with planners who were beginning to grapple with the implications of the spread of automobile ownership.

By the time it was completely built out in the 1920s, Forest Hills Gardens consisted of almost 900 townhouses and free-standing homes, along with 11 apartment buildings, a few churches, a community centre, and the West Side Tennis Club (home to the U.S. Open tennis tournament until 1977), covering an area about 14 blocks long and 8 wide at its widest point.

Today the district houses some 4,500 residents. It looks almost exactly like the original renderings of Olmsted's and Atterbury's 1909 plan, thanks in large measure to the Forest Hills Gardens Corporation, which oversees street paving, sidewalks, security, parking, and landscaping. The corporation is responsible for enforcing the covenants that new owners must sign when buying property, which prevent exterior alterations without express approval. The outcome is a quiet and sequestered but rather snooty and self-consciously upscale district with a distinctive architecture and richly planted landscape.

Further reading on Forest Hills Gardens

Klaus, Susan, *A Modern Arcadia. Frederick Law Olmsted Jr. and the Plan for Forest Hills Gardens*, Boston: University of Amherst Press, 2002. *A carefully researched and nicely illustrated account of the origins of the development and the collaboration between architect Grosvenor Atterbury and landscape architect Frederick Law Olmsted Jr.*

The Ghetto Venezia

The Jewish ghetto in Venice evolved in response to a combination of discrimination, social segregation, religious sensibilities, and commercial needs. Developed on the site of an old foundry (*getto* in Venetian dialect), at a time when Venice was a major world city, its name has become synonymous with districts of segregated ethnic minorities in cities everywhere. The Venetian ghetto was populated by Jews who had been driven from cities across Europe and the Levant by persecution, and who were drawn to Venice by its wealth and commercial vitality. Italian- and French-speaking Jews were joined by Yiddish-speaking Ashkenazim, Spanish- and Portuguese-speaking Sephardim, and, later, by Levantine Jews, creating a distinctive community within a unique city.

The spatial isolation of Jewish communities in European cities was common long before the creation of the Venetian ghetto. Since medieval times, Jews in many parts of Europe had settled in separate streets or quarters. In some cases these districts had been walled off, but this was a defensive rather than an exclusionary arrangement and it was the Jews themselves who controlled entry into their area. Gradually, however, the nature of these Jewish quarters began to change as western Christendom became more insistent on enforcing the exclusion of Jews. The Christian leadership of Venice developed the same exclusionary impulse but it was tempered by recognition of the importance of Jewish bankers and traders to the city's economy. The compromise was to set aside a specific area for Jews.

In 1516 the Venetian ruling council designated the *ghetto nuovo* as the site for the Jewish enclave. It had been an arms foundry district under the administration of a military institution until the end of the fourteenth century. Located as it was on the northern periphery of the city, the *ghetto nuovo* was not especially valuable real estate. The buildings there, set around a large central courtyard and surrounded completely by water, already resembled a walled fortress, and only minor changes were needed to create a block of apartments with only a single entrance, via a small wooden bridge and a narrow *sotopòrtego* (passageway). Jews were allowed only to operate pawn shops, lend money, trade in textiles, and practice medicine, and the gate to the ghetto was locked at night. Nevertheless, the Jewish community prospered, and Jews received better treatment there than in many other European cities at the time.

Population growth, confined to the *ghetto nuovo*, resulted in intense overcrowding. Ground-floor apartments were usually given over to shops, warehouses, or pawnbrokers, but apartments on upper floors were soon subdivided to make room for more tenants. In many cases these divisions were accomplished

Figure-ground diagram of the ghetto district.

horizontally by inserting new flooring halfway between the original floor and ceiling. If the new apartments were dark, extra windows could be cut. The result was a distinctively irregular pattern of fenestration that can still be seen today, even though some of the windows have been bricked up. Another common method of coping with overcrowding was to construct additional floors on top of existing buildings. As a result, the ghetto developed a distinctive element of form: 'skyscrapers' of seven or nine storeys.

Synagogues (known in Venice as *schole*, partly because their function in some ways resembled that of the Christian *scuole* as places of devotion, learning, and charity) were installed on the topmost floors: it is of fundamental ritual importance that those in the *beth-ha-knesset*, the meeting and prayer room of the synagogue, should be able to see the sky and the stars. The Schola Grande Tedesca (1528–1529) and the Schola Canton (1531–1532) were built by central European Ashkenazim, the first group to settle in the ghetto. The Schola Italiana was added in 1571 by the growing Italiani Jewish community. All three synagogues were connected by a system of internal passageways that still exists.

Soon another group of Jews began making their way to Venice. These were Levantines, merchants who brought the spices, raw silk, hides, and currants of the East to the quays of Venice. In 1541, as part of a general move to foster this trade, the Venetian government conceded additional space to the Jewish community: the 'old foundry' or *ghetto vecchio*, which was adjacent to the existing Jewish quarter and linked by a little bridge on the Rio degli Agudi. Walls were built around the new addition to the district and windows facing the outside were walled up, as were any doors of neighbouring Christians that opened on to the ghetto. By the end of the sixteenth century the Jewish population had reached 2,000 or more. Pressure from

The Campo del Ghetto Nuovo in late afternoon. The campo provides an important space for social interaction among community members. Originally, all of the windows of the houses in the *ghetto nuovo* faced this unique focal point.

The Schola Canton, built in the 1530s by central European Ashkenazim, the first group to settle in the ghetto, many of them from Provence, France.

Footbridge across the Rio del Ghetto Nuovo, giving access to the *ghetto nuovo* from the *ghetto nuovissimo*.

Opposite: 'Skyscraper' development around the Campo. Beneath the campo, as elsewhere in Venice, is a cistern, or *pozzo*, that traps and stores fresh water for local consumption.

more affluent Jewish merchants led to the concession in 1663 of additional space, the *ghetto nuovissimo*, just to the east of the *ghetto nuovo* on the south side of the Rio di San Girolamo. Within the Jewish community, synagogues became a primary focus of ethnic identity and rivalry. Nine of them were built, each expressing one or another group's intense need to assert its identity through architecture and architectural adornment. In the *ghetto vecchio*, the Schola Levantina (1683–1700) and Schola Spagnola (1660) were baroque showpieces of the Levantine merchants who practiced the Sephardic rite.

The physical appearance of the district has changed little since the seventeenth century, although the ghetto gates were demolished when Napoleon occupied Venice in 1797, and in the 1830s a group of houses bordering the Rio di San Girolamo in the Campo Ghetto Nuovo was pulled down. The precipitous decline of Venice as a trading centre in the nineteenth century prompted a significant decline in the population of the ghetto and its consequent neglect and decay. Today the district is remarkably ordinary, insofar as anywhere in Venice can be described as ordinary. The Jewish Museum, along with a souvenir shop, a kosher restaurant, a kosher bakery, and a kosher snack bar, serve as reminders of the district's history and draw a steady stream of visitors. A hint of incipient gentrification is provided by several art galleries, two bookstores, and a couple of jewellery studios, but the overall affect of the district is humdrum. The fabric of the district suffers from a slightly

Rear facade of the *ghetto nuovo*, bordering the Rio del Ghetto Nuovo.

A gondolier waits on the bridge leading to the Campo del Ghetto Nuovo from the Calle del Ghetto Vecchio.

more advanced form of the 'noble rot' that has set in across the city. The heart of the district is still the Campo Nuovo, an unusually large open space for Venice. Sequestered to a degree from the city's relentless flow of tourists, it has its own distinctive rhythm. It is at its quietest late in the evenings and in the mornings when it is crisscrossed by housewives en route to and from the shops and markets of the Cannaregio. By afternoon, mothers with infants in strollers take advantage of the open space, and by late afternoon the Campo becomes a vibrant playground, filled with a mixture of after-school children playing football and riding bicycles, returning workers exercising dogs that have been cooped up all day in small apartments, and others stopping to chat en route to an aperitivo before returning home.

Further reading on the Venetian Ghetto

Curiel, Roberta, and Cooperman, Bernard Dov, *The Venetian Ghetto,* New York: Rizzoli, 1990. *An illustrated history of the district.*

Sullam, Anna-Vera, and Calimani, Riccardo, *The Venetian Ghetto,* Milan: Mondadori Electa, 2005. *An illustrated guide to the development of the district and its synagogues.*

Grands Boulevards Paris

The Grands Boulevards district has a strong claim as the cradle of modern consumer society, the place where shopping first became a fashionable activity. In the course of a long history, the district has developed a remarkable set of contrasts, from the exclusive stores of the rue de la Paix (the most expensive street in the Paris version of the Monopoly board game) to the sex shops and peep shows along rue Saint-Denis, and from the carefully preserved apartment buildings around the Opéra to the decaying urban fabric of Le Sentier – a mixture of the chic and the seedy that seems quintessentially Parisian. Threaded through the fabric of the district are the *passages couverts*, or arcades, that revolutionized the experience of shopping and helped to make Paris the epitome of modernity in the nineteenth century.

Situated just to the north of the First Arrondissement and stretching in a long, narrow arc from the Opéra in the west to République in the east, the district is now part of the institutional and commercial core of the metropolis. The boulevards that form the spine of the district were laid out on the site of the city's old ramparts by Louis XIV at the end of the seventeenth century. Once the old walls had been demolished and the ditches filled in, the frontages of the wide carriageway were promptly developed into mansions and pavilions, with a broad sidewalk that attracted strollers.

Over the course of several cycles of property development, the Boulevards acquired a catalogue of Parisian neoclassical architecture, from the regularized massing of the Louis XVI period (1754–1792) through the eclecticism of Empire and Restoration styles in the first quarter of the nineteenth century to the more decorative Italian, French Renaissance, and oriental detailing of the Louis-Philippe era (1830–1848). The Boulevards and their side streets became the setting for a series of innovations of modern city life: the first horse-drawn public omnibus, public urinals, cab ranks, newspaper kiosks, cylindrical advertising columns, gas lighting, covered passages, and cafés with outside seating.

These innovations attracted dandies, journalists, artists, gourmets, and whores, and the café clientele of the west-end Boulevard des Italiens set the trends for all of Paris in terms of manners, dress, and conversation. A new social type also emerged: the *flâneur*, a bourgeois male observer of the patterns and rhythms of city life. The *flâneur* sought out the sights of the city and its tumultuous crowd, on the lookout for the new, exciting, and unfamiliar; window-shopping, wanting to see and be seen, while seemingly remaining aloof and detached.

The first *passages* were built in the late eighteenth century by landlords who wanted to augment their income by exploiting the space within the blocks they owned. In opening up the arcades, developers took advantage of new materials like plate glass and the new cast iron and steel construction techniques that embodied modern progress. With its compact arrangement of diverse retail establishments, the

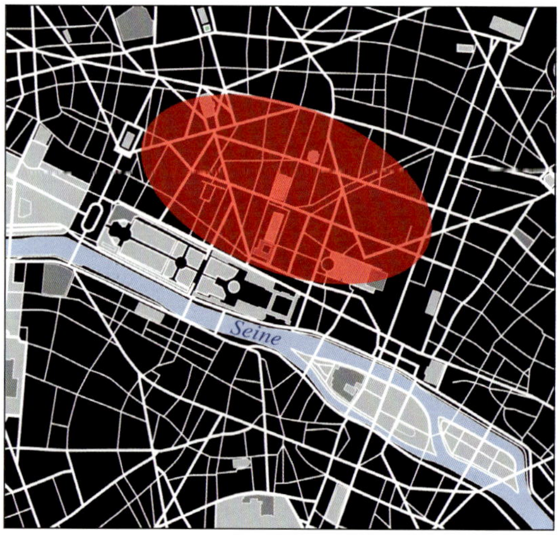

The Grands Boulevards district occupies a densely built-up section of central Paris on the right bank of the River Seine.

Les Grands Boulevards, painted in 1888 by Luigi Loir. Courtesy of the Athenaeum, <http://www.the-athenaeum.org/>.

passage was a new way to display and sell the mass-produced merchandise that was increasingly available in an age of industrialization, along with wave after wave of new commodities from colonial exploitation. Protected from the weather by glass roofs, window shoppers were attracted by a variety of merchants, specialty stores, and exhibitions. Equally important, the *passages* gave bourgeois women a public space that was acceptable for them to occupy – in the daytime, at least. Glowing and magical at night with gaslight, the atmosphere in many *passages* changed, with the covered spaces offering shelter to strolling prostitutes and their customers.

Altogether, some 150 *passages* were built in Paris during the first half of the nineteenth century, the majority of them in the Grands Boulevards district. A few of them specialized in a single commodity, such as fish in the Passage du Saumon and lithographs in Passage du Caire, but most housed a mix of milliners, hosiers, haberdashers, tailors, bookshops, bootmakers, wine merchants, caricaturists, print shops, and cafés.

By mid-century, ambitious developers in several European cities had expanded the scale of the idea of the *passage* to the galleria, a spacious indoor court rather than a narrow passageway. But by the end of the nineteenth century both had been superseded by the department store: larger, more spectacular, and more respectable, with no dubious nightlife to contend with. In Paris, the Printemps department store was founded in 1865 and the Galeries Lafayette in 1893, both located on Boulevard Haussmann. Department stores provided the setting for the rapidly expanding middle class to stake out its cultural identity. Hence the grandly designed halls and the ostentatiously snooty service staff of the department stores – all designed to connote a superior ambience. The introduction of electric lighting allowed for even more dazzling store displays, while the introduction of electric

Galerie Véro-Dodat, restored in the 1980s after a century of neglect. One of the first Parisian *passages* to have gas lighting. Its shops sell a classic mixture of antiques, *objets d'art*, art books, and fashion accessories, but its arcades are nevertheless often deserted.

Opposite: Parisian café at the junction of rue Montorgueil and rue Rambuteau.

street lighting made entire shopping districts much safer and more attractive.

Today, fewer than twenty *passages* remain, most of them having been destroyed between 1853 and 1870 to make way for the modernization and redevelopment of the Parisian street system under the supervision of Baron Haussmann. The surviving *passages*, after

La Pointe Saint Eustache
Buffet Poilane — Café — Brasserie — Vins de Pays
JET LAG
Brasserie

Rue Montorgueil, at the eastern end of the district, was the oyster market of the old *halles*. Today it has a mixture of fresh food stores, cafés, and bars that draws both locals and tourists.

Au Rocher de Cancale café-restaurant on rue Montorgueil has changed little since it opened in 1846. The menu still includes oysters from Cancale, in Brittany.

Sunday flea market on the Place de la Bourse.

Rag trade accessories in the Passage du Caire, the oldest (1798) of all the *passages*, now somewhat run-down. Its proximity to the Sentier has resulted in its being colonized by shops specializing in fabric and rag-trade accessories such as mannequins, busts, and clothes racks.

decades of slow decay, have been rediscovered and as a result, some, like the Galerie Vivienne, have been renovated and restored to something approaching their former glory, colonized by chic boutiques and cafés.

The streets off the western end of the Grands Boulevards constitute the heart of the city's main commercial and financial district, with the Banque de France and the Bourse (stock exchange), the flagship department stores, five-star hotels, and the exclusive premises of top couturiers, jewellers, global-brand specialized luxury stores, and art dealers.

At the other end of the district is the more relaxed and everyday commerce of produce, meat, and fish markets; the fashionable mixture of cafés, patisseries, bistros, boutiques, and bars in the area around the pedestrianised rue Montorgueil; and the traditional heart of the city's sex trade, along the former royal processional route of rue Saint-Denis.

In between, the streets are dominated by the peeling buildings of small prêt-à-porter women's fashion manufacturers and the fabric and haberdashery wholesalers of the Sentier area. The development of the textile industry here dates from the eighteenth century, and it led to the construction of a particular kind of building – tall and high-density, with a neoclassical vocabulary for the facades. The same building had to house the shop, the warehouse on the courtyard, the production workshops on the upper floors, as well as family accommodation.

Today the rag trade labour force is dominated by Turkish, Serb, Bangladeshi, Senegalese, and Malian immigrants, often undocumented. The warren of streets that constitute the Sentier is difficult to enter, physically isolated, socially removed, and little visited, but it nevertheless forms an important component of the commercial life of the Grands Boulevards.

Further reading on Grands Boulevards

de Moncan, Patrice, *Les Grands Boulevards de Paris*, Paris: Du Mecene, 2002. *A standard history of the district (in French).*

Grive, Catherine, *Passages Couverts de Paris*, Paris: Editions Déclics, 2009. *Beautifully photographed documentation of the surviving passages in Paris (in French).*

Schwartz, Vanessa, *Spectacular Realities: Early Mass Culture in Fin-de-Siecle Paris*, Berkeley: University of California Press, 1999. *Describes the emergence of Paris and the Grands Boulevards as a setting for spectacle and consumption.*

Sutcliffe, Anthony, *Paris: An Architectural History*, New Haven: Yale University Press, 1996. *A book that summarizes the architectural development of Paris in the context of its urban and political history.*

Greenbelt Maryland

Greenbelt was a product of the New Deal social experiments that followed the Great Depression of the 1930s. A rare example of centralized urban planning in the United States, it was as aimed at generating jobs and providing affordable housing in a declining national economy as much as it was an attempt to create a better urban community. It was, nevertheless, strongly influenced by the ideals of the Regional Planning Association of America and, as a result, it was a singularly progressive new town. In spite of the deep conservatism of postwar America and the pressures of metropolitan development in the surrounding Washington-Baltimore region, it successfully evolved from a federally managed experiment to a self-directed and highly engaged community.

In response to the Great Depression that began in 1929, President Roosevelt's Federal Housing Administration (FHA) played a key role in stimulating the labour-intensive construction industry by stabilizing the mortgage market and facilitating sound home financing on reasonable terms. Optimistic New Deal administrators saw a further opportunity: to plan urban development through the creation of new towns. Rexford Guy Tugwell, appointed by Roosevelt as head of the Resettlement Administration, envisaged hundreds of 'greenbelt' towns that would contain government-sponsored, low-cost housing, and promptly drew up a list of nineteen towns on which to start. Funds were allocated for only eight, however, and Congress, under strong pressure from the private development industry, whittled this number down to five. Two of the five were blocked by local legal action. The remaining three were built: Greendale, southwest of Milwaukee; Greenhills, near Cincinnati; and Greenbelt, just north of Washington, D.C. A small initiative in the larger framework of New Deal policies and programmes, the greenbelt town experiment was one of Roosevelt's most radical efforts to involve the federal government in urban community development.

Tugwell called on architect/planner Clarence Stein to prepare design guidelines and to serve as the principal planning consultant for Greenbelt. Stein was a proponent of the garden city movement and an influential member of the Regional Planning Association of America (RPAA), formed in 1923 as an association of reform-minded individuals. The RPAA's intellectual roots were distinctly radical for the time, fusing the restorative gospel of the garden city movement with the social engineering ideals of the City Beautiful movement.

From the beginning, Greenbelt was designed as a complete town, with businesses, schools, roads, and facilities for recreation and town government, as well as affordable housing. The layout incorporated Clarence Perry's 'neighbourhood unit' concept, articulated by the catchment area of an elementary school, focused on the school itself, local stores, and a central community space, and bounded by arterial streets wide enough to handle through-traffic. Thus the town's two curving major streets were laid out upon and below a crescent-shaped natural ridge. Shops, school, playing fields, and community buildings were grouped at the centre

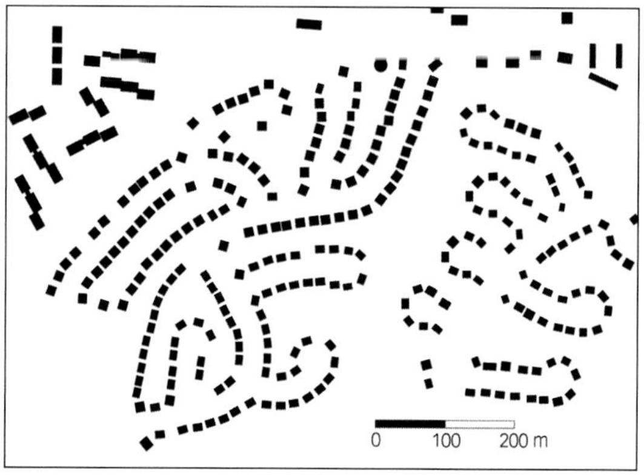

Figure-ground diagram of part of Greenbelt. The curvilinear morphology is based on the district's topography.

of this crescent. Homes, mostly row houses and apartments, were grouped in superblocks, with a system of interior walkways and underpasses permitting residents to go from home to town centre without crossing a major street. All of this was surrounded by a greenbelt of parkland 800 m wide. The town's architecture was heavily influenced by the Art Deco style, with curving lines and glass-brick inserts in the facades of apartment buildings.

Greenbelt was also a social experiment, its population of 3,500 intended to be drawn entirely from low-income households. But because of mounting costs only moderate-income families were admitted when it opened in 1937. More than 5,000 families had applied for the original 885 residences. The successful ones were selected not only because they met income criteria, but also because they were able to demonstrate positive attitudes toward community life and showed an inclination to participate in civic affairs. The FHA was by no means singularly progressive, however. In its 1939 Underwriting Manual the FHA openly recommended that subdivision developers use restrictive covenants to prevent the sale of homes to minorities. It was not until 1949 that discriminatory restrictive covenants were declared unconstitutional. Meanwhile, Greenbelt had more than doubled in size after the Federal Public Housing Administration (FPHA) had located defence-industry housing there.

Greenbelt was distinctly progressive, however, in its residents' appetite for self-governance

Apartment buildings, Crescent Road, featuring glass brick inserts in the facades and wrap-around corner windows, both signature elements of Art Deco style. Photo by Andrew Bossi, used under a creative commons Attribution-Share Alike License at Wikimedia Commons.

Generous amounts of green space between superblocks have come into their own as the district's trees have matured.

Pedestrian underpass in the town centre.

Bas relief sculpture on Greenbelt Community Center, considered one of the best Art Deco style buildings in the United States.

and cooperative institutions. A town government was formed in the first year of operation, along with a citizens' association and a journalism club that developed into a cooperative local newspaper. The latter has proven to be crucial in maintaining Greenbelt's original goals and ideology and in engendering a sense of place and loyalty to the town. Filled with community news, reported and researched by Greenbelt residents, the *Greenbelt News Review* is delivered free to every household, every week. The concept of community as a cooperative endeavour was institutionalized through Greenbelt Consumer Services, Inc., which operated a cooperative food store, petrol station, drug store, barber shop, cinema, valet shop, beauty parlour, general store, and tobacco shop. Residents also formed a cooperative baby-sitting pool, a cooperative nursery school, a cooperative kindergarten, and a cooperative building society.

Not surprisingly, Greenbelt ran rudely against the grain of American conservatism. The Washington press was scathing in its

Row housing. In anticipation of World War II, the federal government developed 1,000 new units of row housing for defence workers. These houses were developed into a neighbourhood unit of superblocks with curving, picturesque streets.

Apartment buildings. The International-style apartments in Greenbelt, with flat roofs and concrete structure, were at the leading edge of architectural design, and ideologically consistent with Roosevelt-era social democracy.

depiction of the town and its goals, while developers in the region saw it as a dangerous precedent. A row over the efforts of one developer to intimidate the town into acceding to his development proposals went all the way to the U.S. Supreme Court (and was resolved in favour of the town's cooperative newspaper). It did not take long before the U.S. Congress voted to sell off the three greenbelt towns to private ownership. Thanks in large measure to the efforts of Clarence Stein, Greenbelt itself was sold not to a private developer but to a homeowners' cooperative (Greenbelt Veterans Housing Corporation, later Greenbelt Homes, Inc.).

By the mid 1960s, Greenbelt found itself hemmed in and partially bisected by the intersection of the Capital Beltway and the Baltimore-Washington Parkway. Greenbelt was now highly accessible within a rapidly growing metropolitan region. As a result, the town came under a great deal of pressure for residential and commercial development. The Greenbelt homeowners' cooperative ran into financial difficulties and was forced to sell several large parcels of land to private developers. The core of the town has been protected from the encroachment of private development and redevelopment, however. In 1997, when Greenbelt celebrated its sixtieth anniversary, the U.S. Department of Interior recognized Historic Greenbelt as a National Historic Landmark. Today, the town is much more diverse demographically – about 25 per cent of the residents in the original residential area are African American – and it retains a strong sense of community along with many of its original cooperatives, including the grocery store.

Further reading on Greenbelt

Arnold, Joseph, *The New Deal in the Suburbs: A History of the Greenbelt Town Program, 1935–1954*, Columbus: Ohio State University Press, 1971. *A comprehensive history of the origins of the new town programme of the Resettlement Administration.*

City of Greenbelt, *History of Greenbelt* <http://www.greenbeltmd.gov/about_greenbelt/history.htm> *Provides a summary of the development of the district.*

Parsons, K. C., 'Clarence Stein and the Greenbelt Towns', *Journal of the American Planning Association* 56.2 (1990), 161–84. *A lengthy article on the influence of Clarence Stein on Greenbelt and other New Deal initiatives.*

Hollywood
Los Angeles

For many people throughout the world, Hollywood has long symbolized glamour, celebrity, and hedonism. Yet the reality of the district is such that it has always been multifaceted. It has also experienced significant changes in its physical and social make-up in response to the changing dynamics of the motion picture and television industries, the cycle of neighbourhood obsolescence and reinvestment, and the movement of different demographic groups in and out of the district.

The glamour, celebrity, and hedonism associated with the district derive, of course, from the motion picture industry. Before the arrival of the industry in Hollywood, the district was an independent suburban township, unexceptional and somewhat remote from the emerging metropolitan economy that was Los Angeles. Things changed radically between 1907 and 1915 as the nascent motion picture industry, based in the northeast of the country, discovered the virtues of Southern California: a variety of landscapes, a warm sunny climate, and plenty of relatively cheap land for the increasingly space-intensive sound stages and back lots. By 1915 there were more than a dozen production companies in Hollywood, including the Famous Players and the Lasky Company, whose merger in 1916 became the forerunner of Paramount, the district's first major studio.

By 1919, 80 per cent of the world's motion pictures were being made in California, most of them in a loosely defined Hollywood that was already extending beyond the core of the district (which extended a couple of miles either side of the now-famous junction of Hollywood Boulevard and Vine Street). The 1920s and 1930s were the Golden Age of the Hollywood movie industry. It was established as a prototypical industrial district, tightly bound by an agglomerative logic among the studios and their ancillary trades and services. The major studios were each vertically integrated enterprises across production, distribution, and exhibition. It also brought glamorous events and drew affluent residents to the hilly northern and northwestern fringes of the district. Low-wage service workers, meanwhile, were relegated to the flatlands to the south and east of the district.

After World War II the basis of Hollywood as an industrial district changed significantly. The advent of television drained off the traditional audiences of the major studios, while a high court antitrust decision forced the major studios to divest themselves of their extensive chains of cinemas. The old system was replaced by a more complex and diffuse agglomeration of film and television studios, together with firms specializing in set design and construction, props supplies, digital visual effects, and so on. Several major studios relocated across the Hollywood Hills to Burbank, creating an extended geography of 'Hollywood' that was home to the entertainment industries' key institutions and agencies, along with their workforce of actors, writers, costume designers, set

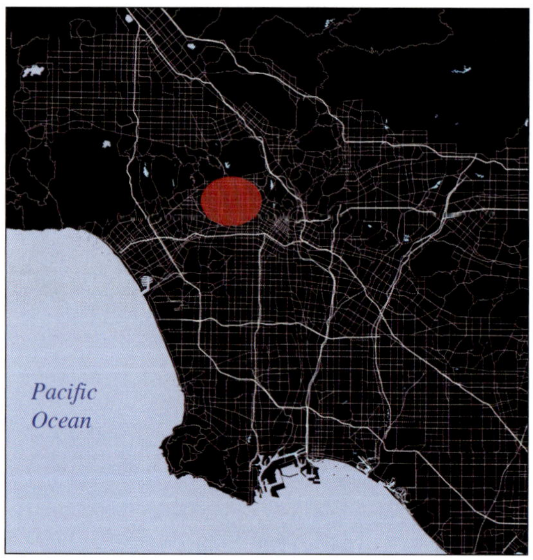

Hollywood is located in north-central Los Angeles, bounded to the north by the Hollywood Hills.

designers, camera technicians, sound engineers, casting directors, and so on.

Meanwhile, in Hollywood proper, the cheap housing of the flatlands had fallen into decay and the district came to be characterized by crime, gang violence, graffiti, and infestations of rats and roaches. The affluent Hollywood hillside communities resorted to walls, gates, security cameras, and 'armed response' placards on their lawns in an attempt to distance themselves from the troubled flatlands. The glittering popular image of the district was only maintained:

... by a calendar of ritual (premieres, the Academy Awards, footprint ceremonies) and the magical investment of a dozen or so locations (the [Hollywood] Bowl, Grauman's Chinese and Egyptian Theaters, Musso and Franks, the corner of Hollywood and Vine) as tourist shrines.

Mike Davis, *Ecology of Fear*. New York: Henry Holt, 1998, p. 395

In the 1980s, major Hollywood landowners won approval from the Los Angeles city council for a $1 billion facelift. In their plan, authored by architect Jon Jerde, Hollywood Boulevard would be transformed into a gated theme park, anchored at each end by entertainment megacomplexes. Poor surrounding neighbourhoods would be kept at arm's length from the Boulevard until they were gentrified or torn down. But before sufficient investment could be secured, the project was usurped by Universal,

Affluent Hollywood. A classic view of the famous sign. Photo by Joseph Plotz, used under a creative commons Attribution-Share Alike License at Wikimedia Commons.

who hired Jerde to design CityWalk, an ersatz urban fragment that links the Universal City parking lot to the entrance to Universal's studio tour. CityWalk – essentially an outdoor shopping mall, postmodern style – incorporates some of the iconic features of Hollywood glamour along with various examples of Southern California architecture and a lot of over-the-top signage. A giant guitar stands in front of the Hard Rock Café, and a huge King Kong hangs from one of the buildings.

Back in Hollywood itself, a combination of neighbourhood watch groups and intensified policing (and the consequent jailing of senior gang leaders) helped to clean up the district, prompting a certain amount of gentrification. New investment brought several new mixed-occupancy high-rise lofts and condominium buildings, while the powerful symbolic capital embodied in the district's name and its landmarks helped to ensure additional investment in tourist attractions and high-end consumption. Nevertheless, Hollywood today remains multifaceted, with a broad spectrum of housing and sociocultural groups and a streetscape punctuated by many striking juxtapositions: neighbourhood parks in which children play while homeless people sleep; upscale restaurants next to decaying buildings; and the very visible presence of police on Hollywood Boulevard and Sunset Strip.

Top: **Sunset Gower Studios**; middle: **Sunset Boulevard**; bottom: **CityWalk**. Photo by Alarhu, released to public domain in Wikimedia Commons.

Further reading on Hollywood

Scott, Allen, *On Hollywood. The Place, The Industry,* Princeton, NJ: Princeton University Press, 2005. *A fine-grained history and analysis of the industrial complex of entertainment industries around which the district has developed.*

Williams, Gregory P., *The Story of Hollywood: An Illustrated History*, Los Angeles: BL Press, 2006. *A carefully researched and profusely illustrated volume that tells the story about how people lived, worked, and made Hollywood one of the most famous districts in the United States.*

Clockwise from top left: **French chateau-style apartments** on Scenic Avenue, low foothills; **Jardinette Apartments**, one of the first Modernist buildings in America, designed in 1927 by Richard Neutra (Photo by 'Los Angeles', used under a creative commons Attribution-Share Alike License at Wikimedia Commons; **The Hollywood Pacific Theatre building** (1928), now converted to a nondenominational church; **Wilcox Avenue**, off Hollywood Boulevard; **Hollywoodland**, a 1920s development that was among the first to attarct movie industry personalities to reside in the district.

Hoxton
London

Like many inner-city districts in large metropolitan areas, Hoxton has gone through a series of transformations in response to structural economic change, to cycles of investment and disinvestment, to its changing situation within the evolving overall framework of the city's infrastructure and spatial organization, and to the movement of different groups of people into and out of the district. In its current phase, it has become widely known as a neobohemian district that is rapidly gentrifying.

In the late seventeenth century Hoxton, just beyond London's city walls, was seen by property developers and London gentry as being far enough away from the dirt and squalor of the city but close enough for a short commute to work. It was duly transformed into a superior sort of district, a phase that is marked by a few surviving Georgian residences and by its formal street pattern featuring Charles Square and Hoxton Square.

The Industrial Revolution brought another transformation. The completion of the Regents Canal in 1820 meant building materials could be shipped into the area quickly and easily, and by the midpoint of the nineteenth century Hoxton had become a working-class district, the centre of the London furniture industry. Workshops and warehouses were surrounded by hastily erected housing for a rapidly increasing population of migrants and immigrants.

By the end of the century, Hoxton had become run-down, its population notorious for poverty and squalor. For much of the twentieth century, despite incremental improvements to infrastructure, the elimination of the worst of the slum housing, and the provision of social housing, Hoxton remained a classic inner-city problem area, its manufacturing base sharply diminished and its population trapped in a cycle of deprivation. Hoxton is still one of the most underprivileged and run-down areas of London, with poor schools, high levels of unemployment, and a built environment dominated by obsolescent and semi-derelict structures. Yet it has famously undergone a double transformation since the mid-1980s as the fickle processes of gentrification have flickered across the landscape.

The trigger for the initial gentrification of Hoxton was that it acquired a neobohemian aspect as aspiring artists and young designers, musicians, and unemployed or entry-level cultural-industry workers found inexpensive live/work spaces in the district's industrial lofts and buildings toward the end of the 1980s. It helped that some of the incomers were key members of a much-heralded new generation of artists led by the likes of Damian Hirst, Rachel Whiteread, Sarah Lucas, and Tracey Emin, and known collectively as Young British Artists (YBA), exponents of BritArt. The streets of Hoxton began to be used for experimental shows and the buzz attracted galleries and dealers. Soon the atmosphere generated around the sociality of the neighbourhood, together with the existence

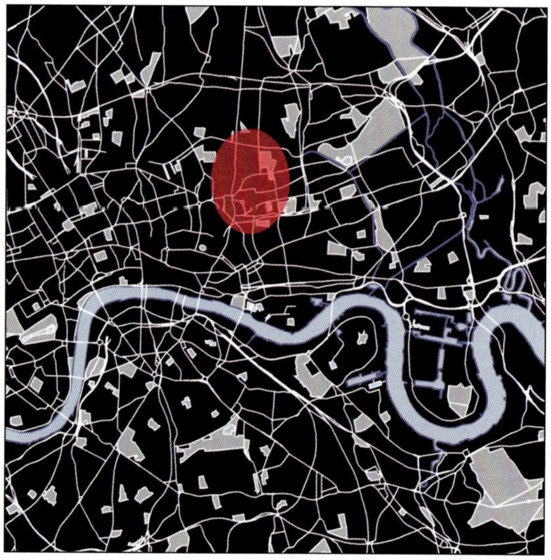

Hoxton is one of London's many inner-city districts that surround the central financial and commercial districts.

of a reserve army of design-oriented workers with economically self-sacrificing dispositions, began to attract an *avant-garde* of graphic design firms, independent music labels and studios, interior design firms, photographic studios and galleries, architecture firms, and new media companies that colonized the old furniture workshops of the district. Disused and obsolescent workshops and warehouses were renovated as offices, galleries, and bookstores/cafés. Loft spaces were renovated as apartments, while as-yet unimproved housing provided cheap accommodation for reinforcements to the reserve army of neobohemians.

Hoxton's neobohemian street atmosphere met important personal identity needs for many artists and design professionals as well as for the image and branding of the firms for which they worked. By moving into a neobohemian scene, designers could signal their radical-progressive commitment to themselves and to others, including clients. They had distinct ideas about what living like a designer should entail, and this in turn influenced the atmosphere of the district. Hoxton's signature identity was fashion rebel: scruffy clothes and daft haircuts. For men, the 'uniform' was vintage Levi jeans paired with T-shirts bearing the names of obscure record labels; the look was completed by a haircut that became known as the Hoxton Fin. The Hoxton-girl look was deliberately trashy, featuring Blondie T-shirts, plastic jewellery, and pixie ankle boots.

Several projects, funded through government inner-city regeneration programmes, helped to reinforce this production-oriented phase of gentrification, including basic refits of warehouses, the remodelling of an old electricity-generating station into Circus Space (large warehouse spaces and studios housing a circus school and flexible and affordable space for artistic companies and corporate clients),

Hoxton: the junction of Old Street and Charlotte Road, in the centre of the district. Photo: Londonstills.com/Alamy.

and a new cinema for the London Film and Video Workshop, the Lux.

Meanwhile, other government policies – fewer controls on development, a reduction in support services for working-class people, and the privatization of the public housing stock – contributed to a gradual displacement of the existing multicultural working-class community. In their place came the pioneer gentrifiers: young creatives of all sorts, attracted by the low rents, the neobohemian affect of the district, and the gritty authenticity of the built environment, with its warehouses and workshops with loading bays and wall cranes for furniture to be hoisted up. Abandoned warehouses began to be converted into lofts and pubs, and clubs, including a pioneering gay club, the London Apprentice, opened around Hoxton Square. The now-famous YBAs socialized a couple of blocks away, in the Bricklayer's Arms on Charlotte Street. Media representations of the district, ignoring its less glamorous aspects and the

The Bricklayer's Arms public house, famous as the preferred watering hole of the Young British Artists (YBA) in the district. Photo: Michael Sparrow/Alamy.

The White Cube art gallery, Hoxton Square.

Leonard Street, where former furniture workshops, built in the 1870s, have been colonized by photography studios, media companies, printers, and commercial artists.

The Comedy Cafe, a bar, restaurant, and comedy club in converted workshop space on Rivington Street.

Gentrified housing in Hoxton Square, now a highly desirable location, no longer affordable by pioneer gentrifiers.

displacement of disadvantaged households, helped to promote Hoxton as the exemplar of an edgy and innovative cultural quarter. *Time Magazine*, for example, referred to Hoxton as one of the 'coolest places on the planet' in 1996. With the advent of Tony Blair's government in 1997, Hoxton was widely trumpeted as an example of New Labour's 'Cool Britannia'.

By the late 1990s the incoming Labour government had put the propagation of creative industries and urban culture at the heart of urban policy, with Hoxton often held up as an example of how inner-city districts could experience an 'urban renaissance'. In Hoxton itself, gentrification was reinforced by the appearance of several key 'cultural incubators', including the prestigious White Cube art gallery, opened in 2000 in a 1920s light industrial building on Hoxton Square and, nearby, the Prince's Drawing School, founded in 2000 by The Prince of Wales. Ultra-cool clubs and celebrity-chef restaurants also began to appear, notably the Shoreditch Electricity Showrooms, the Cantaloupe bar and restaurant, the Cargo club, and Fifteen and the Hoxton Apprentice (both training restaurants under the tutelage of celebrity chefs).

These developments strengthened the reputation of Hoxton as a cultural quarter but made it unaffordable for the neobohemians at the heart of its initial transformation, since most of them never had the capital or the creditworthiness to purchase their property and protect themselves from rent increases. As property prices began to rise, many of the neobohemians and 'cultural proletariat' left for cheaper space farther east, around Brick Lane and, farther still, Dalston and Hackney Wick. In their place has come a more affluent cohort of gentrifiers with the capital and creditworthiness to purchase and renovate loft apartments and to patronize

Social Housing: St Luke's Estate, Peerless Street. Built and managed by the local authority at subsidised rents for low-income households, and now run by a housing association. Many of the households that formerly rented flats from the local authority were able to buy their property when the management of the estate was transferred to the housing association.

an increased number of galleries, upscale cafés, noodle bars, sushi restaurants, and Italian delicatessens. Near enough (just over 1 km) to the expanding fringe of London's banking and financial quarter, Hoxton has also developed an embryonic night-time economy, its restaurants, clubs, and bars catering increasingly to affluent office workers.

As a result, a second transformation has occurred, tipping Hoxton from a district of cultural production to one of cultural consumption, and from an *avant-garde* neobohemia to just another gentrifying district. In addition to the arrival of white-collar gentrifiers, the social mix of the district has been upgraded as local government agencies and nonprofit institutions targeted a new 'worthy poor' of key workers (such as nurses, firemen, and teachers) for their new and refurbished social housing. For example, in the Peabody Trust's Nile Street project, completed in 2005, there are three kinds of affordable homes: rented flats and studios for key workers; flats for Peabody's own tenants; and shared-ownership flats where it is possible to take out a mortgage for some of the value

Hoxton Square, a small public park in what is one of the oldest squares in London. It was laid out in the late seventeenth century.

Social Housing: the Nile Street Peabody Trust building, completed in 2005, provides 175 homes with a communal courtyard, roof gardens, and a youth centre. The Peabody Trust, founded in 1862 by the American banker, diplomat and philanthropist George Peabody, owns and manages more than 19,000 homes in London.

of the flat and pay a subsidized rent on the remainder. Of the 175 homes in the project, 128 are 'affordable', the remainder having been sold privately to cross-subsidize the affordable units.

One way or another, Hoxton is no longer the real frontier of cool. In the hands of local designers House of Jazz, the Hoxton-girl look had reached the catwalk and gone on to be reproduced for chain stores. The Hoxton Fin had been adopted by professional footballers and, through their influence on popular culture, by trend-conscious youth everywhere.

Further reading on Hoxton

Pratt, Andy C., 'Urban Regeneration: From the Arts "Feel Good" Factor to the Cultural Economy: A Case Study of Hoxton, London', *Urban Studies* 46.5/6 (2009), 1042–61. *A detailed case study of the transformation of Hoxton as a seminal 'cultural quarter'.*

Hufeisensiedlung Berlin

The Hufeisensiedlung, in Berlin's outlying borough of Neukölln, was a milestone in the history of Modernist housing construction and a classic example of a modern housing estate. Since 2008 the district has been part of a UNESCO World Heritage site that covers six Modernist housing estates in Berlin, the legacy of the *Neues Bauen* ('new way of building') during the Weimar Republic (1919–1933), when Berlin was particularly progressive socially, politically, and culturally.

The housing situation in Berlin after World War I was catastrophic: acute shortages, with an existing stock dominated by bleak and unhealthy tenements. By the mid-1920s a measure of economic and political stability had returned to Weimar Germany and a debate began to emerge over the future shape of German society. The concept of community was an important focus of the debate, thanks in large part to the influence of the book *Gemeinschaft und Gesellschaft* ('Community and Society') by sociologist Ferdinand Tönnies. Originally published in 1887 and reprinted in revised form in 1912, the book's popularity surged during the Weimar years when it saw five editions between 1920 and 1926.

The idea of fostering community within an enclosed spatial framework of close interpersonal relations became a rallying point for visionary architectural schemes, especially among progressive architectural pressure groups like Der Ring. Architecture and urban design should no longer be dominated by bourgeois values of civil refinement, historicism, privacy, and individualization, they argued. Rather, there should be a *Neues Bauen*, a new way of building, encompassing a mixture of social classes and encouraging the formation of communities on the green periphery of the city. This kind of urban development, it was believed, would produce a new, socially able kind of person (*neuer Mensch*) suited to the progressive development of the future republic.

Martin Wagner, appointed as Planning Director for Greater Berlin in 1925, was a key member of this architectural *avant-garde*, along with Peter Behrens, Walter Gropius, Ernst May, Ludwig Mies van der Rohe, Hans Scharoun, and Bruno Taut. He was also deeply committed to the Social Democratic Party and to socialism. The Hufeisensiedlung, designed by Wagner in association with Bruno Taut and built between 1925 and 1933, was a seminal example of the *Neues Bauen*. Once built, many Berlin residents complained that the development was too nice for the working class.

Wagner was an early proponent of the application of new approaches to construction: using inexpensive nontraditional materials such as concrete panel construction, avoiding labour-intensive practices (such as building interior walls with small, hand-laid bricks), and using the newest materials-handling techniques such as travelling cranes. Only this way, he argued, would it be economically feasible to provide

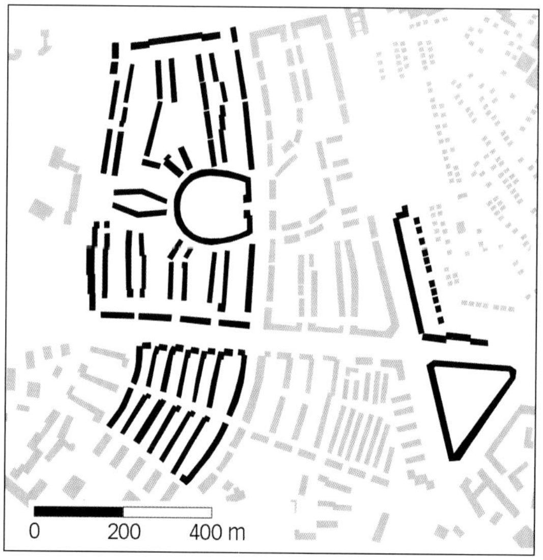

Figure-ground diagram of the Hufeisensiedlung estate. The innovative horseshoe-shaped element is surrounded by short terraces that were conventional in plan but radical in design.

Outer face of the horseshoe element of the estate. The position of the stairs on the street side of the buildings results in a repeating pattern of vertical glazed zones alternating with zones of regular windows.

'light and air, dignity and order' for working-class households.

These modern construction techniques were all applied in the Hufeisensiedlung. The core of the project, from which the entire district takes its name, is a three-storey, horseshoe-shaped group of apartments built around a natural pond. It was commissioned by GEHAG (*Gemeinnützige Heimstätten Aktiengesellschaft*), a trades union housing association, to provide housing for its members. GEHAG also commissioned several streets of row houses to the east of the Hufeisen apartments, while DeGeWo, a municipal facilities management company, commissioned several more streets of row housing to the west.

Taut brought a combination of garden city ideas and rational planning to the ensemble. The broad open space in the centre of the horseshoe provided an arcadian landscape, an innovative space that Taut saw as serving the residents' need for a place where children could play and adults could socialize. The four basic apartment designs have what were, for the time, unprecedented amenities: recessed balconies, and attic space that could be used for washing and for storage. The larger units were provided with rooms that had no designated use, in order to accommodate and encourage diverse lifestyles. The row housing also had laundry rooms and attic space, along with cellars. The terraces were laid out asymmetrically with a staggered arrangement of the blocks of buildings that provided visual diversity. The houses were provided with generous garden space. The back gardens, facing one another and separated only by pedestrian pathways, created broad avenues of green space.

The district epitomized the radical spirit of the Weimar Republic, not only in terms of the progressive amenities of the housing but also in terms of the semiotics of the design. The Hufeisensiedlung's flat-roofed apartments had political overtones, while much of the row housing was painted red, an overt reference to the socialist ideals of Wagner, Taut, and the

Inner face of the horseshoe element, showing the recessed balconies.

Right: **Doorways and stair windows** of terraced apartments echo those of the horseshoe element.

64 64

Terraced apartments on Fritz-Reuter-Allee. The use of colour was innovative in itself, while the choice of red tones was an overt reference to socialistic ideals. The flat roofs and lack of ornamentation were also intended to carry semantic meaning that was anti-bourgeois.

developers, and a provocative demarcation from the neighbouring Eierteich Settlement with its traditionalistic design and pitched roofs. The original Hufeisensiedlung development amounted to more than 1,000 dwellings, while a further 2,000 were added before the Nazi takeover ended socialist progressivism and proscribed Modernist design. The district survived World War II without significant damage and wound up – just – in West Berlin during the geopolitical partition of the city.

Today, UNESCO recognition has ensured the integrity of the district and prompted investment in some much-needed maintenance. The Hufeisensiedlung is now a quiet, leafy suburban district, its streets lined with old cherry trees. The only clue to its larger significance is the occasional knot of architecture or planning students wandering through to sketch and take photographs. Although well-established as a working-class neighbourhood, there is little sense of radicalism. Rather, UNESCO

Clockwise from top left: **Hufeisensiedlung outer face**, Photo: Bloomberg via Getty Images; **Corner element** of the Hufeisensiedlung, showing the embedded retail space; **apartment building** rear facade; **town home terracing** on Hüsung.

recognition has increased the desirability of the district among design-aware households, not necessarily the *neue Mensch* that Wagner and Taut had in mind so much as a new bourgeoisie for whom design is part of consumerism rather than community. Signs of incipient gentrification in the district include a few expensive new models among the vehicles parked on the streets, together with glimpses of expensive interior furnishings and décor.

Further reading on Hufeisensiedlung

Hake, Sabine, *Topographies of Class: Modern Architecture and Mass Society in Weimar Berlin*, Ann Arbor: University of Michigan Press, 2008. *This book approaches Weimar architectural culture from the perspective of mass discourse and class analysis, exploring the way in which architectural projects such as* Neues Bauen *related to wider debates and to representations in literature, photography, and film.*

White, Ian Boyd, *Bruno Taut and the Architecture of Activism*, Cambridge: Cambridge University Press, 2010. *Explores the work of Bruno Taut and his influence on the development of modern architecture in Germany.*

Isle of Dogs London

Until the nineteenth century the Isle of Dogs existed as sparsely settled marshland, bounded by a big, looping meander of the River Thames. Then, at the beginning of the nineteenth century, the area was developed to accommodate the docks and warehouses needed for the transoceanic shipping that sustained Britain's commercial empire. By the early 1970s the docks had become obsolete and by 1980 they had all closed, the wharves abandoned and the warehouses derelict. Today, the Isle of Dogs is dominated by the skyscrapers and office complexes of global financial services, surrounded by the sharply contrasting landscapes of social housing.

At their peak, London's docklands employed more than 30,000 labourers. On the Isle of Dogs, the West India and Millwall Docks handled bananas from the Canary Islands, sugar from the West Indies, vegetable oils, spices, and tropical fruit and vegetables from Africa and Asia, grain from North America, timber from Scandinavia, and wine from France and the Mediterranean. Much of the workforce initially lived off the island in the nearby districts of Wapping, Limehouse, and Stepney, but the busy docks prompted a housing boom on the island in the first half of the nineteenth century.

Built for rent by working-class families, and severely damaged by German bombing in World War II, most of the housing was replaced between 1950 and 1970 by social housing in the form of three-, four- and five-storey apartment blocks, maisonettes, and terraces in what were intended to be self-contained neighbourhoods in the Modernist town planning idiom. But the economic basis of these communities was undermined as the docklands fell into a steep decline, first as a result of competition from Rotterdam and other European ports, and then as a result of the introduction of containerization, which shifted London's port facilities to Tilbury, 25 km farther downstream. The abandoned docklands and marooned neighbourhoods were widely regarded as emblematic of the decline of Britain's traditional economic base, a very visible source of embarrassment to the government.

At the same time the vast amount of vacant land was readily identified by the private sector as the basis for a potentially lucrative regeneration of the island, replacing old industries with new, and building upscale river-view condominiums for affluent households in place of the working-class population.

Following a series of plans and reports, the central government, under Prime Minister Margaret Thatcher, took some 2,000 hectares of

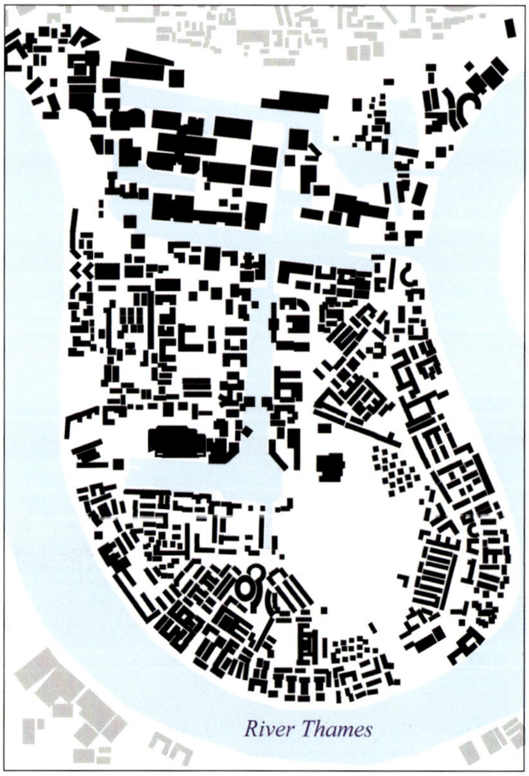

Figure-ground diagram of the Isle of Dogs. Not really an island, the district is surrounded on three sides by the River Thames. The larger structures of the financial precinct are to the north of the district, while the southern tip of the district consists mostly of residential development.

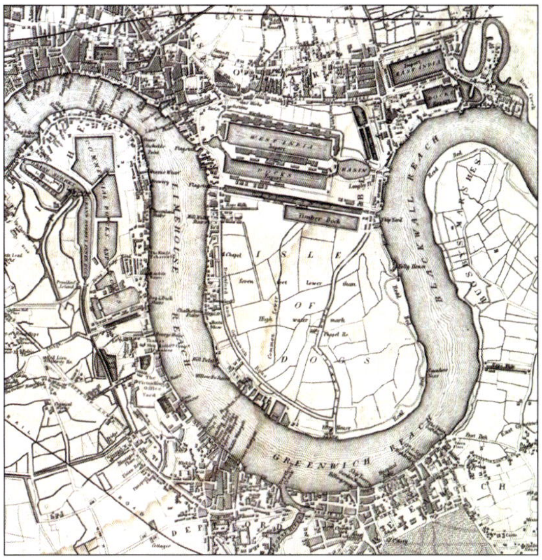

The Isle of Dogs in 1845. This map shows the first of the modern docks, the West India Dock and the Timber Docks, in the north of the district; most of the rest of the district remained marshy, more than 2 m lower than the high-water mark. Map extract from the David Rumsey Map Collection, <www.davidrumsey.com>.

land out of the hands of the local governments and the Port Authority in 1981 and gave it to a specially created corporation with extensive powers, the London Docklands Development Corporation (LDDC). The regeneration of the Docklands was a deliberate attempt not simply to market this part of London to global investors, but also to sell the whole idea of the United Kingdom as a rejuvenated, postindustrial economy. The Docklands were to become the spatial expression of neoliberal enterprise culture, fostering the growth of London's advanced business services and replacing a redundant – both literally and figuratively redundant – working-class population with a middle-class one. The LDDC promptly designated the area around the West India and Millwall Docks as the Isle of Dogs Enterprise Zone, giving developers freedom from local property taxes for a ten-year period, with no development land tax, and a 100 per cent capital allowance for new commercial and industrial buildings, to be offset

Docklands townscape, looking west. Once the commercial heart of Britain's empire, employing more than 30,000 dockyard labourers, the docklands are now recognized as the largest single urban redevelopment scheme in the world, with hundreds of thousands of square metres of office and retail space and substantial amounts of new housing. Photo: The Image Bank/Getty.

Docklands riverscape. Cesar Pelli's Canary Wharf tower building – One Canada Square – is to the left. Riverside apartment buildings are designed to take maximum advantage of river views.

against corporation and income taxes. Within a few years hundreds of companies had taken advantage of these tax perks to move onto the Isle of Dogs.

In 1985 Canada-based Olympia & York, the world's largest property development company at the time, put together an ambitious redevelopment scheme that would provide several hundred thousand square metres of new office space. The government committed to furnish a new transportation infrastructure: a driverless light railway line – the Docklands Light Railway (DLR) – and a £3.5 billion extension to the underground subway system. The centrepiece of the development was Canary Wharf, its flagship structure, a sleek fifty-storey tower (One Canada Square) designed by Cesar Pelli. Beneath the development was an underground shopping mall and beneath that was a multilayered service spine for the whole development, including parking. The first phase of the development was completed in 1991, just in time for the collapse of the global property market. It led to the bankruptcy of Olympia & York, and it took until 1997 for the development to regain momentum under new owners (the Canary Wharf Group). The revival of the property market on the Isle of Dogs was driven by rising demand for deep floor-plate, grade A office accommodation (which was not available in the City of London, given the conservation constraints there at the time) and boosted by the opening of the London Underground's Jubilee Line extension in 1999, with Norman Foster's signature-style Canary Wharf station. By 2005 the Isle of Dogs finally had the skyline profile that the Thatcher government had sought as a highly visual and symbolic manifestation of the renaissance of London's role in the global economy.

The LDDC, having been widely criticized for being unaccountable and for increasing social polarisation and encouraging gentrification, was wound up in 1998. The subsequent opportunism of developers and local government agencies has resulted in a mixture of residential, commercial, exhibition, and light industrial space that is the

Cabot Square, named after explorer John Cabot, provides one of the few formally designated public open spaces in the financial precinct.

The Docklands Light Railway was critical to the early redevelopment of the district, which had long suffered from poor accessibility from other parts of London.

largest single urban regeneration scheme in the world. It is, though, fragmented and polarised, with no civic spaces, no public buildings, few parks, and an inadequate transport infrastructure. The buildings are, for the most part, architecturally unremarkable. Ironically, the LDDC had seen architecture and urban design as a means to establish a marketable sense of place for the Docklands. Landscaping and street furniture were deliberately chosen to contrast as far as possible with the deindustrialized legacy of the district, but have ended up lending only a generic sense of placelessness. The water, originally held untouchable by the LDDC, has meanwhile gradually been encroached by piecemeal development, with much of the remaining waterfront now inaccessible to the public.

As development has unfolded, a broad layering has become evident in the built environment. The core of the initial development around Canary Wharf unfortunately coincided with a fashion for postmodern styling, so that – Pelli's tower excepted – the big cornerstone corporate office buildings were dressed up with the vestigial columns and pediments and overscaled entrances of precast postmodern classicism. Meanwhile, smaller commercial developments on the periphery of the Canary Wharf project typically took the form of single- or two-storey lightweight structures arranged around parking courts and embellished with nautical references and bright colours. Later developments, catering increasingly to international financial and publishing companies, have opted more for glassy, International Style towers. The first residential developments aimed at the Island's new white-collar workers gravitated to the riverfront, using stepped and angled forms to

Clockwise, from top left **Canary Wharf commuters** (photo: iStock Exclusive/Getty); **pontoon bridge** across West India Docks, with converted banana warehouses in the background; **Jubilee Line** underground station entrance at Canary Wharf, designed by Foster + Partners; **office workers** on lunch break in Cabot Square.

maximize the number of apartments with a river view (and thereby maximizing the price premium for developers and landlords).

The best sites having been taken, subsequent residential developments exploited remaining dockside sites, deploying renovated dockside cranes, ships' anchors, and buoys as embellishment in an attempt to restore the authenticity that had been eschewed by the LDDC's original design guidelines. Elsewhere, on land-bound sites, residential development has been in the form of high-density enclaves, mostly gated and/or walled. All are aimed, of course, at the upper end of the housing market. They have attracted a disproportionate number of single persons and couples who have not yet had children, are not contemplating them, or have had them long ago. For many of them the Island is a second home; they spend their work week in central London, often socializing with colleagues or clients before retiring to the Island simply to sleep, and then resume a life elsewhere at weekends. The result is a lifelessness that contrasts dramatically with the lively bustle of the cramped public spaces around the Island's office developments.

An even greater contrast, though, is with the Island's social housing estates, whose 13,500 residents remain largely excluded from the surrounding economy and whose neighbourhoods have remained largely untouched by the physical and economic regeneration of the island. As private developers have picked off sites around Millwall Docks and in Blackwall and Cubitt

Town in the south of the island, social housing built in the 1950s and 1960s has been encircled and isolated. Today, the Isle of Dogs is the most extremely polarised district in the country, with multiple pockets of population among the 10 per cent most prosperous in the country literally interspersed among those that are among the 10 per cent most impoverished, according to the Department for Communities and Local Government's index of multiple deprivation.

Invicta Wharf. New housing on the Isle of Dogs, viewed from Greenwich. Photo by Richard Croft, used under a creative commons Attribution-Share Alike License at Wikimedia Commons.

Further reading on the Isle of Dogs

Butler, Tim, 'Re-Urbanizing London Docklands: Gentrification, Suburbanization or New Urbanism?' *International Journal of Urban and Regional Research* 31.4 (2007), 759–81. *A study of gentrification in the docklands.*

Carmona, Matthew, 'The Isle of Dogs: Four Development Waves, Five Planning Models, Twelve Plans, Thirty-Five Years, and a Renaissance … of Sorts', *Progress in Planning* 71 (2009), 87–151. *A comprehensive account of the redevelopment of the district.*

Cox, Alan, *Docklands in the Making: The Redevelopment of Isle of Dogs, 1981–1999*, London: Athlone Press, 1996. *A review of architecture in the district, based on a survey conducted for the Royal Commission on Historical Monuments.*

Social Polarisation. The district's social housing stands in stark contrast to the office buildings of the financial precinct. Photo: Dan Kitwood/Getty.

New housing on Ferry Street, at the southern tip of the district. Photo by Peter Trimmimg, used under a creative commons Attribution-Share Alike License at Wikimedia Commons.

Cubitt Town. Photo by J. Nigel Cox, used under a creative commons Attribution-Share Alike License at Wikimedia Commons.

Kentlands Gaithersburg

Kentlands is an ambitious subdivision on the southwestern edge of Gaithersburg, Maryland. Built on a greenfield site, it was developed as a private, master-planned community, a packaged and branded landscape of upper-middle-class housing with carefully controlled landscaping, a 'downtown' commercial district, and community amenities. It has gained notoriety as the earliest and most complete example of a New Urbanist subdivision, in which carefully prescribed design codes are deployed in an attempt to generate a built environment that is redolent of traditional small-town values, conducive to a sense of community, a sense of place, and sustainable urban development.

The Kentlands subdivision stands on part of what was once prosperous farmland. The property was purchased in 1942 by Otis Kent, a wealthy tax lawyer, who set it up as an upscale family estate. In the 1960s, part of the property was deeded as a wildlife sanctuary and the remainder of the property – 142 hectares – was eventually sold by the family in 1988 to a property developer, Joseph Alfandre. A portion of the site was quickly sold on to shopping centre magnate Mel Simon for the development of a conventional regional mall. Alfandre then hired Andres Duany and Elizabeth Plater-Zyberk to conduct a week-long charette on the design of his proposed subdivision. Duany and Plater-Zyberk were enjoying a significant amount of critical acclaim for their retro design of the tiny resort town of Seaside, Florida; the Kentlands project gave them the opportunity to develop what they later came to call the 'principles of the New Urbanism'.

New Urbanism is founded on the belief that good urbanism can be propagated through the codification of design principles. The principles are based on precedents and typologies derived from observations of patterns exhibited in traditional communities. Citing the enduring popularity of walkable, diverse, urban atmospheres in places like Nantucket, Massachusetts; Old Town, Alexandria, Virginia; Georgetown, D.C.; historic Charleston, South Carolina; and Savannah, Georgia, Duany and Plater-Zyberk placed special emphasis on a traditional vocabulary of urban design, with a typology that includes boulevards, perimeter blocks, plazas, monuments, and the pedestrian scale of streets and public spaces.

The physical configuration of streets is key to New Urbanism, as is the role of building mass as a definer of urban space, the need for clear patterns among elements of built form and public spaces, and the importance of having identifiable, functionally integrated quarters. The assumption is that both civic architecture and pedestrian-oriented streets can act as catalysts of sociability and community. Tree-lined streets are designed with a comparatively narrow width and lined with stoops or front porches as social buffer zones between the public realm of the street and the private realm of the home. Culs-de-sac are avoided; small lots, mixed uses, and side alleys are encouraged. A

Figure-ground diagram of part of Kentlands.

Main Street, Kentlands. Neotraditional design evokes a small-town atmosphere, but there is a narrow range of shops and offices and consequently there are few people around to animate the space.

traditional small-town neighbourhood flavour is pursued through strict design codes that result in housing that mimics pre-World War II housing styles, relegating garages to the back lot, and placing houses on small lots.

In their charette for Kentlands, Duany and Plater-Zyberk were able to craft a plan that appealed to Alfandre because its closely written codes promised to maintain the character of the development until build-out and beyond. The plan also had a strong brand identity with sensibilities – a vision of community and a sense of certainty, respectability, and predictability – likely to appeal to the key market segment of upper-middle-class households. In crafting the neotraditional character of the subdivision, Alfandre, Duany, and Plater-Zyberk were able to take advantage of several historic buildings, including Kentlands Mansion, the main residence of the former owners. The adjacent Kentlands Barn has been converted into an exhibit space and public arts centre; the former farm manager's house has been transformed into a private residence; another farm building became the project architect's office; and the firehouse and garden buildings have been left, presumably in an optimistic attempt to signal authenticity, legacy, or identity.

Surrounded by a system of artificial lakes and jogging trails, the first model homes in Kentlands were opened in 1990. One of these included a small accessory apartment, carriage-house style, over the garage, something that proved to be popular among buyers. The first residents moved into new homes in 1991, just as Alfandre, overextended in the midst of an economic downturn and facing foreclosure, was forced to execute a deed in favour of a subsidiary of his bankers.

The neotraditional character of the project was nevertheless largely assured by the zoning, subdivision, and planning approvals that had already been completed. And in spite of its financial problems, Kentlands quickly began

Parking lots behind Main Street expose the failure of New Urbanist principles. The extensive parking lots – along with several others – are for the adjacent suburban supermarkets and shopping malls that serve the district's automobile-dependent population.

to attract design awards and media attention. The principles of New Urbanism that were supposedly embodied in Kentlands enlivened interest in planning and urban design and brought fresh ideas to what had become routinized and bureaucratized issues of land use and zoning. They also reinforced sense of place, liveability, sustainability, and quality of life as important policy issues, and helped to resurrect the idea of a definable public interest.

Meanwhile, in Kentlands itself there were in reality persistent problems in terms of fostering the economic vitality of the project that would, in theory, make it a sustainable urban community rather than merely a slickly packaged residential subdivision. A Wal-Mart complex was proposed for Kentlands in the mid-1990s but was successfully opposed by the Citizens Alliance for Planning Excellence, an umbrella group that drew members from surrounding communities in and around Gaithersburg as well as from Kentlands itself. Similarly, a proposed 'fast-food park' collapsed in the face of community opposition. The corporate developers who had taken over from Alfandre did build a gas station/convenience store/carwash complex, and a retail strip ('Boulevard Shops'), but the vision was floundering. A second charette led to a revised district plan in 1996. This provided for a commercial Market Square with a Market Street spine road, a plaza, and a major cross street. Among the first businesses to move in were a toy store, a diner, and a cinema; other specialty stores, restaurants, and coffee and dessert shops have followed.

Today Kentlands has been completely built out, with about 1,800 residential units that include single-family homes, urban cottages (i.e. smaller single-family homes), townhouses, garage townhouses, rental apartments, and condominium units. In addition to the retailing and storefront offices of Main Street and Market Street, the district has a church, a school, and a community centre. It is well endowed with sidewalks, a series of beautifully landscaped small parks, and plenty of playgrounds, pools, basketball courts, and clubhouses. Surveys of residents have elicited relatively high levels of satisfaction with their environs, but critics have pointed out that, its mix of housing types notwithstanding, Kentlands is an enclave of affluent upper-middle-class households. Although it has been adopted as a seminal example of New Urbanism, it does not meet many of the principles that have since been articulated by the movement. It is only tenuously related to the surrounding metropolitan region and has no significant relationship to its immediate hinterland. None of the housing is affordable by lower-income households and there is little diversity in the demographics of the district. It is highly automobile-dependent and few jobs are located within its immediate hinterland. It does match up well, though, in terms of visual aesthetics – the pedestrian network, architecture, and streetscape.

What Kentlands, and New Urbanism in general, have got right is market appeal as a premium space: a lifestyle enclave to accommodate the secession of the successful. Beyond this market appeal, Kentlands and New Urbanism should be seen as an architectural *derriere-garde*, a New Age urbanism that is part conventional wisdom and part fuzzy poetic, commercially resonant but ultimately meaningless. Real urbanism emerges from a city- or metropolitan-wide physical infrastructure and political economy. Developments of 5,000 or 10,000 people cannot support economically viable 'town centres' that will adequately serve the needs of their populace, and the antiseptic products of form-based codes preclude the close-grained diversity and unexpected encounters – both visual and social – that are the true glory of cities and a fundamental component of any real urbanism.

It might be concluded, then, that Kentlands is not so much a seminal example of New Urbanism but, rather, a seminal example of a regressive kind of suburban development, with an intrinsic bias in favour of the middlebrow consumer preferences of upper-middle-class fractions. It is a district that adopts the rhetoric of social diversity and affordability even as it deliberately caters to a mix of residents with above-average incomes, and that is fundamentally anti-urban in its overall impact.

Above, Top: **Neotraditional housing**; middle: **the Arts Barn**, originally built in 1900 as a stable, now includes four artist-in-resident studios, an art gallery, a shop, and a ninety-nine-seat theatre in the former barn loft; bottom: **rear-alley garage access** to single-family homes.

Further reading on Kentlands

Lee, Chang-Moo, and Ahn, Kun Hyuck, 'Is Kentlands Better than Radburn? The American Garden City and New Urbanist Paradigms', *Journal of the American Planning Association* 69.1 (2003), 50–71. *Provides morphological case studies and quantitative analyses in comparing and contrasting Kentlands with Radburn in terms of how their goals and prescriptions have been realized.*

The Kuip
Gent

The late-medieval core of Gent (Ghent), known locally as the 'Kuip', is testament to the city's changing role within the European urban system. At one time a cornerstone of the most important protoindustrial region in Europe and second only to Paris in total population, the Kuip developed a skyline and morphology commensurate with its wealth. Gent's fortunes rose and fell with the complex cross-currents of European geopolitics as well as with changing patterns of trade and economic development, but it maintained its position as one of Europe's most important cities for more than 500 years. On the eve of World War I the city hosted the World Exhibition, tidying up the Kuip and restoring its medieval architecture. In the twentieth century the significance of the city's strategic location as a market centre and its comparative advantages as a manufacturing centre were diminished in the context of the European space-economy, leaving the Kuip as a beautifully preserved example of medieval European urbanism.

The Kuip stands close to the site of a Roman settlement at the strategically important point where the River Leie enters the Scheldt. The Roman settlement lasted into the late fourth century and was replaced in the seventh century by a small ecclesiastical centre that grew up around two abbeys. That settlement was laid waste in 879 C.E. by raiding Vikings, who pitched their camp there for a year, pillaged the abbeys, and razed them to the ground. The new commercial settlement that subsequently grew up some 500 m upstream on the left bank of the Scheldt was Gent.

By the eleventh century Gent was flourishing, mainly on the basis of woollen cloth production, using wool from the sheep kept on the newly enclosed Flemish polder land. By the twelfth century, demand for Flemish cloth was such that local wool merchants were importing large quantities of top-quality wool from England, allowing manufacturers in Gent to produce luxury-quality cloths that were traded across Europe, into Russia, and around the Mediterranean.

The town's economic links with England led to a shrewd political alliance that allowed it – and by extension the whole of Flanders – to remain largely neutral and to continue to thrive during the great economic depression that brought most European urban development to a halt during the Hundred Years War (1337–1453) between France and England. The architect of the alliance, Jacob Van Artevelde, proclaimed King Edward II of England as King of France in 1340 in the Kuip's Vrijdagmarkt (Friday Market). The spiritual heart of the city, the market square has retained a frontage of medieval residences, interrupted only by an out-of-scale trade union building in Art Nouveau style in the northwest corner. In the centre of the square is a statue of Van Artevelde, pointing toward England.

Figure-ground diagram of the Kuip. Surrounded on three sides by the River Leie and associated waterways, the district combines dense massing with generous public open spaces.

To accommodate the town's cloth trade, the town dug canals, developed small harbours on both the Scheldt and the Leie, and built ramparts and town walls that established the lineaments of the Kuip. Between the thirteenth and fifteenth centuries the town held a population of some 65,000, slightly less than Paris but considerably more than London or any other European city. In the Kuip the wealthy élite of the town built themselves large residences complete with turrets and crenellations, while craftsmen organized themselves into guilds and built elaborate guild houses. Over the course of several generations their prosperity resulted in a spectacular cityscape.

An early landmark was the church of Saint Nicholas, rebuilt between 1220 and 1250 in imposing 'Scheldt Gothic' style using blue-gray stone from the Tournai area after an earlier wooden version burnt down. The 98-metre belfry tower was completed in 1338. Belfry towers were a classic element of medieval towns in the Low Countries, serving as fortified lookouts as well as symbols of civic pride in the flat landscape. Gent's tower was one of the most impressive and functioned as a treasury as well as a watchtower. It has been rebuilt or restored six times since its original construction and was added to the UNESCO World Heritage list of protected monuments in 1999.

The long meat hall in Gothic style that stands on the right bank of the Leie was built between 1425 and 1445 and now serves as a showcase for the region's culinary specialties. The town's cloth hall, built between 1426 and 1441 adjacent to the Belfry tower, was the trading place of the wool and cloth merchants and is now a café-restaurant popular with tourists. The nearby

The Graslei, fronting part of Gent's original harbour on the River Leie, one of the best-preserved medieval cityscapes in northern Europe. This group of buildings, dating from between the twelfth and sixteenth centuries, reflects the wealth and power of city's medieval guilds. Even after the decay of the Flemish trade, the guilds were still affluent enough to change their original wooden houses into splendid stone mansions. Photo: Tibor Bognar/Corbis.

town hall reflects the growing significance of civil society in Gent as well as the city's wealth. Initially constructed in elaborate late-Gothic style between 1482 and 1535, it was massively extended in 1635 in Renaissance style, resulting in a jarring juxtaposition of architectonic language. Completing the ensemble of institutional structures in the Kuip is the Gothic cathedral of St Bavo, consecrated in 1569. Yet it is the commercial cityscape of the Graslei, fronting the old city harbour on the Leie, that provides one of the finest sights in the district – and, for that matter, in all of northern Europe. Here, alongside the grain warehouse that dates from 1200, is a group of structures that reflects the wealth and power of the medieval guilds, including the House of Free Sailors (1531), the House of Masons (1527), and the House of Grainweighers (1698).

The religious wars of the late sixteenth and the seventeenth century ended the role of Gent as a centre of international importance. The Calvinist republic that had developed in Gent

The Belfry Tower. Built in the fourteenth century, the tower served as a bell tower, a fortified watchtower, and town treasury.

The town hall. The southeastern wing of the town hall, seen here, was built at the beginning of the eighteenth century in Renaissance style, in stark contrast to the adjoining original north wing, which had been built between 1518 and 1535 in late-Gothic style.

St Nicholas Church, begun in the thirteenth century and constructed in 'Scheldt Gothic' style, viewed from the Belfry Tower.

was overwhelmed by the Spanish army, and between 1600 and 1660 the public life of the city was dedicated to the Catholic reconstruction. In addition to the repair and restoration of damaged monasteries, convents, churches, and chapels, the Catholic leadership encouraged the citizenry to embellish the city with triumphant Baroque architecture, in direct contrast to the austere functionalism favoured by Protestants. The prosperity of the guilds was undercut as textile manufacturers shifted to cotton imported from the New World, thanks to a new, direct connection to the sea. The new cotton barons, meanwhile, built themselves patrician residences in the French style.

After a local entrepreneur, Lieven Bauwens, famously pulled off a feat of industrial espionage in the 1780s by stealing cotton textile technology from English manufacturers, Gent grew at a spectacular rate, its population jumping from 61,000 in 1815 to more than 175,000 in 1930. The built environment spread well beyond the Kuip, which then became subject to an urban renewal programme in order to showcase the city centre for the World Exhibition of 1913. The modern development of the city has taken place well beyond the Kuip, while a combination of historic preservation legislation, tourist-related capital investment, and gentrification has allowed the Kuip to retain its medieval cityscape.

Further reading on the Kuip

de Vries, Andre, *Flanders: A Cultural History*, New York: Oxford University Press, 2007. *Traces the development of a civic culture based on both trade and ideas, with a chapter on Gent and its role in the region's identity.*

Verhulst, Adriaan, *The Rise of Cities in North-West Europe*, Cambridge: Cambridge University Press, 1999. *Details the impact of political, military, ecclesiastical, economic, and social factors on the development of Gent and fourteen other towns, mainly situated on the rivers Meuse and Scheldt and along the North Sea coast of present-day Belgium, Holland, and France.*

La Défense
Paris

In less than sixty-five years since the district was an anonymous suburban lacuna of small factories, shanties, and a few farms, La Défense has become the prime high-rise office district of Paris, a nodal concentration of head offices, advanced business services, and ancillary educational, retailing and personal services. In the process, the district has been recast several times, each iteration bringing taller skyscrapers and a greater concentration of French business administration and finance. Meanwhile, La Défense became a monumental symbol of contemporary France, emblematic of the aspirations of Paris to compete as a major world city in the global economy.

On axis with the Louvre, the Place de la Concorde, the Arc de Triomphe, and the Champs Elysées, its orientation alone assigns La Défense unmistakable importance. This *axe historique* dates from 1640 when André Le Nôtre, Louis XIV's landscape architect, planted rows of elm trees westward from the Louvre. With France on the winning side after World War I, plans began to be made to extend the axis into a *Voie Triumphale*. Renowned architects like Le Corbusier and Auguste Perret submitted plans for rows of impressive skyscrapers in Modernist style, but none of the plans was realized, mainly due to the onset of the Great Depression of the 1930s.

The mood after World War II was less triumphal and more concerned with modernization and economic recovery. In 1950 the Federation of Engineering Industries selected La Défense as the future site for a large exhibition hall, the Centre des Nouvelles Industries et Technologies (CNIT), and the following year the central government identified La Défense as the location for a modern new office centre.

In 1958 the government created the *Etablissement Public pour l'Aménagement de la Région de La Défense* (EPAD) to plan and regulate the development of the district: part of a broader strategy of metropolitan decentralization. Almost 1,000 hectares of land were allocated from three different neighbouring municipalities: Courbevoie, Puteaux, and Nanterre, and the district was given a name – La Défense – after a statue called 'La Défense de Paris' that had been standing there since 1883, commemorating the soldiers who had defended Paris during the Franco-Prussian War (1870–1871). EPAD's plan echoed the principles embodied in Le Corbusier's visionary plans of the 1920s. Two rows of ten office towers were to border a central pedestrian plaza that would cover a network of roads and services underneath. To maintain architectural unity, all office buildings would have to respect the same rules: office towers would be twenty-five storeys, while residential buildings were to be no more than ten floors high.

By the late 1960s the first generation of skyscrapers began to rise. In 1970 La Défense was connected to the regional rail system (the RER), and the central government, having installed the telecommunications, highway, and railway infrastructure, encouraged private companies to build their own office towers. Most of the interested companies and speculative developers, however, wanted taller and more distinctive

Figure-ground diagram of La Défense. The district is dominated by a central plaza that is on axis with the Arc de Triomphe, 5 km away.

towers. As a result, the restrictions of the original plan were abandoned and a second generation of towers began to appear in the 1970s. The visibility of the towers from as far away as the Louvre prompted a heated public debate, with detractors asserting that they disturbed the classic view of the Arc de Triomphe as seen from the Champs Elysées.

Partly in response to this architectural *scandale*, an international competition for the design of a project for the city end of the plaza – the Tête Défense – was held in 1982. The initiative was also emblematic of President Francois Mitterrand's strategy of signalling French progressivism by sponsoring a number of *grands projets* for Paris. Others included the completion of the Musée d'Orsay, the construction of the Institut du Monde Arabe, the creation of a centre for science and industry in the north-eastern sector of Paris at La Villette, the enlargement of the Louvre, and the construction of a new opera house at the Bastille. The result of the competition for the Tête Défense was an arch of monumental size, designed by Danish architect Otto von Spreckelsen and created by joining two 106-m-high office blocks at roof level. The Grande Arche reasserted the significance of the entire district.

At the same time, the giant corporations spawned by globalization were seeking ever-larger office complexes with the capacity for computer networks and telecommunications. Downtown Paris is geologically unsuitable for tall buildings and is subject to historic preservation policies. The result was a third generation of towers at La Défense, taller than ever and with an increasing use of glass and steel. Among these were the EDF Tower, the Egée tower, the Adria Tower, and the forty-five-storey Coeur Défense, which was built on the site of the eleven-storey Esso tower that had been one of the district's first-generation towers.

Today more than 35,000 people live in La Défense and 175,000 people work there. There is a cineplex, together with 210,000 m^2 of shops (including the Quatre Temps shopping mall, the largest in continental Europe), and 2,600 hotel rooms. Apart from quiet Sunday mornings, streams of people coming and going give the district a busy and purposeful air. Nevertheless,

The monumental scale of the central plaza of La Défense dwarfs pedestrians. Beneath the plaza is a gallery with shops, restaurants and and express cafés, a metro station, and parking.

New generations of towers. The towers to the left and right in the photograph are third-generation towers, the Tour Egée (1999) and the Tour Sequoia (1990); in the centre is a fourth-generation tower, Tour T1, completed in 2008.

Right: **Tête Défense**: the Grande Arche, designed by Otto von Spreckelsen and completed in 1989.

the monumental space can seem bleak and windswept. The large-scale sculptures that have been placed around the plaza seem to intensify the feeling, dwarfing pedestrians. The affect of bleakness is somehow underscored by the knots of office workers that cluster outside the entrances of buildings for their cigarette breaks. It is alleviated by an allé of trees along the esplanade that descends to the southeastern end of the district, where there is an attractive and sequestered water feature in the Parc Diderot.

La Défense has become the undisputed centre of French corporate power with more than 3 million m^2 of office space, much of it devoted to corporate headquarters. Now established as an address of global importance, it boasts more than 1,500 businesses, including a dozen or so from the global top 50. Nevertheless, some of the buildings are aging, others have a dated appearance, and, from a strategic planning perspective, the entire district has outgrown its situation. La Défense has lost some of its lustre, threatening its role as a key element in the 'brand identity' of modern France. As a result, the entire district is scheduled for a government-sponsored makeover and extension. Recognizing the symbolic value of signature buildings commissioned from 'starchitects' and of the importance of architecture and design in city branding and inward investment,

Monumental in scale but inhospitable at ground level, the towers of La Défense have become emblematic of Parisian claims to global city status. Below: the **Boulevard Circulaire** around the core of the district, with the fifty-six-storey Tour First (2010), also known as the Axa Tower, in the background.

The statue commemorating the defence of Paris in the Franco-Prussian war of 1870–1871. Behind: Tour Total Fina Elf, a complex consisting of three connected towers.

Coeur Défense, a forty-five-storey tower completed in 2001, on the north side of the plaza. It replaced one of the first-generation towers, the Immueble Esso.

President Nicolas Sarkozy has mandated that new towers will be iconic buildings associated with starchitects like Norman Foster and Jean Nouvel. Design stardom and city branding, it is hoped, will become mutually self-reinforcing, keeping Paris on the map of world cities as the signature buildings of star architects provide the backdrop for fashion shoots, movie scenes, TV commercials, music videos, and news broadcasts. Already approved are the Tour Sans Fins (425 m tall), Hermitage Plaza towers (323 m), the Generali tower, (308 m) the Tour Signal (301 m), and the Osmose Tower (284 m). La Défense will be divided into four main axes, mimicking the layout of other buildings along the triumphal way.

Further reading on La Défense

Berry, Ian, et al., *Les Grands Traveaux*, Paris: Editions de la Reunion des Musees Nationaux, 1989. *Provides photographic coverage of the Grande Arche.*

Noin, Daniel, and White, Paul, *Paris*, London: Wiley, 1997. *A comprehensive review of the development of the city, with a strong emphasis on spatial planning, including the grands projets and La Défense.*

Sutcliffe, Anthony, *Paris: An Architectural History*, New Haven, CT: Yale University Press, 1996. *Situates the development of La Défense in the context of the urban and political history of Paris.*

Levittown
New York

Levittown is arguably the most famous suburb of all, the prototype model for the 'democratic utopia' of mid-twentieth-century American suburbia. Its fame derives in part from its scale: at the time of its construction it was the largest-ever suburban subdivision. But the principal reason for its fame derives from the way that it made suburban lifestyles affordable for working-class families as a result of innovations in construction. These innovations were the result of introducing Fordism to urban development: assembly-line mass production for a mass market. Levittown's immediate success made it the precursor of hundreds of sprawling subdivisions that rapidly came to encircle every U.S. city of any significance.

Levittown was famously built on potato fields. The land was purchased in 1945 by Abraham Levitt and his sons, Alfred and William, who were able to get it at a knockdown price because the region's farmers were selling out after of years of pest damage to their potato crops. Situated equidistant between New York City and the growing defence-related industrial plants on Long Island, the site was targeted by the Levitts as an ideal place to capitalize on the housing crunch of the immediate postwar years. Demobilized soldiers, sailors, and airmen and their families were living with their parents or in rented attics or basements, and the country had an overall shortage of about five million houses.

In addition to the sheer backlog of housing, there were several important factors that facilitated mass-produced suburban housing in the years following World War II. Automobiles had become increasingly affordable, while federal policy had required every state, as a condition of federal aid, to establish a state highway department to plan, build, and maintain interurban highways. The Federal Housing Administration (FHA) had stabilized the mortgage market by introducing mortgage insurance, while exclusionary zoning – legitimized by the U.S. Supreme Court in its landmark case, *Village of Euclid, Ohio v. Ambler Realty Co.*, 1926 – resulted in municipal zoning maps that conferred stability on local land markets and emboldened developers to lay out ever-larger subdivisions.

Taking advantage of all this, the Levitts drew on Fordist principles of economies of scale, the standardization of products, modular prefabrication, and assembly-line techniques in developing their potato fields. Abraham Levitt, the father, was the financier; Alfred Levitt was the architect (who had at one point served a paid apprenticeship under Frank Lloyd Wright), and William Levitt was the salesman and production manager.

In order to build their homes cheaper and faster, they decided to eliminate basements and build their new homes on concrete slabs, as they had in an innovative earlier project. This required a modification to the local building codes, which the municipality allowed in recognition of the severity of the housing shortage. William Levitt streamlined the company's procurement as well as its production processes. The company was not simply a development

Figure-ground diagram of part of Levittown.

Cape Cod style house, Cherrytree Lane. The Cape Cod was the basic model until 1949, when ranch-style homes were added. Most of the basic models, both Cape Cod and ranch style, have been modified and refurbished over the years.

and construction company, but a vertically integrated chain, from timber yards to appliance wholesalers. All of the lumber was precut and shipped from a timber yard they owned in California, and an abandoned railway line was reopened to bring other construction materials to the site. Nonunion contractors were used for the actual assembly of the homes, a move that met with heavy opposition. By July 1948 the Levitts were turning out thirty houses a day.

The first 2,000 homes were built for rent. They were boxy Cape Cod-style houses with a very simple interior plan. Backyards were not fenced, making for common open spaces and a sense of liberation that contrasted sharply with the rental tenements of prewar cities. The kitchen and living room looked out on the street, allowing mothers to oversee children playing and to observe their neighbours.

The popularity of these homes prompted the Levitts to switch to building homes for sale, offering slightly larger houses in Ranch style. These measured 10 m by 7.5 m and came in five different models, differing only by exterior colour, roof line, and the placement of windows. They had no garage but came with an expandable attic. The kitchens were outfitted with a Bendix washer and a General Electric stove and refrigerator. The demand for homes in Levittown was so great that even the procedure for purchasing them had to be modified to incorporate assembly-line methods. As the U.S. economy began to boom, the Levitts responded by modifying their houses annually, echoing the practice of automobile companies. The Levitts' 1950 model ranches came with a carport and a television set built into the living room staircase. The 1951 model included a partially finished attic.

By the end of 1951 the Levitts had unrolled more than 17,000 homes onto the Long Island suburban fringe. This was urban morphogenesis on a heroic scale, and it marked the end of urban development as a process dominated by

Modified Cape Cod home, Azalea Road. Bay windows have been added, along with a small extension and a paved driveway.

Original style Cape Cod, Blue Spruce Road. Apart from the addition of a free-standing garage, this house has not been modified.

fine-grained accretion and infill and the beginning of a process dominated by the mass production of suburbia.

It did not take long before Levittown became synonymous with people's disenchantment with mass-produced suburbia. The editors of influential *Fortune* magazine sponsored a conference that staged a bitter attack on postwar suburban development, while Lewis Mumford, the leading public intellectual of the time, saw it all as aimless and discontinuous, diffuse and unfocused:

> *A multitude of uniform, unidentifiable houses, lined up inflexibly, at uniform distances, on uniform roads, in a treeless communal waste, inhabited by people of the same class, the same income, the same age group, witnessing the same television performances, eating the same tasteless pre-fabricated foods, from the same freezers, conforming in every outward and inward respect to a common mold.*
>
> *The City in History*, New York: Harcourt, Brace & World, 1961, p. 486

In popular music, Pete Seeger sang about little boxes made of 'ticky-tacky' that all looked just the same; and it did not take long for academics, architects, planners, and social commentators to document the nexus of negative attributes of sprawling Fordist subdivisions. Rationalized, standardized, and tightly zoned suburban developments, it was pointed out, result in placeless neighbourhoods that lack visual, demographic, and social diversity. Residents must surely lead lives of quiet desperation in districts that are characterized by conformity, shallowness, and isolation. The economics of private Fordist subdivision inevitably result in a lack of public open spaces, urban infrastructure, and civic amenities. Sprawling 'off-ramp' subdivisions result in increased traffic, long commutes, and a chronic dependence on automobiles. Automobile-dependent lifestyles, meanwhile, lead to increases in rates of asthma, lung cancer, and heart problems. Stress resulting from commuting leads to adverse effects on marriages and family life. And so on: as historian Jon Teaford succinctly puts it, 'Sexual intercourse, connubial affection, motherly devotion, atmospheric purity, flora and fauna, civic loyalty, and individual happiness all seemed to be victims of the relentless sprawl of the edgeless city' (*The Metropolitan Revolution*, New York: Columbia University Press, 2006, p. 248).

Levittowners, however, understood their new environment in the context of the affordable alternatives: substandard tenement housing, trailer homes, crowded apartment complexes, and bed-sit apartments in converted houses. In comparison with the shortcomings of these options, aesthetic and philosophical objections

Home improvements, along with the maturing of trees, have created, a degree of diversity in what had originally been a highly standardized suburban landscape. This photograph shows part of Blue Spruce Road.

to Levittown seemed irrelevant. Moreover, as people settled in to the district they developed new ways of life and a new sense of community. Eminent sociologist Herbert Gans authored a landmark book – *The Levittowners* – which demonstrated that within fifteen years of its creation the district had developed a significant degree of social cohesion:

> *The critics have argued that long commutation by the father is helping to create a suburban matriarchy with deleterious effects on the children, and that homogeneity, social hyperactivity, and the absence of urban stimuli create depression, boredom, loneliness, and ultimately mental illness. The findings from Levittown suggest just the opposite – that suburban life has produced more family cohesion and a significant boost in morale through the reduction of boredom and loneliness.*
>
> 1967, p. 220

Over time, Levittown houses have changed character in response to the changing profile of the district's residents. Garages and dormers have been added and interior spaces remodelled. Some houses have become run-down while others have been made palatial. Mature trees and gardens – some overgrown, others beautifully kept – have softened the district's original affect of sterility. Today, Levittown is a multiclass, multiethnic community with little to hint of its radical impact on American urbanization.

Further reading on Levittown

Gans, Herbert, *The Levittowners: Ways of Life and Politics in a New Suburban Community*, New York: Vintage, 1967. *A seminal study of the social dimensions of the district.*

Kelley, Barbara, *Expanding the American Dream: Building and Rebuilding Levittown*, Albany, NY: State University of New York Press, 1993. *A comprehensive coverage of the construction, design, and politics of the district, and the way it provided a ladder for blue-collar Americans to get a stake in the American Dream, largely through sweat equity and do-it-yourself improvements.*

Lundrigan, Margaret, and Navarra, Tova, *Levittown: Volume II (NY)*, New York: Arcadia, 1999. *An illustrated history of the district.*

Matarrese, Lynne, *The History of Levittown, New York*, Levittown, NY: Levittown Historical Society, 2005. *The official history of the district's historical society.*

Little Saigon
Los Angeles

Little Saigon is located in the southeastern periphery of the Los Angeles metropolitan area in Orange County, straddling the cities of Westminster, Garden Grove, and Santa Ana. The conventional image of Orange County, as portrayed in the media, is one of affluent white suburbia. Indeed, it once was, like Encino far to the north of the metro region (see page 76), classic California Suburbia territory, with affluent subdivisions interspersed among more modest 1950s and 1960s sitcom suburbs, all occupied by a relatively homogeneous white population – the very manifestation of the American Dream. From the mid-1970s, Vietnamese immigrants and Vietnamese Americans settled in the district, eventually creating an 'ethnoburb' with distinctive elements to its businesses and its built environment.

The district was subdivided into neat rows of tract homes after World War II. The district was developed in response to a backlog of unfulfilled demand for housing from the Depression and war years, high rates of migration into southern California from the rest of the country, and the establishment of nearby military bases that brought personnel who settled permanently, attracted by the warm weather, the low cost of housing, and a booming economy. The non-white population of the district was barely 1 per cent in 1950 and only about 3 per cent by 1970, a classic example of California Suburbia. But the mid-1970s recession that had been triggered by the OPEC oil cartel brought the boom to a halt. By the late 1970s the district had become economically depressed, with clusters of run-down strip malls, auto repair shops, machine shops, and aging mobile home parks.

The stalled economy and depressed house prices in the district coincided with the arrival of Vietnamese war veterans and refugees to the United States in large numbers with the fall of Saigon in 1975. At first the federal government dispersed refugees to four relocation centres, one of which was Camp Pendleton, just 50 km to the southeast of Westminster. A second wave of refugees – the Vietnamese 'boat people' – arrived in the United States between the late 1970s and early 1980s, seeking to escape Vietnam's new communist regime. Altogether, almost a million Vietnamese refugees and war veterans arrived in the United States between 1975 and 1985. As they began to settle in the United States, Orange County was not only conveniently close to the refugee processing operations in Camp Pendleton but was also appealing because of its relatively low commercial and residential rents. The first Vietnamese businesses in the district appeared in 1978: a produce market, a real estate office, a medical office, a pharmacy, and a restaurant on Bolsa Avenue, at the heart of what is now Little Saigon.

Like European immigrants before them, Vietnamese families sought out the familiar linguistic and cultural comforts of their compatriots. In Westminster they were able to regroup

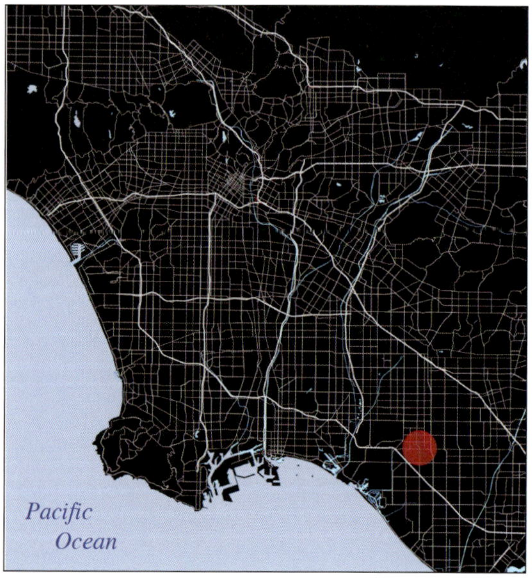

Little Saigon is located some 55 km southeast from downtown Los Angeles.

Placeless suburbia. Large expanses of Little Saigon look just like the rest of suburban Los Angeles – even along Bolsa Avenue, shown here, the commercial heart of the district.

with family and friends, forge social networks, appropriate new places, and build a sense of community. Ethnic businesses, meanwhile, provided an initial occupational niche. Today Little Saigon is home to between 75,000 and 100,000 Vietnamese and Vietnamese Americans. The number is imprecise because the district sprawls over an extensive area and across several municipalities: Westminster, Garden Grove, and Santa Ana. Throughout the district there are still many remaining white residents as well as some Cambodian and Laotian immigrants. Overall, the Vietnamese population amounts to some 20 to 30 per cent of the total. As such, Little Saigon is not a segregated ethnic enclave but an 'ethnoburb' – a multiethnic community in which one ethnic group has a significant concentration but does not comprise the majority. Unlike ethnic enclaves, ethnoburbs are not a result of forced segregation, but a relatively voluntary concentration of ethnic people who want to maximize their personal and social ethnic networks as well as business connections.

What began in the 1970s with a produce market and few shops and services has grown today to include more than 2,000 businesses. Bolsa Avenue is lined with suburban-style strip malls, Vietnamese restaurants, supermarkets, professional offices, nail salons, flower shops, and bakeries. The business district is anchored by the Asian Garden Mall, which incorporates a large jewellery centre with wholesale as well as retail outlets, along with a food court with *pho* restaurants that serve traditional Vietnamese noodle soup.

Throughout Little Saigon there are hundreds of mom-and-pop stores and coffee shops and restaurants specializing in French-style coffee and baguette sandwiches, many of them in formerly white-owned storefronts. There are also professional offices of doctors, dentists, lawyers, and accountants who speak Vietnamese, along with several Vietnamese-language television stations, radio stations, and newspapers. Little Saigon has also become a prominent centre of the Vietnamese pop music industry, with several recording studios. The corollary of all these ethnic businesses is the absence of the fast-food chains and convenience chain stores that are so typical of American suburbia.

Residential landscapes. Top: gated community; middle: Saigon Villas apartment complex; bottom: mobile home estate.

This specialized area provides a place for immigrants to experience solidarity, a sense of identity, and a sense of belonging. Immigrants with limited English can meet, interact, and talk in their native language, and gain employment, while older immigrants can find support and 'Americanized' immigrants and their children can connect with their ancestral culture. Because of its concentration of ethnic businesses, Little Saigon has become a destination district for Vietnamese Americans, an emotional focal point and a place where visitors can combine shopping with retreat to a community where their people and culture are the norm. The district takes on a hectic atmosphere at weekends as visitors from across the metropolitan area and beyond arrive to browse in shops for traditional Vietnamese attire, Vietnamese videos, music CDs, or herbal medicines, to purchase jewellery, eat *pho*, enjoy the sound of the Vietnamese language, and buy a Vietnamese-language newspaper and perhaps a few cultural treats, such as pickled celery, pickled lettuce, carambola juice, jackfruit, lychees, and moon cakes.

Although Little Saigon is by no means completely Vietnamese in its character, the built environment contributes significantly to a Vietnamese sense of place, with covered colonnades, gateways, open archways, curved roofs with overhanging eaves, ornate glazed red, blue, and green roof tiles, dragons and other symbolic motifs, and landscaping with miniature trees – all directly inspired by the imperial palaces of central Vietnam as well as by traditional temple architecture. The most distinctive structures are the Asian Garden Mall and the T&K supermarket complex on Bolsa Avenue. The roof of the Asian Garden Mall has an ornate gateway with ridge ornaments and a roof of green tiles. At the entrance is a statue of Buddha, behind which are statues representing the gods of Prosperity, Longevity, and Good

Cultural landscapes. Top: Buddhist monastery in converted suburban residential garage space; bottom: Vietnamese and Asian businesses on Bolsa Avenue.

Luck (*Phuc Loc Tho* in Vietnamese, the mall's Vietnamese name). The landscaping includes bonsai trees and the interior decor incorporates Vietnamese symbols such as red paper lanterns, fans, statues, and figurines. More generally, the city of Westminster's Design Standards Manual explicitly requires the incorporation and use of Vietnamese design features and motifs in certain structures and stipulates the exclusion of design styles (such as Mediterranean, Spanish, Colonial, or Old English) that would undermine the consolidation of Vietnamese identity. The city has also sanctioned the official designation of the district as Little Saigon, adding welcome signs on the streets leading to the district and placing exit signs along nearby major freeways.

Further reading on Little Saigon

Aquilar-San Juan, Karin, *Little Saigons: Staying Vietnamese in America*, Minneapolis: University of Minnesota Press, 2009. *Shows how Little Saigon is a site for the simultaneous preservation and redefinition of Vietnamese identity.*

Trinh Vo, Linda, and Yu Danico, Mary, 'The Formation of Post-Suburban Communities: Koreatown and Little Saigon, Orange County', *International Journal of Sociology and Social Policy* 24.7/8 (2004), 15–45. *Examines the demographic transformation of Little Saigon and its economic, political, social, and cultural development in comparison with nearby Koreatown.*

Wei, Li, *'Ethnoburb', The New Ethnic Community in Urban America*, Honolulu: University of Hawaii Press, 2009. *Describes the new phenomenon of suburban ethnic clusters of residential and business districts in large metropolitan areas that are multiracial, multiethnic, multicultural, and multilingual communities in which one ethnic minority group has a significant concentration but does not necessarily constitute a majority.*

The Loop
Chicago

The Loop is the archetype of the classic central business districts (CBDs) of North American cities. Its cluster of office towers has come to symbolize the city itself – brash and confident. It was in the Loop that the skyscraper was born, and over time the district has acquired buildings designed by many of the world's most celebrated architects. A direct product of the commercial specialization resulting from nineteenth-century urban growth, the Loop has changed in character in response to the sequential changes in Chicago's economy and spatial organization. After a period of decline associated with the decentralization of many commercial functions, the Loop has been revitalized as a result of extensive urban regeneration programmes.

Chicago's unprecedented spurt of growth (from under 30,000 in 1850 to 500,000 in 1880, and 1.7 million in 1900) coincided with a revolution in transportation technologies that rearranged cities around railway and electric streetcar and cable car systems. It also coincided with a revolution in building technologies and communications technologies that allowed cities to build upward as well as outward. Much of downtown Chicago had been devastated by fire in 1871, so the subsequent rebuilding of the city was able to give expression not only to the logic of the new technologies but also to the to the spirit of the age. The result was a district that that gave visual expression to the growth and dynamics of the twentieth-century city, a symbol of progress, modernity, and affluence.

In Chicago the railways were especially important, allowing the city to become a major regional transportation hub. As the city grew, the location of railway stations and the subsequent confluence of streetcar lines shaped the early development of Chicago's business district. The conventional wisdom is that it came to be known as the Loop because of a turning loop in the cable car system that served the district. As the single most accessible area in the dramatically expanding city, competition for sites in the Loop was fierce, and so the price of land in and around the district was significantly higher than anywhere else. The outcome of competition for these premium spaces was a distinctive clustering of high-end retailing, specialized office buildings, and important civic buildings. As new and innovative buildings appeared, the Loop became a symbol of Chicago's energy and prosperity.

Initially, it was retailing activities that came to dominate, especially the more specialized and exclusive retailers that could generate sufficient profits to outbid any other potential user of downtown space. Because most shoppers were reluctant to walk very far from their starting point, the result was a distinct and compact shopping area, an elliptical zone on the axis of State Street in which retailing was practically the only activity along street frontages

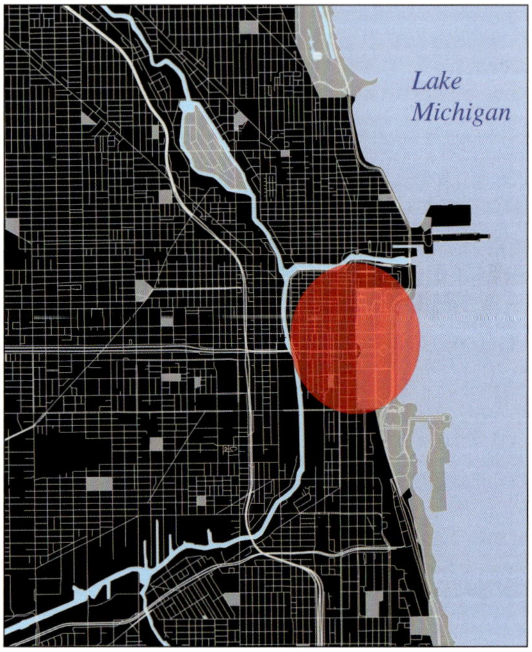

The Loop has developed around the site of the early settlement, a lakeshore site that became an inland transportation hub.

at ground level. Dominating the entire retail scene were the palatial department stores of Carson's and Marshall Field's, brimming with wave after wave of new commodities from the flood of industrial mass production and international trade. The stores provided the material means for the middle class in particular to stake out their cultural identity. In keeping with the emerging bourgeois taste of Middle America, the stores were given elaborate decorative detail and an air of grandeur and civility that masked vulgar commercialization. The introduction of electric lighting toward the end of the nineteenth century allowed for even more dazzling displays of luxury goods, while the introduction of electric street lighting made the entire shopping zone much safer and more attractive.

As the city grew, the reluctance of shoppers to walk very far created a series of 'walking zones' that evolved into specialized retail subareas, a theatre subarea and specialized clusters of high-order services such as banks, law offices, and medical arts buildings. It did not take speculators long to realise the value of central office space to smaller companies. Speculatively built office blocks provided an 'address' for small offices, which could also share in the splendour of marbled lobbies and concierge services that such settings provided. The Loop's office district bordered the shopping subarea for it, too, had a functional dependence on the nexus of transportation at routes that brought office workers on commuter trains and streetcars along with out-of-town business

High land values are reflected in tall buildings. Land values drop off sharply at the edge of the central business district. Photo by Kmf164, used under a creative commons Attribution-Share Alike License at Wikimedia Commons.

visitors by long-distance trains. The office subarea gave the Loop its most prominent landmarks, with taller and taller office buildings.

What made the Loop distinctive were the skyscrapers that were purpose-built for insurance companies and publishing houses. In addition to their need for personal intercommunication among large numbers of employees, these organizations found skyscrapers a valuable means of advertising. The new enabling technologies of elevators and iron-cage construction were exactly suited to the inflated land values and increasingly specialized patterns of land use in the Loop. Even so, it took another technological innovation – the telephone – to make skyscrapers practicable settings for businesses. The telephone allowed firms to dispense with human messengers, who would otherwise have clogged the elevators of tall buildings.

The first architect to conceive a distinctive style for skyscraper construction was Louis Sullivan, working in Chicago in conjunction with his partner Dankmar Adler. Sullivan, influenced by Arcadian Classicism and its conviction that nature should be made manifest through structure and ornamentation in art and architecture, was the author of the now-famous dictum, 'Form follows function'. Sullivan and Adler's first significant contribution to the cityscape of the Loop was the seventeen-storey Auditorium Building (1889) with a facade in Romanesque Revival style.

Ever since, Chicago – and in particular the Loop district – has been associated with landmark architecture. In 1885, William Le Baron Jenney designed the ten-storey Home Insurance Building, generally regarded as the first skyscraper in the world because of its load-carrying structural frame. Thereafter, the Loop sprouted ever-taller – and, for a time, more elaborate – skyscrapers. For a long time after its completion in 1973 the Sears Tower (now known as the Willis Tower) was the tallest building in the

Chicago Gothic: the Wrigley Building, left, and Tribune Tower, right. Photo by hibino, used under a creative commons Attribution-Share Alike License at Wikimedia Commons.

Right: **Chicago Modern**: Trump Tower. Photo by Stephen Hanafin, used under a creative commons Attribution-Share Alike License at Wikimedia Commons.

world. The most recent addition to the Loop's skyline is the Trump International Hotel and Tower, a Skidmore, Owings and Merrill building that stands just 27 m short of the Willis Tower.

Another characteristic element of the Loop (as with CBDs in general) has been that of the city hall and its associated functions, including the main library, the central post office, and the courthouse, museum, assembly hall, and opera house that make up the classic tableau of civic amenities. It was convenient for the offices of city bureaucrats and officials to be at the hub of things: convenient both for them and for their constituents, given that the Loop was by far the single most accessible place in the city. In 1911

CHASE

the city opened an imposing new eleven-storey city hall, occupying an entire city block and designed by Holabird & Roche in Classic Revival style.

Investment in the Loop fell away dramatically after the mid-point of the twentieth century as expressway building and suburban sprawl drew retailing into regional shopping malls, back-office jobs to suburban office parks, and downtown residents to suburban subdivisions. Industrial buildings on the fringes of the Loop fell into disrepair and railway yards fell into disuse. By the 1970s the Loop had lost a great deal of its vitality while showing, in places, deep scars of neglect and malaise.

In the mid-1980s the riverfront zone of the Loop came to be the focus of the city's revitalization strategy under Mayor Richard J. Daley. The Navy Pier, a popular destination spot with theatres and restaurants which had fallen into disrepair and disuse, was redeveloped at a cost of more than $225 million. It reopened in 1995 with attractions that include the Chicago Children's Museum, an indoor botanical garden, a fifteen-storey Ferris wheel, street entertainment areas with outdoor stages, an IMAX theatre, the Chicago Shakespeare Theatre, and 20 hectares of parks and promenades. Just to the south, the $450 million Lakefront Millennium Project redeveloped another 10 hectares, with a Great Lawn, a commuter bicycle centre, an ice skating rink, and concession stands. The centrepiece of the Park is an outdoor Music Pavilion with a seating area for 11,000 spectators and a massive overhead trellis designed by Frank Gehry. A third key element in the redevelopment of the lakeshore was the Museum Campus, at the southeastern end of the Loop. Here, the project required the rerouting of five-lane Lake Shore Drive in order to join the grounds of the Field Museum of

Millennium Park. Photo: J. Crocker, used under a creative commons Attribution-Share Alike License at Wikimedia Commons.

Clockwise from top left (all photos used under a creative commons Attribution-Share Alike License at Wikimedia Commons): **Michigan Avenue**. Photo: Dudesleeper; **Dearborn Park**. Photo: TonytheTiger; **Chinatown**. Photo: Daniel Schwen; **Lakefront Trail**. Photo: Alan Scott Walker.

Natural History, the Shedd Aquarium, and the Adler Planetarium.

Together with the city's Tax Increment Financing initiatives and the extensive tree-planting programme of Mayor Daley and his successors, the lakeshore projects have been an important precondition for the residential repopulation of the Loop. Outdated office buildings have been converted into luxury residential use, while neglected railway property owned by a partnership of three rail companies has been redeveloped as Dearborn Park, a mixture of townhouses, apartment buildings, and high-rise rentals. Inevitably, residential repopulation has also meant gentrification, displacing the district's low-income and minority households.

Further reading on the Loop

Wille, Lois, *At Home in the Loop: How Clout and Community Built Chicago's Dearborn Park*, Carbondale: Southern Illinois University Press, 1997. *An account of the transformation of urban decay in the Loop into an integrated and thriving community.*

Wolfe, Gerard, *Chicago In and Around the Loop*, New York: McGraw-Hill, 2004. *A detailed guide to the history and architecture of the Loop, organized in terms of a series of walking tours.*

Lower 9th District New Orleans

The Lower 9th District takes its name from the southern part of the city's ninth electoral ward. It is also 'lower' in the sense that it is mostly below sea level, tucked into a deep depression between the Mississippi River, the Industrial Canal, and Lake Borgne. Originally a cypress swamp, the district has always been an African American neighbourhood, home to clerks, policemen, labourers, and the maids, bellhops, and busboys who care for New Orleans tourists. Within the city, the Lower 9th has also always been a metaphor for poverty and neglect, known for both its bad luck and its resilience. According to the 2000 census, more than a third of the Lower 9th's 20,000 residents were below the poverty line, nearly 14 per cent were unemployed, and half of the households were headed by women.

Laid out on a simple grid, the architecture of the district has always been dominated by classic 'shotgun' houses: narrow wooden structures, usually no more than 3.5 m wide, with three to five rooms in sequence with no hallways, and doors at each end. The Holy Cross section of the district, fronting the river, was placed on the National Register of Historic Places in the 1980s because of its shotgun houses and its idiosyncratic 'steamboat houses', built in the early 1900s by a riverboat captain in elaborate riverboat style.

The district was devastated by Hurricane Katrina, which made landfall on August 29, 2005. Sections of the levees protecting New Orleans were breached from storm surges, flooding 80 per cent of the city, including all of the Lower 9th, where dozens of people drowned and the water stood for up to six weeks. In the Holy Cross section it was about a metre deep, while in northern sections of the district the flooding was more than 3 m deep, the water lapping at rooftops. Altogether more than 4,000 homes in the Lower 9th were destroyed. Entire houses were knocked off foundations, barbershops and corner grocery stores flattened, and cars floated onto porches. What remained was coated in muck: a toxic layer of sewage and dirt. Mould rapidly devoured interiors and the inevitable outcome was the largest demolition of a community in modern U.S. history.

Unlike most poor African American districts, nearly two-thirds of the residents of the Lower 9th Ward were homeowners. Many of these families had lived in their shotgun-style houses for generations and owned them outright. Almost none, though, had flood insurance. The Federal Emergency Management Agency (FEMA) had zoned the Lower 9th Ward as low risk because it was expected to be protected by the levees. In fact, the Lower 9th was the city district hardest hit by the storm, a result, it was widely believed in the aftermath, of negligence on the part of the U.S. Army Corps of Engineers, the agency that built and was supposed to maintain the surrounding levees. Past experience led many

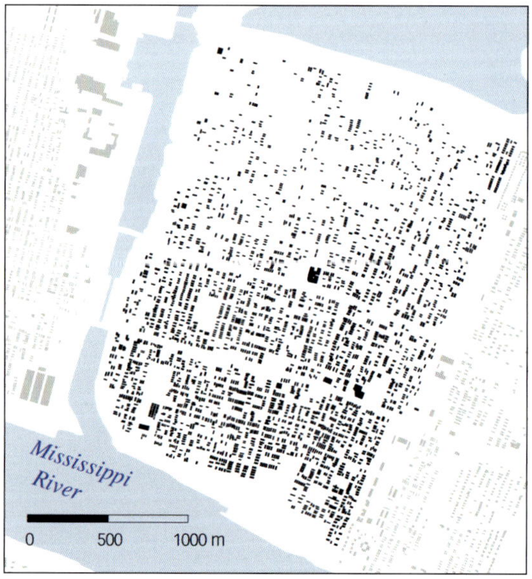

Figure-ground diagram of the Lower 9th District. The northern sector remains sparsely developed more than six years after the hurricane.

residents to suspect that the breaches of the levees had in fact been intentional:

In the context of these historical precedents – systematic federal policy failures, the experience of African Americans during the 1927 flood, and the city's proven willingness to breach the levees to protect one part of the region at the expense of another – many residents in New Orleans believe, or at least find it probable, that the breaches along the New Orleans Industrial Canal that flooded the Lower 9th Ward when Hurricane Katrina struck were intentional. Although this belief might appear irrational to outsiders and government officials, it highlights a powerful distrust regarding government protection of African Americans' interests.

Nelson et al., 2007, p. 39

Only a fifth of the district's residents have returned to live in the district since 2005, in part because of inadequate reconstruction funding compared with assistance that homeowners in other New Orleans neighbourhoods have received, and in part because the Unified New Orleans Plan developed by the city's Office of Recovery Management emphasized the district's continuing vulnerability to flooding. Some of the surviving houses remain abandoned and boarded-up, still bearing the ominous fluorescent orange X's on their facades that disaster officials used to indicate they were uninhabitable. A nonprofit organization, the Preservation Resource Center, has worked to help restore and repopulate the Holy Cross section, purchasing, renovating, and reselling vacant historic properties community. The Center also has a salvage program that recovers reusable ornamental items such as mantels, doors, windows, and wrought iron from historic buildings that cannot be saved.

The Lower 9th two weeks after Hurricane Katrina, in September 2005. The storm hit New Orleans on 29 August and, before long, 80 per cent of the city was under water. Thousands of people who failed or were unable to evacuate, mostly poor and elderly, were trapped on bridges, overpasses, and rooftops, and in the Louisiana Superdome (now the Mercedes-Benz Superdome). A total of 1,833 people died in the disaster. Photo: Marvin Nauman/FEMA.

Five years after Katrina, a teenager and her rescued dog walk past a new home in the Make It Right housing complex. Photo: Bevil Knap/EPA/Corbis.

Below: **Little change** in much of the Lower 9th Ward. Photo by David Haberthür, used under a creative commons Attribution-Share Alike License at Wikimedia Commons.

In the northern reaches of the district, where the Industrial Canal flood wall collapsed and virtually everything was destroyed, there is a very different approach to recovery. Rather than restoration and renovation, the focus is on providing new homes. Here, the key agency is the Make It Right Foundation, established in 2007 by the actor Brad Pitt. The foundation invites architects to donate designs for sustainable contemporary homes based on traditional shotgun and duplex styles; using the existing narrow lots; elevating houses to avoid future flooding, including rooftop access to simplify rescue; and featuring prominent porches or front stoops for socializing. The standard house was to be 112 m^2, have three bedrooms and two baths, and cost no more than $150,000. Homeowners would pay what they could and the foundation would help with the rest. By 2011 several dozen homes had been completed, toward a goal of 150. One of the most innovative homes, designed by Pritzker prizewinner Thom Mayne, is built to rise up to 4 m with surging flood waters, with guideposts that will keep it from floating away.

Newly constructed home in the Make It Right housing complex in the Lower 9th District. Photo: Julie Dermansky/Corbis.

Because all of the homes built to date have been certified by the U.S. Green Building Council as Leadership in Energy and Environmental Design (LEED) platinum for their energy efficiency and sustainability, the Make It Right area is now the 'largest, greenest neighborhood of single family homes in America', according to the Council.

Another home in the Make It Right housing complex. Photo: Julie Dermansky/Corbis.

Further reading on the Lower 9th

Hartman, Chester, and Squires, Gregory, eds., *There Is No Such Thing as a Natural Disaster: Race, Class, and Hurricane Katrina*, New York: Routledge, 2006. *This book covers the roles that race and class played in the response to Hurricane Katrina, the storm's impact on housing and redevelopment, and the implications for government agencies, financial institutions, and neighbourhood organizations.*

Nelson, Marla, Ehrenfeucht, Renia, and Laska, Shirley, 'Planning, Plans, and People: Professional Expertise, Local Knowledge, and Governmental Action in Post-Hurricane Katrina New Orleans', *Cityscape: A Journal of Policy Development and Research* 9.3 (2007), 23–52. *Examines the planning processes and the difficulties the city has faced in developing its recovery plans, post-Katrina.*

Le Marais
Paris

The landscape of the Marais is a product of centuries of layered development. Initially the site of horticultural gardens run by religious orders on marshland drained in the tenth century, the district was at its prime as an élite residential area from the middle of the fifteenth century to the beginning of the eighteenth century, after which the Marais gradually deteriorated. Spared the radical surgery of Baron Haussmann's modernization schemes in the nineteenth century, it retained much of its medieval and Renaissance fabric but developed into a backwater of slums. After World War II, historic preservation triggered investment and gentrification, bringing the district into the mainstream of central Paris as both a residential area and a destination district.

The district's name stems from the region of watered gardens (*maraîchers*) tended by several different religious orders for several hundred years. The Knights Templar also held agricultural land in the district, where they built a fortress for their headquarters. After the Order of the Knights Templar was abolished early in the fourteenth century, the eastern end of the Marais was developed around two royal complexes, the Hôtel Saint-Pol and the Hôtel des Tournelles. Both consisted of groups of buildings surrounded by gardens and a succession of courtyards and galleries along with ornamental gardens, orchards, vineyards, and aviaries.

The complexion of the district changed decisively in the mid-sixteenth century as the religious orders began to sell off their horticultural gardens and the royal complexes were abandoned. The Hôtel des Tournelles was famously razed by order of Catherine de Médici after her husband, Henry II, had died there as a result of a jousting accident. The Hôtel Saint-Pol was sold off as building plots by Francois I, who was short of money for the renovation of the Louvre as his principal royal palace. The new streets were laid out in a grid that became the Saint-Paul village. The rest of the Marais, just over a kilometre from the Louvre, now became an attractive location for the new town mansions – *hôtels particuliers* – of affluent aristocrats. Dozens of *hôtels* were built, most of them in architectural styles that

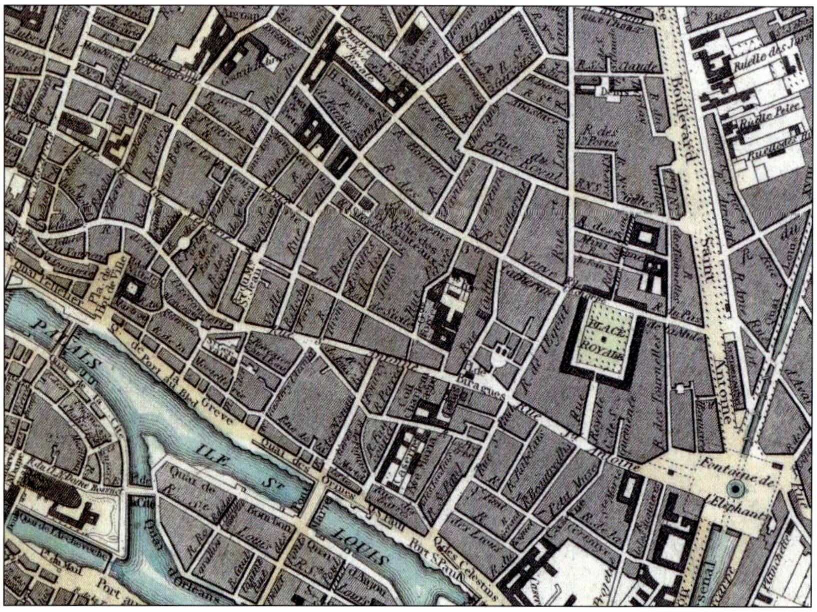

The Marais in 1834. Map extract courtesy of the David Rumsey Map Collection <www.davidrumsey.com>

came from Italy. Larger *hôtels* were typically fronted by a courtyard, with a garden behind; parallel wings on either side linked the house to a screen on the street frontage, pierced by a *porte cochère*. The Hôtel Carnavalet is a splendid example. Like most *hôtels*, the street frontage is austere, its most imposing facades reserved for the interior courtyard.

By the early seventeenth century, Henri IV had begun to modernize Paris, bringing progressive ideas about building and ambitious urban design projects conceived in the grand manner that characterized Renaissance city planning. A key element in Henri's schema was the Place Royale (now the Place des Vosges, one of the great public spaces of Europe) on the site of the old Parc des Tournelles. The nine pavilions around the central square were built with delicate brickwork, and the two tallest pavilions – at either end – were intended for the king and queen, but were never used. Similarly, a manufactory for silk textiles was planned for the north side, with showrooms and elegant shops under the arches. But the silk workshops were never installed; the buildings were immediately bought up and fitted out as residences for the wealthy and titled, the apartments kitted out with sumptuous interiors, fine panelling, elaborate tapestries, costly paintings, and rare cabinetry. The Marais became a centre of elegance and sophistication, drawing in high government officials, Italian bankers, judges, royal officials, and the occasional landed aristocrat. It was where the Parisian intelligentsia had their gatherings, where women held fashionable salons, and where artists were drawn to live close to their secular or religious patrons.

When the old city wall was demolished in the late seventeenth century, the Marais became part of the fabric of the city instead of a dead end, but in the process it began to lose some of its identity and exclusiveness. The nobles and bourgeois owners of the *hôtels particuliers* and the Place Royale began to find

Place des Vosges. Originally called the Place Royale when it was built by Henry IV in 1605, its well-proportioned facades, shadowed arcades, and balanced colour scheme led to the Marais becoming a centre of elegance and fashionability.

themselves hemmed in among shopkeepers and the petite bourgeoisie. When Louis XIV and his court choose to reside at Versailles, there was a westward movement of wealth and fashion, with the nobility abandoning the Marais for spacious mansions across the river in the Faubourg Saint-Germain.

During the Revolution the Marais was emptied of aristocracy; those who escaped the guillotine moved to the provinces. The *hôtels* began to be subdivided. Servants' quarters were let out as furnished rooms, while ground-floor apartments were taken over by small-scale industry, wholesale commerce, and cheap housing.

Over the next century the Marais gradually descended into poverty and decay. But it escaped the radical surgery of Baron Haussmann who, between 1853 and 1870, demolished large sections of old Paris to make way for broad, new tree-lined avenues, with numerous public open spaces and monuments. Haussmann installed a new water supply system, a gigantic system of sewers, and street lighting. He built new bridges, a new opera house, and other public buildings, and made extensive improvements in smaller urban parks that turned them into places of sociality and leisure, but he skirted the Marais and left it intact. A couple of generations later, Le Corbusier's totalitarian plan for Paris, the Plan Voisin (1925), proposed razing the entire district, replacing it with rows of sixty-storey towers set between freeways and tracts of open space. While Le Corbusier's proposals gained worldwide attention among Modernists, they were met with scorn by Parisian intellectuals and politicians.

Meanwhile, Jewish immigrants from Eastern Europe had settled in the Marais, in rue des Rosiers and adjacent streets, creating a community that flourished until the Nazi occupation of

The Rue des Barres, at the western end of the district, with the Eglise Saint Gervais Communion de Jérusalem to the left.

The bars and cafés of the Marais have become emblematic of a Parisian lifestyle that is recognized around the world. Shown here is the Cafe-Restaurant Camille, on the corner of rue Elzevir and rue des Francs Bourgeois.

Paris in 1940. The legacy of the community is still very visible today, especially in the delicatessens specializing in halvah, challah, bagels, knishes, and other Jewish delicacies.

In the immediate postwar years the Marais was still a poor quarter, the courtyards of its great hôtels covered with galvanized steel roofs and clogged up with piles of boxes and pallets. In the 1950s parts of the Marais were declared *îlots insalubres* ('unhealthy districts') and condemned, the inhabitants moved out and the windows boarded up. Many of the working-class households moved to new social housing projects constructed in the outer suburbs.

The rehabilitation of the Marais began in the 1960s. The key turning point was the appointment of the writer André Malraux as Minister of Culture by Charles de Gaulle in 1958. Malraux instigated an aggressive programme of historic restoration and in 1964 the Marais became the first entire district to be designated for clean-up and preservation. The district's blackened buildings revealed tawny stonework and bricks of soft red, and its remaining *hôtels* were reclaimed as part of the national patrimony. The Hôtel de Sully, for example, was restored in 1965 to house the Centre des Monuments Nationaux. The Hôtel Carnavalet is now home to the Museum of the History of Paris, the Hôtel de Soubise houses the Museum of French History and part of the French National Archives, while the Hôtel Sâle houses the Picasso Museum.

Others, such as the Hôtel de Sens, had to be more or less reconstructed. A rare example of medieval domestic architecture, the rebuilt Hôtel de Sens acquired the appearance of a Gothic hall on an American Ivy League campus. Structures that were beyond repair

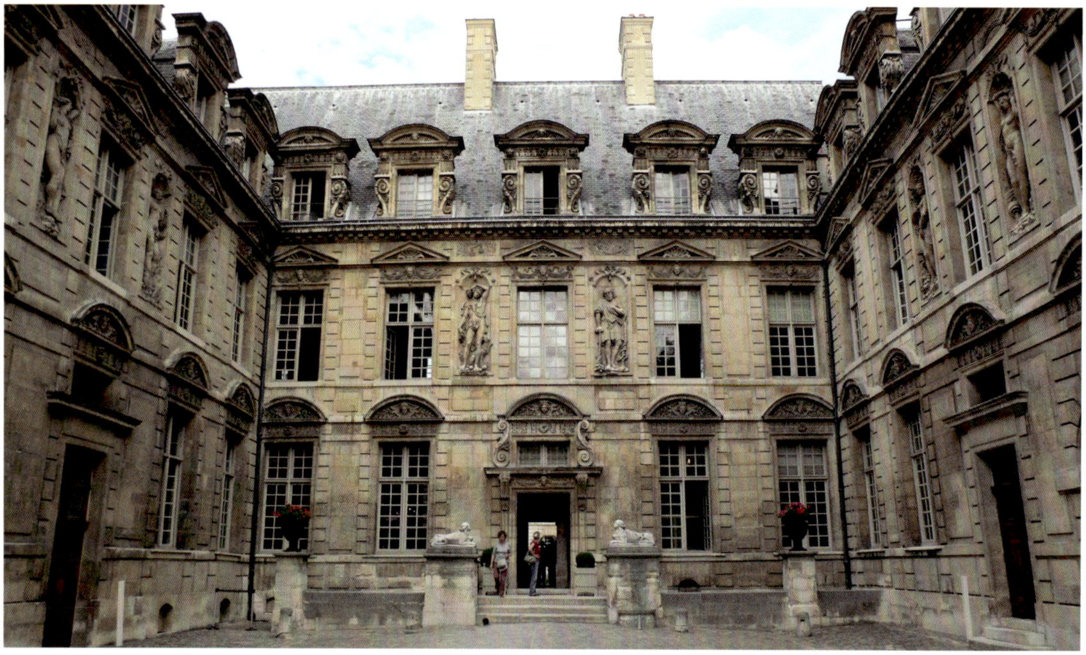

The Hôtel de Sully, built as a private mansion between 1625 and 1630 and now the Centre des Monuments Nationaux, responsible for the management of historic buildings and monuments in state care.

or restoration were replaced by modern apartment houses, built in the style of *architecture d'accompagnement*, conforming in terms of massing and general appearance to the traditional apartment blocks of the district.

Not surprisingly, these changes promptly led to the gentrification of the Marais, a process that was accelerated by a 1977 Housing Act designed to encourage owner-occupancy through low-interest loans, and by the abolition of rent controls in 1986. White-collar workers moved into renovated apartments, bars and bistros were given makeovers, and patisseries and grocery stores were converted into designer clothing stores. Beginning in the late 1970s, the district also attracted gay businesses: bars, clubs, and bookstores whose owners consciously set out to create a new gay quarter. Gay businesses are clustered along relatively few streets, principally in the southwestern corner of the district, but the district as a whole has attracted an increasing number of gay residents who have established a distinctive community through shared tastes, cultural preferences in music and food, and even by a distinct 'Marais look' among the gay male inhabitants.

It did not take long for the historic legacy of the district, along with its bistros, delicatessens, and boutiques, to appear on tourists' itineraries. Today the Marais is at once a destination district of international standing, a gentrifying district, a gay district, a Jewish district, and a heritage district.

Further reading on Le Marais

Gady, Alexandre, *Le Marais: Guide Historique et Architectural*, Paris: Le Passage, 2002. *An extended guide with an emphasis on the architectural legacy of the district.*

Karmel, Alex, *A Corner in the Marais*, Boston: David Godine, 1998. *A personal memoir of living in the district, emphasizing the history of the author's neighbourhood.*

The Hôtel de Sens. Built between 1475 and 1507, it was originally owned by the archbishops of Sens, 100 km southeast of Paris. It houses an art library but remains a private residence.

Old-fashioned pharmacy on rue des Francs Bourgeois, in the heart of the Marais.

Sacha Finkelsztajn, a delicatessen on rue des Rosiers specializing in Jewish cuisine from central Europe and Russia.

Timbered medieval building (left) at the intersection of rue des Barres and rue du Grenier Sur L'Eau.

Mission District San Francisco

The Mission District is both multilayered and multicultural. The original settlers, Yelamu Indians, were displaced by Spanish missionaries during the late eighteenth century. The Mission San Francisco de Asis, built in 1776, is San Francisco's oldest building. The district became an extensive shantytown during the California Gold Rush (1848–1855) but was redeveloped as a Victorian suburb in the last quarter of the nineteenth century. Partially destroyed by the earthquake and fire of 1906, the district gradually acquired a mixed population of migrants and immigrants, a distinctive gay population, and increasing numbers of affluent young professionals.

San Francisco's civic landscapes are distinctive, a product of the composition of the city's distinctive class structure and cultural sensibilities: relatively wealthy, petty bourgeois, bohemian, cosmopolitan, egalitarian, environmentalist, and tolerant. Geographer Richard Walker, in an illuminating essay on the city, has identified four dominant residential ecologies:

> *The oldest and most famous is the nineteenth-century Victorian townhouse realm. The most recent and extensive is the vast domain of single-family homes, mass suburbia of the twentieth century. The dominant element setting the cultural tone of the Bay Area is a middle-class suburbia of a peculiar sort: the ecotopian middle landscape. The most overlooked, yet vital, realm of all is the hotel and apartment districts of San Francisco and the inner East Bay.*
>
> 1995, p. 35

The Mission, located just over 1.5 km to the southwest of the city's central business district, contains extensive elements of two of these – the Victorian townhouse realm and the hotel and apartment realm – along with a smattering of early twentieth-century single-family homes. It was developed in the mid to late nineteenth century to accommodate the city's growing population of petit bourgeoisie, its lower-paid white-collar workforce, and, increasingly, its labouring classes.

In the first decades after the mid-century Gold Rush, Yankee migrants and German, Polish, and Scandinavian immigrants moved into the flatlands of the Mission district, occupying cheap wooden buildings, mostly unpainted with plain facades. The northern part of the district featured a racetrack, restaurants, a zoo, and a two-block 'pleasure resort', Woodward's Gardens. But from the 1860s the district was redeveloped. As Walker notes (p. 36), the Victorian landscape was 'thrown up in one titanic 30-year spasm of capitalist property development that erased most of the earlier terrain of the Gold Rush city'.

It was laid out on a simple grid and developed mainly by small builder-developers on lots that were 7.5 to 9 m wide and 30 to 36 m deep in groups of five to fifty buildings. Less spacious than the Victorian mansions of Nob Hill and Van Ness Avenue and not as flamboyant as the single-family homes of Pacific Heights, the Mission's Victorian row houses, duplexes, and hotels nevertheless exhibited the classic

The Mission is located a short distance to the south of the city's central business district.

Italianate styling, with flat roofs, bay windows (or tall narrow double-paned windows on flat-front buildings), overhanging eaves, and elaborate cornices.

Apart from an area between Dolores Street and Van Ness Avenue as far south as 20th Street, most of the Mission District survived the 1906 earthquake and subsequent fire. Nevertheless, the Mission experienced significant change as working-class Irish and Italian families moved in, displaced from destroyed central neighbourhoods. Many of the larger Victorian buildings were converted into apartments, while new residential building in the district after World War I was mostly infill in the form of smaller, more modest homes.

Through the twentieth century the district's dense supply of affordable housing attracted successive waves of immigrants. Since the 1950s the Latino population in the Mission District has doubled every ten years, lending the neighbourhood much of its current character. Latino culture is particularly evident in the district's famous street art, which combines elements of Mexican mural painting, surrealism, pop art, urban punk, eco-warrior, cartoon, and graffiti. Rooted in the tradition of Mexican mural work associated with Diego Rivera, Jose Clemente Orozco, and David Alfaro Siqueiros, the Mission's street art took off in the 1960s when the development of bright, weather-resistant acrylic paint coincided with the Chicano movement's embrace of Latino heritage. Early murals had a strong focus on social struggle, while more recent trends are for life-affirming, positive themes inspired by Las Mujeres Muralistas, a group of women muralists active in the 1970s.

The district also attracted a neobohemian population and in the 1970s developed a multicultural and pansexual diversity. Filipino and Vietnamese immigrants arrived, while the Valencia Street corridor became a lesbian-feminist zone featuring a lesbian bar (Amelia's), a bath house, a sex toy store (Good Vibrations), and the Valencia Rose, a gay and lesbian performance space. A little to the west, the upper

Mission Street, one of several commercial strips running through the district. Photo: Charles O. Cecil/Alamy.

Victorian houses. There are more than 2,500 Victorian houses in the district. More than 900 are Italianate houses of the 1870s (as in the example on the left). Another 800 are the Stick-style houses popular in the 1880s (middle). Queen Anne-style houses (right) from the 1890s are in the minority, for by the 1890s most Inner Mission land was already built upon.

section of Dolores Park near 19th and Church (known as Dolores Beach), which affords fine views of the downtown district, has become a favourite spot for muscled gay sunbathers. From here, on the last Saturday each June, the anarchist Dyke March takes place.

The combination of a central location, Victorian architecture, relatively low rents, and the charming irreverence and live-and-let-live atmosphere of the district led inevitably to gentrification. The process was supercharged by the dot-com wealth of young San Francisco and Silicon Valley professionals in the 1980s and 1990s. Many Latino households were displaced as the district acquired multiple juxtapositions of the shabby and the glossy, with porn shops, hourly motels, and peep-show joints next door to home décor boutiques, vegan bakeries, and restaurants serving sushi and $15 martinis.

Vacant workshops were converted into loft apartments and abandoned lots were transformed into community gardens. The broad avenues of Dolores Street, Mission Street, Guerrero Street, and Van Ness Avenue acquired a rich mixture of taquerias, pupuserias, produce markets, Salvadoran bakeries, beauty salons, auto-repair shops, and check-cashing centres along with hotels, apartment buildings, independent cafés, thrift shops, used-book stores, and hip bars and restaurants. The Valencia Corridor became a trendy neighbourhood drawing people from across the city to enjoy the nightlife and the thriving arts scene.

These corridors, suggests Richard Walker, are the most vital element in the city's social ecology. For residents of small homes and apartments in dense districts like the Mission,

... home life stretches out along the street: dining in a neighbourhood eatery, reading in a coffee shop, playing in an arcade, going out to the movies. Here lies the everyday substrate for a public life in urban places, making for congregations of people, assemblages of diverse activities, and the flow of feet along the pavement. ... These commercial zones of dense housing, cheap entertainment and public life have served as the great free spaces of the city, the key nodes of urbanism in the sense of promiscuous mingling of

Balmy Street. The first murals in this narrow street were created in 1971 by schoolchildren from a local tutoring centre. In the 1980s a group of artists calling for peace in Central America collaborated on a series of murals portraying peasant struggles for land and dignity. Many of the Mission District's best artists have painted here and the scenes have changed over time.

diverse people, activities and ideas. They provide the moving panorama enjoyed by Baudelaire's flâneur; the porous spaces in which flourish the experimental lives of the bohemians, or their more recent equivalents, beatniks, jazzmen, hippies, gays, punks; and the gathering spots for political rebels and public intellectuals.

1995, p. 48

Murals on apartments above the House of Brakes on 24th Street. Photo by House of Brakes, used under a creative commons Attribution-Share Alike License at Wikimedia Commons.

Further reading on the Mission District

Godfrey, Brian, 'Urban Development and Redevelopment in San Francisco', *Geographical Review* 87.3 (1997), 309–33. *Describes the pivotal periods of intense city building, each about twenty-five years in duration, that have shaped the city.*

Jacoby, Annice, *Street Art San Francisco: Mission Muralismo*, San Francisco: Abrams, 2009. *With 600 photographs, this comprehensive book showcases more than three decades of street art in San Francisco's legendary Mission District.*

Walker, Richard, 'Landscapes and City Life: Four Ecologies of Residence in the San Francisco Bay Area', *Ecumene* 2.1 (1995), 33–64. *An insightful essay on the dominant civic ecologies – social and physical – of San Francisco.*

New Town Edinburgh

In a city famous within Scotland for its social snobbery, Edinburgh's New Town presents a particularly snooty air of privilege and refinement. The New Town is also symbolic of the city's – and to a certain extent, Scotland's – aspirations toward international standing in terms of art, architecture, literature, and philosophy. While the tourist image of the city is typically of a kilted bagpiper set against the backdrop of Edinburgh Castle, the city's own self-image is framed around the Georgian squares and crescents of the New Town and its Victorian-era monuments, statues, and Greek Revival institutions. Together with the Old Town, situated across Princes Street Gardens along the volcanic crag-and-tail that is crowned by Edinburgh Castle, the New Town is a UNESCO World Heritage site.

The basis of the New Town was constructed between 1767 and 1890 as an aggregation of seven successive planned residential developments to the north of the city's historic core. In broad context, the New Town should be seen as an example of the urban design and planning that swept across Europe in the late Renaissance. These projects involved the regeneration of major public buildings, the restructuring of primary city streets, the creation of enclosed squares, plazas, and piazzas, and the addition of extensive new residential districts, typically laid out to a rectilinear plan.

Important exemplars of restructured primary streets include Unter den Linden in Berlin; the Via Leonina (now the Via di Ripetta) and the Strada Felice in Rome; and the Champs Elysées and the rue Royale in Paris, their articulation achieved by the spacious Place Louis XV (the present Place de la Concorde). Important exemplars of enclosed squares, plazas, and piazzas include the Place Dauphine, the Place Vendôme, and the Place Royale (renamed the Place des Vosges after the French Revolution) in Paris; Potsdamer Platz and Leipziger Platz, in Berlin; Covent Garden, Leicester Square, and Bloomsbury Square in London; the Piazza

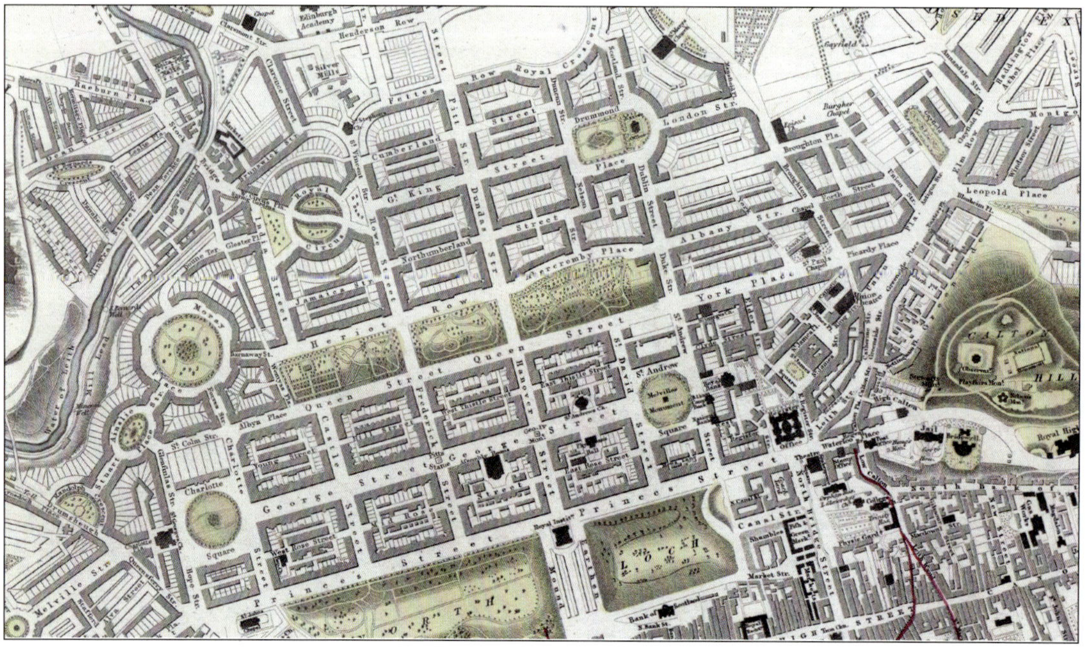

The New Town in 1834. Map extract courtesy of the David Rumsey Map Collection, <www.davidrumsey.com>.

Charlotte Square. The final part of the initial phase of the New Town, completed in 1820. Much of the housing was designed by architect Robert Adam. The memorial in the centre of the garden commemorates Prince Albert, consort to Queen Victoria. Photo: Bill Miller/Alamy.

Navona in Rome; the Plaza Mayor in Madrid, and the Piazza San Marco in Venice. The New Town in Edinburgh was an important exemplar of a planned new residential district; other examples include Dorotheenstadt and Friedrichstadt in Berlin, and Georgian Bath.

Until the mid-eighteenth century, Edinburgh had been confined to the Old Town, jammed into a narrow site along the High Street ridge because of surrounding marshy ground on both sides of the ridge. Draining the deep, marshy valley of North Loch area began in the 1750s and the city built a bridge across the valley in 1772, allowing the higher land to the north of the Old Town to be developed. Spurred by a desire to compensate for the city's loss of status (as a national capital as a result of Scotland's 1707 Union with England and Wales), Edinburgh's large and well-educated middle-class community vigorously pursued the late-Renaissance ideals of 'progress, prosperity, order, and elegance'. In 1766, nearly two decades after the competition for the design of the Place Louis XV in Paris and three years after a competition had been held for a plan for St Petersburg, the city held a competition to design the layout of about 40 hectares of city-owned land. The winner was the young architect James Craig. His design was based on a simple grid-iron plan with formal enclosed squares at either end of the principal street, George Street (after the then monarch, George III). Parallel with George Street and bounding the development were Queen Street to the north and Princes Street to the south.

The speed of subsequent development of the plan and the quality of the architecture ensured that this first phase of the New Town quickly became the apogee of stylish sophistication, drawing the city's élite from their cramped quarters in the Old Town. The New

New Town Residences on Heriot Row. Photo: Urbanmyth/Alamy.

Town was built in neoclassical style, with finely dressed, locally quarried sandstone and with many buildings having grandiose pillars and wrought-iron railings outside and tall ceilings and decorative friezes and trimmings inside.

Financial and aesthetic success prompted further developments and grander schemes with broad streets, gardens, terraces, and crescents. By the beginning of the nineteenth century, extensions to the New Town had been built to the north, east, and west, with crescents and circuses replacing terraces and enclosed squares as the dominant layout. Many of the later extensions, however, lacked the Georgian élan, and elegant style became a matter of unimaginative convention. The North Loch, finally completely drained by the 1820s, was transformed into a public park, Princes Street Gardens. Princes Street itself, originally entirely residential, began to change as shops, department stores, and hotels spread along its length, drawn by the amenity of the park, the view of the dramatic skyline of the Old Town, and the coming of the railway and the clientele of grand railway hotels. By 1900 Princes Street had become Scotland's most fashionable shopping street, widely considered to be among the most attractive in the world.

Meanwhile, vast quantities of fill from the development of the New Town were used to create an artificial causeway – the Mound – between Princes Street and the Old Town, and a site for the Royal Scottish Academy and the National Gallery of Scotland. The neoclassical style adopted for these buildings reflected Edinburgh's aspiration to be thought of as the Athens of the North – one of the major centres of the international Greek Revival architecture and a hearth of progressive philosophy. The wealth that Edinburgh acquired as a financial centre in the latter part of the nineteenth century allowed the Victorians to launch an ambitious phase of civic improvement, with extravagant public buildings, monuments, and statuary in an eclectic mixture of romantic, Gothic, baronial, and neoclassical styles.

The core of the New Town has survived virtually intact, though the interiors of many residences have been modernized as flats and office spaces, while the mews buildings that once housed servants and stables have been converted into desirable residences. The exterior appearance of the Georgian architecture was, of course, meant to be socially intimidating

Opposite, clockwise from top left: **Georgian residences**, Rothesay Terrace; **stabling converted into apartments**, Rothesay Mews, Photo by M. J. Richardson, used under a creative commons Attribution-Share Alike License at Wikimedia Commons; **residential terrace**, Chester Street; **Charlotte Square**, west side, the National Archives of Scotland in the domed building; **North Charlotte Street**; **Charlotte Square**, northwestern corner; **Buchan House** (1772), St Andrew Square, now IBM offices; **Melville Street** and the statue of Robert Dundas, 2nd Viscount Melville, statesman.

Princes Street Gardens. In the distance is the Balmoral Hotel, formerly the North British Hotel, a classic railway hotel; to the left is the Scott Monument, a Victorian tribute to author Sir Walter Scott.

as well as refined and elegant, but on a dull day the regimented streets and uniform black iron railings can seem rather charmless.

What makes the New Town special is its setting. The main axis, George Street, was built along a ridge, with dramatic views down side streets: south to the Castle and the skyline of the Old Town, and north to the Firth of Forth and the distant hills of Fife. Within the New Town, the massing of built form is relieved by a series of formal gardens, each with its own character. Moray Place Garden, for example, is flat, with a perfectly manicured formal layout and year-round colour from geometric-shaped flower beds; Bank Gardens is 2.5 hectares of steep grassy slope with zigzag pathways through mature trees, holly bushes, and a rockery filled with shade-loving grasses; while Queen Street Gardens consists of park-like lawns, lined by trees and bushes that screen the central area from public view. The gardens are all private, accessible only to residents of adjacent residences.

The exception is Princes Street Gardens, an old-fashioned city park with bedding plants and terraced walks, war memorials, statues to civic dignitaries, and benches with commemorative plaques. In good weather its restful setting and opportunities for people-watching draw crowds of tourists, shoppers, and office workers.

Princes Street itself has become a clone of other British high streets, most of its distinctive independent shops and department stores having been displaced in the 1960s and 1970s by national chains, and most of the Victorian buildings – or at least their street-level facades – replaced by bland and often cheap-looking retail architecture. An additional array of cloned retailing has been installed in Princes Mall, formerly a market and exhibition hall (Waverly Market), but at least it is tucked away discreetly, below the level of the street. The notable exception to cloned stores and bland architecture is Jenners, an old-fashioned department store founded in 1838 whose current building, with a three-storey interior hall and elaborate wood panelling, was built in 1895.

The locus of fashionable, high-end retailing has shifted to George Street, where there is also a concentration of smart auction houses and fashionable bars. Queen Street, the northern limit of the original New Town, still retains much of its original appearance, but it has become a major traffic artery with an alienating affect for pedestrians. In contrast, Rose Street, a traffic-free back route between Charlotte Square and St Andrew Square, has a very different character, lined with modest houses, quirky little shops, restaurants, and innumerable pubs and bars.

Further reading on Edinburgh New Town

Cant, Malcolm, *Edinburgh's New Town and Its Environs*, Edinburgh: Stenlake, 2009. *An illustrated guide.*

Edwards, Brian, and Jenkins, Paul, eds., *Edinburgh: The Making of a Capital City*, Edinburgh: Edinburgh University Press, 2005. *A comprehensive review of the making and remaking of Edinburgh from the Renaissance city to the present.*

Youngson, A. J., *The Making of Classical Edinburgh*, Edinburgh: Edinburgh University Press, 2002. *A well-written account, with excellent photographs and beautiful reproductions of James Craig's plans of the New Town.*

Old Town Alexandria, Virginia

Old Town Alexandria is situated on the west bank of the Potomac River, 10 km south of Washington, D.C. Much of its fabric dates from colonial and early Federal periods, but Old Town also bears the imprint of successive roles as a trading port, a manufacturing centre, a railway depot, a tourist destination, and an office centre. Eighteenth-century prosperity was reflected in substantial brick townhouses that lined streets that were laid out in a simple grid with the principal axis, King Street, running east to west from the river. Much of this fabric has long been protected by strict historic preservation, but it is interlaced with a broad spectrum of other buildings and land uses.

In the early eighteenth century much of the area around Alexandria had been cleared and was under tobacco cultivation. By the mid-eighteenth century, the settlement was known for its tobacco warehouses, and by the early 1770s Alexandria had become one of the principal colonial trading centres and ports, exporting tobacco to Britain and corn, barley, wheat, and oats from the Shenandoah Valley to the West Indies and to Britain. After independence from Britain, Alexandria was incorporated as a city and developed as an important entrepôt, importing manufacturing equipment and luxury goods as well as exporting agricultural staples. It also developed one of the largest slave markets in the United States. Alexandria's wharfside expanded as ships from Spain, Britain, Portugal, the West Indies, and the Caribbean unloaded their precious cargoes of imported china, Antigua rum, Puerto Rico coffee, and Lisbon wines, as well as an assortment of consumer goods from Great Britain. Alexandria also developed an important coastal trade with New England, sending cargoes of flour and tobacco and receiving preserved meats, grain, and forest products.

Beyond the wharfside, the Old Town developed as a straightforward grid, with seven parallel streets leading to the river, secondary streets set at right angles, and a market square set in the centre. The same grid plan of 1-hectare blocks was subsequently extended several times. The principal streets were named in hierarchical fashion, reflecting the town's colonial origins. At the centre of the original plan were King Street and Queen Street. Parallel to King Street going south were Prince and Duke streets, while to the north of Queen was Princess Street. Beyond Princess was Oronoco, named in honour of a type of tobacco leaf originating from the

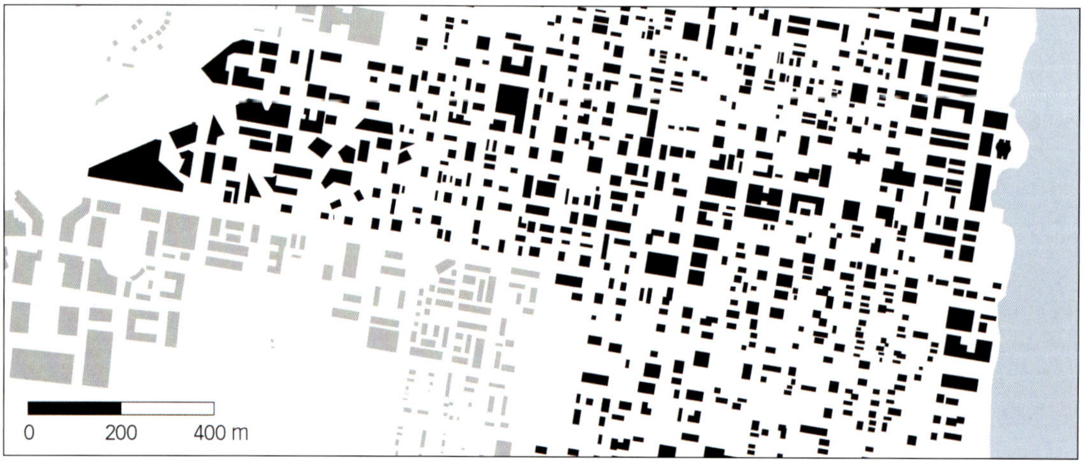

Figure-ground diagram of Old Town Alexandria. The simple grid plan is typical of towns in colonial Virginia.

region of the great river in South America. Streets laid out after independence were named after heroes of the Revolution: Virginia patriots and Englishmen sympathetic to the American cause, including Nathaniel Greene, Gilbert du Motier (the Marquis de LaFayette), Benjamin Franklin, Thomas Jefferson, Patrick Henry, George Washington, George Wythe, and John Wilkes.

The streets were lined with substantial brick houses, the wealthiest merchants paying a premium for waterfront lots that gave them the ability to construct homes with private wharves and warehouses below. Georgian-style townhouses were predominant, and where brick was too expensive the style was replicated in clapboard. By the late eighteenth century, architectural taste had begun to reflect both British precedents and the desire to express an independent national identity. As a result, larger civic and commercial buildings were built in a new 'Federal style' of architecture that drew on a neoclassical vocabulary. The Federal style, in turn, was superseded in the 1830s and 1840s by a 'Grecian mode' of architecture, with colonnaded porticos, gable and hipped roofs of low pitch, and doors surrounded by narrow sidelights.

By the mid-nineteenth century Old Town Alexandria had added manufacturing to its entrepôt industries, with two shipyards, a foundry, a brewery, several tanneries and engineering works, and several cigar factories. During the 1850s Alexandria was transformed into a major railway hub, with wheat and flour deliveries coming in from the mid-Atlantic Piedmont along with coal from West Virginia, while guano fertilizer, imported from South

Old Town, looking east from the George Washington Masonic National Memorial. Photo by Ben Schumin, used under a creative commons Attribution-Share Alike License at Wikimedia Commons.

Architectural styles in Old Town changed according to both fashion and construction techniques. Virginians began to build with brick earlier than the New England colonists, partly because of the availability of suitable clay and partly because of the susceptibility of wood frame structures to rot in the more humid climate. Clockwise, from top left: Georgian town house, Prince Street; eighteenth-century clapboard row houses, Duke Street; eighteenth-century mixed clapboard and brick row housing, Duke Street; early nineteenth-century brick row housing, King Street.

The Torpedo Factory, built during World War I and now the centrepiece of a lively waterfront with a marina, shops, public parks, and walkways. An award-winning example of adaptive reuse.

America, was delivered to the agricultural interior. The building boom sparked by the railways added more than 700 dwellings in less than five years, most of them spacious three-storey Greek Revival town dwellings of pressed brick with ornate moulded brick cornices.

During the Civil War (1861–1865), the Old Town was occupied by Union military forces and became a logistical supply centre for the federal army. After the war, the Old Town thrived for several decades as a manufacturing centre, and during World War I a specialized munitions industry developed along the Alexandria waterfront, featuring a torpedo factory that is now an award-winning example of adaptive reuse and the focal point of the district's redeveloped waterfront.

After World War II the Old Town began to experience a degree of social polarisation, with the gentrification of brick townhouses in the core of the district contrasting with decaying row housing toward the western edge of the district and bleak social housing projects on its northern periphery. The opening of a Metro stop at the western end of King Street in 1983 changed the dynamic entirely. Now highly accessible from both downtown Washington, D.C., and suburban Virginia, the district began to attract both office development and an increased flow of tourists. Residential and commercial gentrification crept steadily westward along King Street toward the Metro station, around which large-scale property redevelopment has resulted in an extensive office and hotel complex.

Proximity to the federal agencies located in downtown Washington, D.C., and in suburban Virginia has made Old Town an attractive setting for more than 200 nonprofit organizations and professional associations, from the American Diabetes Association to Voices for Global Change. Meanwhile, recognizing the economic and cultural importance of the district's historic fabric, the City of Alexandria has passed strong historic preservation and zoning

Christ Church, designed by James Wren and completed in 1773. Its location at what was then the upper end of Cameron Street, away from the built-up section of town, caused it to be referred to as the 'Church in the Woods'.

Gadsby's Tavern, completed in 1792, was a centre of political, business, and social life in early Alexandria.

The Athenaeum. Originally a bank, built in Greek Revival style in 1852, it is now a fine arts centre.

legislation, sponsored several local museums, and invested in a major clean-up and redevelopment of the district's waterfront. Together with the architecture and museums of the district, the marina, shops, restaurants, and public parks of the redeveloped waterfront have made Alexandria an important destination for more than 1.5 million tourists each year.

In the process, the eastern end of King Street has been overwhelmed by tourist-oriented restaurants and gift shops. The ambience of the Old Town and waterfront have also attracted a

Alexandria City Hall was erected on the site designated for the market and city hall when Alexandria was founded in 1749. The current building was designed by Adolph Cluss and built in the 1870s, with major additions and renovations in the 1960s. The Saturday farmers' market at City Hall is thought to be one of the oldest continually operating farmers' markets in the United States.

large amount of new, upscale residential development, much of it in the form of large townhouses and condominium complexes whose faux colonial facades have brought a creeping inauthenticity to large tracts of the 'Old' Town.

Further reading on Old Town

City of Alexandria, 'Alexandria History', <http://alexandriava.gov/index_quicklinks.aspx?id=7666>. *An extensive decade-by-decade account of the principal changes in the district.*

Smith, Peter H., 'Historic Preservation in Alexandria, Virginia, and the Creation of the Old and Historic Alexandria District', *Historic Preservation Forum* 13.1 (1998), 22–9. *An account of the conservation and preservation movement in the district.*

Pike Place
Seattle

The Pike Place market district in Seattle is important as an archetype and exemplar of what has become a widespread and critical component of contemporary urbanism: farmers' markets. Having established some important organizational principles in the early twentieth century, the market has retained much of its original spirit and character in spite of a series of attempts to 'improve' the market by bringing it into conformity with the development trend of the moment or to raze it and replace it with more modern facilities. As a result, it carries a sense of place powerful enough to have become iconic in the identity branding of the city as a whole. Commercially successful, it is also the centre of a strong neighbourhood community that provides homes for nearly 500 residents and a range of social services that includes a medical clinic, childcare facilities, a preschool, a food bank, and a senior centre.

Much of the food supply for Seattle's early development came from farms in the surrounding valleys of the Rainier, Duwamish, Black, and White rivers. All the farmers were at the mercy of 'commission houses' – wholesalers who then sold the produce to the city's retail grocers and restaurants after a steep markup. By the early 1900s some farmers and consumers had already begun to rendezvous informally in order to circumvent this system. But when the price of onions increased tenfold between 1906 and 1907, the cost of fresh produce became a central issue in the city's politics. The result was a city-sponsored experiment to help local farmers sell their produce directly to consumers, bypassing the wholesalers suspected of inflating prices. Customers would 'Meet the Producer' directly, a philosophy that is not only the foundation of Pike Place Market businesses today but also of the tens of thousands of farmers' markets in Europe and North America that are thriving as a result of contemporary demand for fresh, locally grown produce.

By the end of 1907 the first market building had opened, with every space filled; within ten years the market's ensemble of core buildings was complete. The Outlook Hotel and the Triangle Market were built in 1908 with an extension ('Flower Row') in 1911; the Sanitary Public Market (its name justified by barring horses from its interior) opened in 1910, and the adjacent Corner Market opened in 1912. Two years later real estate developer Frank Goodwin erected the vertical labyrinth of the Main Market (the Fairley Building). The market complex stood on the face of a bluff, descending storey by storey toward the waterfront, with windows open to vistas of Puget Sound and the Olympic Mountains. The atmosphere of the market was created early on by a few basic rules. The city hired a Market Master charged with running a daily lottery for assigning stalls to competing farmers and vendors, which made for both variety and a sense of fair play. The size of the stalls was kept small and sales were limited to food and food products raised or produced by the seller. Because almost half of the farmers in the region were recent immigrants – mostly

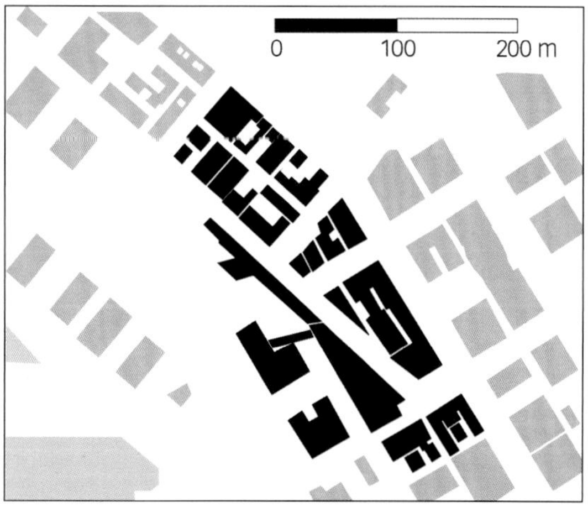

Figure-ground diagram of Pike Place. The market district occupies just a few blocks, adjacent to Puget Sound.

Germans, Italians, and Chinese, with a growing number of Japanese and Filipinos – the market also acquired a sense of liberal cosmopolitanism that attracted artists, political radicals, and miscellaneous characters. Within a few years the area beneath the Main Market's neon sign and giant clock became an informal Speaker's Corner.

The first real threat to the market district was posed by the automobile: the market's location and its sprawling site immediately began to be seen as an impediment to the new technology, and in 1921 there was a proposal to relocate the market to a more peripheral location. When this idea foundered, a developer proposed to tear the market buildings down and replace them with a giant new structure complete with a civic auditorium and radio station. The Depression of the 1930s precluded any action on such proposals, while the economy made consumers increasingly appreciative of the market. The 1941 Japanese attack on Pearl Harbor had a particular impact on the market, since by that time more than three-quarters of the market stalls were taken each day by Japanese American farmers. For many months, scores of market stalls stood empty after every Japanese American on the West Coast had been forced to abandon house and home (and farm and school) and move inland to concentration camps. During World War II the 1st Avenue area adjacent to the market became Seattle's red light district. The Outlook Hotel, renamed the LaSalle, became a brothel, catering with Fordist efficiency to thousands of sailors.

The postwar decentralization of the city and the advent of supermarket chains linked to national agribusiness corporations led to a

Market entrance, 1st Avenue and Pike Street. The market's signature clock was erected during the Great Depression. Together with the neon sign, it has become emblematic not only of the district but of the city itself.

Fish stall. Fresh seafood, in great variety, has always been a hallmark and one of the most popular attractions of the market.

Flower stalls, another hallmark of the market. The flower vendors occupy the North Arcade of the market.

period of decline for the market. Meanwhile, technological advances in farming and transport changed the local farming economy, with contract farming for agribusiness and food processing corporations displacing much of the truck farming activity that had supplied the market.

Pike Place deteriorated, but its location at the western edge of downtown Seattle made it an attractive piece of real estate. In the view of Seattle's downtown establishment, the market had become an eyesore and an obstacle to 'progress'. The completion of the Alaskan Way viaduct in 1953 compounded the situation by effectively walling off the market district from the waterfront. The city eventually declared the district 'blighted' and scheduled it for redevelopment. By the mid-1960s, the Pike Plaza Redevelopment Project was integrated into Seattle's first application for federal urban renewal funds.

But citizen opposition, rallied by young architect Victor Steinbrueck, managed to persuade the federal government's newly created Advisory Council on Historic Preservation to approve a Pike Place Market Historic District that would block use of federal funds for demolition. Downtown real estate interests then persuaded the Advisory Council to reduce the size of the Historic District by 90 per cent, prompting the U.S. Department of Housing and Urban Development to give the go-ahead for extensive demolition. In the end, a compromise mid-sized preservation zone was established and the city established a public Preservation and Development Authority to rehabilitate and manage the market's core buildings.

The district has continued to serve as a gateway for immigrants such as the Hmong flower growers from Laos who arrived during and after the Vietnam War. More recently the market has grown in popularity with the increased desirability of locally sourced food, and with popular appetite for 'authentic' urban settings with a bit of character. Now pedestrian-friendly and tidied up, Pike Place Market, with its familiar neon-lit clock, is the centre of a landmark district that attracts about 10 million visitors every year, tourists as well as local customers. It has become internationally recognized as North America's premier farmers' market, housing approximately 100 farmers who rent table space by the day, and more than 200 year-round commercial businesses, 190 craftspeople, and scores of street performers and musicians.

Victor Steinbrueck Park. This pleasant expanse above a large parking garage offers spectacular views of Elliott Bay and the Olympic Mountains beyond. Designed by Richard Haag and completed in 1978, its name honours the crusading architect who campaigned for the market's preservation.

The Corner Market and the Sanitary Market. The Corner Market was designed by Harlan Thomas and opened in 1912; the Sanitary Market was designed by Daniel Huntington in 1910 and expanded in 1942. It took its name from the fact that horsedrawn carts were not allowed inside.

Further reading on Pike Place

Crowley, Walt, 'Pike Place Market', HistoryLink.org. *A brief and clearly written account of the history of the district.*

Shorett, Alice, and Morgan, Murray, *Soul of the City: The Pike Place Public Market*, Seattle: University of Washington Press, 2007. *A book that tells the story of the reformers and entrepreneurs who conceived of the market, the truck farmers who brought in their produce, and the recurring battles to keep modernization from paving and reshaping it.*

Prenzlauer Berg
Berlin

Prenzlauer Berg is an old working-class district located just to the northeast of Berlin's central area, the Mitte. Initially a predominantly Jewish district, it was subject to the 'de-Judification' of real estate between 1933 and 1945 under the Nazis' Aryanization policies, by which Jewish owners were robbed of their property. After World War II the district was incorporated into the Soviet zone and subject to further seizure of property from private owners, this time by the East German state (the GDR), which took the best sites and allowed the bulk of the district's nineteenth-century housing to decay. It was colonized by dissidents and dropouts who were not awarded state housing. After the reunification of Germany in 1990, an embittered GDR population fled west, while West Germans, with the capital to renovate the old apartment buildings, moved in. By 2010, Prenzlauer Berg had become one of the most thoroughly gentrified districts of any Western city.

Prenzlauer Berg is dominated by five-storey, pre-1918 tenement buildings that front the streets, hiding rows of back buildings and side buildings that virtually fill entire city blocks. The district came through World War II relatively unscathed, but Communist-era policy neglected the old tenements in favour of the construction farther east of new high-rise housing districts that were held to embody socialist ideals. Abandoned buildings eventually attracted squatters and the district gradually became an enclave of countercultural lifestyles, populated by artists, intellectuals, dissidents, and the East German version of Punks. Gethsemane Church, in the northern part of the district, served as a gathering point for the 1989 demonstrations that helped lead to the fall of the Berlin Wall.

In 1990, after the fall of the Wall, Prenzlauer Berg stood at the centre of reunited Berlin, facing enormous pressure for urban renewal or upgrading. Almost every building needed repairs and modernization. About 15 per cent of the district's dwellings were vacant, while more than 80 per cent were inadequately heated, with individual coal-fed ceramic tile ovens that posed severe pollution and health problems. More than 40 per cent lacked a private bathroom and more than 20 per cent had only an outdoor toilet.

But renewal and upgrading were precluded by the legal entanglements of restitution claims that affected more than 80 per cent of Prezlauer Berg's properties. According to the law, owners whose property was expropriated first are awarded ultimate ownership. Thus, the claims of pre-World War II Jewish owners are given preferential treatment over owners who bought the property from Jewish

Figure-ground diagram of Prenzlauer Berg, showing the distinctive block morphology of the district.

landlords and subsequently had their property expropriated by the GDR. This made the clarification of the property rights a slow and complex task. Meanwhile, housing management became almost impossible and the neglect of the housing stock continued. With its cheap housing, 'hip' reputation, its central location only 2 km from Alexanderplatz, and its excellent public transport connectivity by U-Bahn and S-Bahn, the district was ripe for gentrification. The distinctive first wave of gentrifiers was spearheaded by young West Berliners: students, young professionals, and creative workers who brought cosmetic improvements to the tenements and added street art to the graffiti. Before long they were joined by young urban professionals moving to Berlin from elsewhere in Germany.

As restitution claims began to be resolved, an important shift in the gentrification process occurred. For a variety of reasons – differences among heirs, insufficient financial resources to renovate their property, no experience as landlords, or places of residence far away from Berlin – most of the original owners or their heirs decided to sell their property. Meanwhile, the city's pressing need for renewal coincided with a budgetary crisis that led to the introduction of tax incentives for private capital investment, giving professional investors an advantage over individual or cooperative owners. Dilapidated buildings were sold off to developers at bargain prices, interiors were revamped and modernized, and new waves of more affluent gentrifiers moved into the district, not just from Berlin but also from wealthy southern

Roof party. Prenzlauer Berg has become notorious as a gentrified district, now dominated by affluent young professionals, many of them having moved into Berlin from southern regions of the country. Photo: Johaentges/Getty Images.

German states like Baden-Württemberg and Bavaria. The city encouraged this second-wave gentrification by transforming World War II bomb sites into leafy parks and turning a strip of no-man's-land between Prenzlauer Berg and the former West Berlin district of Wedding into a public park, Mauerpark. The city also invested in childcare facilities, neighbourhood arts programmes, social services, and improved schools in Prenzlauer Berg. A 'Hundred Courtyards' programme sought to create new play spaces and gardens in the district's central courtyards, many of which, over the years, had been filled with workshop structures or paved and used for parking. Three localities – Helmholtzplatz, Winsstraße, and Bötzowstraße – were formally designated as renewal areas, while the city's bid to host the 2000 Olympics (that were ultimately awarded to Sydney), brought two new sports facilities to the district: a boxing arena in a Sportpark adjacent to Mauerpark, and a velodrome and swimming facility in the southeastern corner of the district.

Gentrification was also reinforced by some significant private developments. The district's landmark water tower building (that notoriously had been used by Nazi police auxiliaries to imprison, torture, and execute opponents) was converted into nine wedge-shaped luxury apartments. A massive bakery complex at the

'Frank und Amanda' hair salon, Rodenbergstraße, decorated inside and out in offbeat fashion, preserving something of the neobohemian atmosphere that has drawn gentrifiers to the district.

Solid apartment buildings that had long been neglected when the district was part of the GDR have now been comprehensively renovated.

southern end of the district was converted into an office complex containing 24,000 m² of loft spaces with a central piazza, bistros, restaurants, galleries, and exhibition spaces, designed to attract smaller, innovative firms in the media, advertising, computer, and telecommunications industries. And a nineteenth-century brewery complex is now a cultural centre – the *Kulturbrauerei* – with bars, restaurants, clubs, galleries, and a cinema.

Although there are still a few decaying tenement buildings, Prenzlauer Berg today bears all the hallmarks of a thoroughly gentrified district. Its population is overwhelmingly dominated by young adults, while all other age groups, except children under ten, are underrepresented. Many of the pioneer neobohemians and hipsters have been priced out of the district, replaced by more affluent young singles and by young parents who can be seen pushing expensive baby buggies around the farmers' market, through the weekly fleamarket in Mauerpark, or to one of the district's *kinder boutiques* or one of its many trendy sidewalk cafés. Kastanienallee, with its upscale boutiques, is widely regarded as the trendiest street for Berlin's fashion-conscious, and the entire district is peppered with wine shops, upscale restaurants, organic food markets, funky fashion stores, travel agents, retro bars, cocktail bars, and independent shops selling everything from ethnic furniture to baby clothes and antiques.

As Prenzlauer Berg has gone from being one of the cheapest neighbourhoods in Berlin to one of the most expensive – with rents increasing tenfold – it has become notorious as the archetypal gentrified district. The process has become highly politicized in Berlin, prompting occasional demonstrations and outbreaks of vandalism as well as isolated protests by tenants resisting eviction from old buildings: 'Capitalism destroys, kills, normalizes'. Anti-gentrification groups have launched poster campaigns: 'Swabians in Prenzlauer Berg … what do you actually want here?' Meanwhile, the real gentrification frontier has moved on to Neukölln (in southern Berlin) and Potsdamer Straße in Schöneberg (in western Berlin).

Further reading on Prenzlauer Berg

Grosinski, Klaus, *Prenzlauer Berg. Eine Chronik*, Berlin: Dietz Verlag, 2008. *An extended biography of the district (in German).*

Levine, Myron, 'Government Policy, the Local State, and Gentrification: The Case of Prenzlauer Berg', *Journal of Urban Affairs* 26.1 (2004), 89–108. *A detailed analysis of the policies that have shaped and promoted the gentrification of the district.*

Quadrilatero della moda Milano

The Quadrilatero della moda – sometimes referred to as the Quadrilatero d'oro, or Block of Gold – is a product of the supercharged materialism that has grown steadily in its influence around the world since the 1970s. More specifically, it is the product of Milan's emphasis on fashion and design as a strategy of postindustrial change. It is located just to the northeast of the city's downtown retail centre in an area formerly dominated by a dense complex of eighteenth- and nineteenth-century apartment buildings set around several of the city's grand seventeenth-century mansions. Now a branded district characterized by self-consciously upscale retailing and exclusive hotels, the Quadrilatero was, until relatively recently, simply a fashionable neighbourhood with some of the city's most exclusive banks and antique stores, along with some of its finest bakeries and food stores.

Milan has always had a fashion and clothing industry, based around the historic textile production of upper Lombardy and the silk industries of the Brianza and the élite seamstresses, hat makers, and tailors of the city itself. Indeed, the (now rather archaic) English term 'millinery' derives from the city's eighteenth- and nineteenth-century specializations in women's fashion accessories. Since the mid-1980s, however, the strategic alliance between the city's administration and the fashion and design industries has resulted in significant levels of investment in facilitating and promoting fashion and design as the basis of both its postindustrial economy and of its brand identity as a world city.

A crucial step was to lure the Italian couture showrooms and catwalk shows from what had become the stuffiness and rigidity of their traditional home in Florence. The process began in the 1970s, with Milan making its public spaces available for the fashion shows of up-and-coming Milanese designers. Political scientist John Foot notes that:

> *Many fashion designers worked directly for PSI* [Partito Socialista Italiano] *politicians and in return received the go-ahead for a series of economic and urban projects, and permission to hold fashion shows in a wide range of urban institutions, from* La Scala *to the* Triennale *to the Stock Exchange to the Racing Track to the Central Station. This alliance worked at all levels, from the design of clothes for the opening night of La Scala, to advice over political presentation and congress organization.*
>
> 2001, p. 129

Among Milan's new generation of designers were Giorgio Armani, Stefano Dolce, Domenico Gabbana, Gianfranco Ferré, Elio Fiorucci, Miuccia Prada, Nicola Trussardi, and Gianni Versace. They were oriented much less to the traditional – and rather narrow – market for high couture and more to the emerging market for the affordable luxury of prêt-à-porter clothing that looks custom-tailored. As such, they

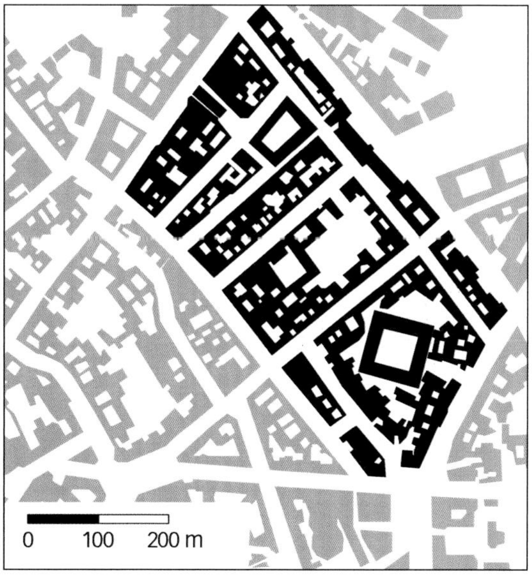

Figure-ground diagram of the Quadrilatero della moda, a very compact district in central Milan.

were well placed to exploit the 'luxury fever' and 'affluenza' of the 1980s and 1990s that accompanied the expansion of the new class of highly paid workers who were pivotal to postindustrial economies: management consultants, lawyers, software and design engineers, research scientists, medical specialists, therapists, corporate executives, financial advisers, strategic planners, advertising executives, and all manner of consultants. For this new international class fraction, traditional markers of status had lost much of their meaning. In their place, instructed by glossy lifestyle magazines and television shows, they opted for the potent symbolism of luxury brands – of pens, watches, cars, luggage, and domestic equipment as well as clothes – as signifiers of distinction and cultural capital.

It was part of what sociologists have characterized as a 'dream economy' with its 'spirit of modern consumerism' and 'self-illusory hedonism' driven by casual vulgarity, spectacle, and extravagance. Tapping into this trend, several of Milan's leading fashion houses established themselves in the exclusive district bounded by Via Manzoni, Via Montenapoleone, Via della Spiga, and Corso Venezia. Their presence, along with the district's high-end antique shops and art galleries, attracted the flagship stores of other leading global brands of ready-to-wear clothing, accessories, jewellery, shoes, and so on. Before long, the district became known as the Quadrilatero della moda. John Foot observed that:

> *This zone appeared and felt differently to other central zones, it gave off a strong image of wealth and (expensive) style. The shops themselves were unlike normal shops. They were unwelcoming and exclusive. They were not meant for 'normal' shoppers, or even for shopping – but for show, or for very rich tourists.*
>
> 2001, p. 128

Via della Spiga. The narrow, cobbled street, combined with luxuriously appointed boutiques, carries the signature affect of contemporary Milanese fashion and design: elegance with a Modernist flavour, ideally suited to the 'dream economy' of the 1980s and 1990s.

High-end consumption. Designer stores on Via della Spiga, Via Montenapoleone, and Via Sant'Andrea.
Bottom row, left: Over-the-top street furniture: planters in the shape of the Fiat 500; right: where it all started, the Galleria Vittorio Emanuele II, just 250 m from the Quadrilatero della moda.

Milanese style in practice. Along the Corso Vittorio Emanuele II, a few metres from the Quadrilatero itself, the importance of fashion is clearly in evidence.

It had become what industrial designer Ilpo Koskinen calls a 'semiotic district' because of its specialization in goods with high semiotic content, that is, products whose economic value is based in large part on the meanings people give them rather than their functionality (*Design Issues*, 21, 2005, pp. 13–27). Agnès Rocamora has another apposite term: *griffe spaciale* – a 'griffe', in the language of fashion, being the designer label affixed to a branded product.

The high-end 'brandscape' of the Quadrilatero della moda now includes Armani, Blumarine, Chanel, Coach, Dolce & Gabbana, Ermenegildo Zegna, Ferragamo, Furla, Hermés, Jimmy Cho, Krizia, Laura Biagiotti, Max Mara, Mila Schön, Missoni, Miu Miu, Moschino, Prada, Tod's, Trussardi, Valentino, and Versace. Embedded discreetly among the stores and showrooms is the Four Seasons Hotel, occupying a renovated fifteenth-century convent. More ostentatious is the Grand Hotel et de Milan, on Via Manzoni, just across from the Armani megastore and hotel complex: 750 m^2 of Armani retailing, including Armani home furnishings as well as flower, book, and art shops; a Sony electronics boutique in the basement; an Emporio Café and a branch of New York's Nobu sushi bar; and the five-star Armani hotel on the top floors. The Quadrilatero's externality effects have spilled over to nearby streets, drawing more high-end fashion retailing and designer hotels, and reinvigorating the magnificent Galleria Vittorio Emanuele II.

The streets of the Quadrilatero are immaculately kept, with carpets, plants, and expensive street furniture. As a semiotic district, it ranks alongside the 'Triangle d'Or' in Paris (between the Avenue des Champs-Elysées, the Avenue Montaigne, and Avenue George V in the 8th Arrondissement) and Bond Street and Mayfair in London, attracting shoppers from Japan and North America as well as from all over Europe. Overall, the Quadrilatero has coloured the atmosphere and shaped the imagined geography and media representation of the entire city, a major achievement of the city's postindustrial strategy of advancing Milan's identity as a centre of design. The Quadrilatero is Milan's 'front region', providing the city with a kind of monopoly rent as a result of its association with the agglomeration of semiotic products and firms of the district.

Further reading on the Quadrilatero della moda

John Foot, *Milan Since the Miracle*, Oxford: Berg (2001). *This book has an informative chapter on Milan as a capital of design and capital of fashion.*

Riverside
Chicago

Riverside is widely recognized not only as one of the first planned suburban communities in the United States but also as one of the first railway commuter suburbs and, more importantly, as a landmark district in urban planning. Designed by Frederick Law Olmsted and his partner Calvert Vaux, Riverside was remarkable for its innovative street plan and carefully crafted public open spaces. Its success as a suburban subdivision with an attractive arcadian aesthetic made it one of the most influential examples of speculative suburban development. Built to generous specifications as an élite district, it has stood the test of time: Olmsted would have been proud of its mature landscapes.

In addition to being the leading landscape architect of his generation (acclaimed, with Vaux, for the design of New York's Central Park in 1858), Olmsted was also one of the country's leading public intellectuals. His many writings appeared in publications such as *Putnam's Monthly*, alongside writings by Henry David Thoreau, Nathaniel Hawthorne, and Charles Dickens. Olmsted brought to Riverside his reputation, his experience of travelling around the English country parks that he so admired, and his close connection with the ideals of the American Renaissance and the Transcendentalists, as expressed by writers such as Ralph Waldo Emerson and Henry David Thoreau. The Transcendentalists were explicitly anti-urban, viewing cities as

General Plan of Riverside by Olmsted, Vaux & Co. Landscape Architects, 1869. Image courtesy of the Riverside Historical Museum.

Riverside still functions as a railway suburb, served by the BNSF Railway, part of the Chicago Metra system.

diseased and dangerous. Emerson had drawn, in the 1830s, on the European Romantics' notion of the pastoral ideal in arguing for settlements that incorporated the benefits of both city and country. Thoreau, a disciple of Emerson's, famously observed that in industrial cities 'the mass of men lead lives of quiet desperation'. He advocated accessibility to Nature as a spiritual wellspring for city dwellers in his book *Walden* (1854). By the mid-nineteenth century Americans had come to think of their relationship with Nature and the 'Great Outdoors' as something distinctively American.

Against this intellectual backdrop, Olmsted sought in his design work to create what has since been described as a 'middle landscape' of pastoral and picturesque settings, in which man and Nature could achieve a state of balance. Olmsted hoped further that '… the natural simplicity of pastoral landscape would inspire communal feelings among all urban classes, muting resentments over disparities of wealth and fashion' (Blodgett, p. 878). But he also acknowledged the desire for people of 'more intelligent and more fortunate classes' to remove themselves from the conditions present in the city. This was just as well, since this was in fact the basis of his client's vision for Riverside.

The immediate context for the Riverside project was the construction of the Chicago, Burlington & Quincy Railroad in 1863, which brought a significant housing boom to what was once farmland west of the city of Chicago. Soon after the completion of the railway, a developer named Emery E. Childs brought together a group of associates to form the Riverside Improvement Company and purchased a 650-hectare tract of land adjacent to the railway's western terminus, 18 km from downtown Chicago. It was an attractive site on the undulating terrain of oak and hickory woodland, bisected by the Des Plaines River.

Olmsted and Vaux, having been commissioned to design a 'suburban village', completed their plan in 1869. It was an exercise in the naturalistic style of landscape design that had its origins in England. Olmsted and Vaux used the floodplain and the riverbanks as an organizing element and reserved the best of the site for public use, taking advantage of topography to enhance the perception of open space and to choreograph the vistas and views inside the district. Two open areas of upland became the principal elements of the district's park system, which also included some forty-one small triangular parks, created by the intersections of the curvilinear streets that carefully followed the area's natural contours. Houses were allocated 30-m lot frontages and a minimum 9-m setback from the tree-lined streets.

Generous lot sizes, sidewalks, public parks, and landscaped intersections have ensured Riverside's arcadian ambience.

The F. F. Tomek House, designed by Frank Lloyd Wright in 1905. It was instrumental in the creation and development of Wright's Prairie School Style of Architecture. The house was designated a National Historic Landmark in 1999.

The Avery Coonley Residence, also designed by Frank Lloyd Wright (in 1908) and regarded by the architect as one of his most successful houses. It was designated a National Historic Landmark in 1975.

Riverside was marketed to Chicago's élite and, by the autumn of 1871, a number of large, expensive houses were occupied or under construction. But in October of that year a disastrous fire laid waste to much of downtown Chicago, leaving 90,000 people homeless. Both capital and construction crews were diverted from the Riverside project as the reconstruction of Chicago took priority. Then, just two years later, land values in Riverside fell by almost 90 per cent as a result of what became known as the Panic of 1873. The Panic itself was triggered by the financial failure of banks that had overextended themselves in selling bonds to fund the railway boom that had followed the end of the Civil War in 1865. In the consequent recession, the Riverside Improvement Company went bankrupt, and it was not until the 1890s that investment in Riverside began to pick up again. When it did, it promptly attracted some of Chicago's wealthiest families and provided commissions for some of the country's leading architects, including Frank Lloyd Wright, Louis Sullivan, and William Le Baron Jenney.

The élite character of the district was reinforced by the establishment, in 1893, of one of the country's first golf courses. Two years later the community built a Township Hall, in rather pretentious Chateau style. But Riverside's fashionability diminished after World War I as

Riverside station and the district's landmark Water Tower, built in 1871 (architect William LeBaron Jenney).

Above: **Domestic architecture** in Riverside ranges from Tudor Revival to Arts and Crafts to Victorian to Colonial Revival style homes.

automobility made for many new élite suburban and exurban subdivisions around Chicago. In the 1920s and 1930s the original 30 x 60-m lots specified by Olmsted and Vaux were subdivided into smaller lots. As a result, housing densities increased and houses themselves were more modest in character. By 1940 the population of the district had grown to 7,935, composed primarily of Chicago's petit bourgeoisie. By 1960 the district was built out and by 1970 its population had peaked at 10,357.

Riverside was designated a National Historic Landmark in 1970, mainly for its significance in terms of landscape planning. The architecture of the district, however, is by no means insignificant. Among the notable buildings in Riverside are the Avery Coonley Residence and the F. F. Tomek House, both designed by Frank Lloyd Wright in Prairie style, and both with National Historic Landmark status. More than fifty other structures have been designated as local landmarks, ranging from Tudor Revival to Arts and Crafts to Victorian to Colonial Revival-style homes. Overall the district has a mixture of small, well-maintained bungalows and larger comfortable houses from the 1920s and 1950s, along with Victorian and Modern residences that attract architectural tours. The continuing prosperity of the district is reflected in the village centre with its chic restaurants, cappuccino bars, and stores selling antiques and Victorian house fixtures.

Further reading on Riverside

Bassman, Herbert, ed., *Riverside: Then and Now*, 3rd ed., Riverside: Riverside Historical Commission, 1995. *A detailed and comprehensive documentation of the history of the district.*

Blodgett, Geoffery, 'Frederick Law Olmsted: Landscape Architecture as Conservative Reform', *Journal of American History* 62.4 (1976), 869–89. *Situates the ideas and practice of Olmsted in the context of the intellectual climate of the time.*

Scharnhauser Park Stuttgart

Scharnhauser Park has been developed on a brownfield site as a New Town district that was created to address housing shortages in the prosperous exurbs of the Stuttgart metropolitan area. Completed in 2012, it bears the imprint of mid-twentieth-century urban design, along with twenty-first-century ecological principles.

Planning model of the district, illustrating the salience of the central spine of 'landscape stairs'.

Scharnhauser Park is a direct descendant of the New Town movement that sprang up in the quarter-century after World War II. In the climate of economic recovery and reconstruction after the war, there was an opportunity to rethink the design of settlements and a strong sense of optimism that planning and urban design could make a significant contribution to progressive social change. This was the golden age of planned technocratic modernization and it saw the implementation of extensive slum clearance and social housing programmes, large-scale civic and commercial renewal projects, and the construction of new towns. It was all very much in the spirit of the Modernism of the 1920s that was founded on the idea of architecture and design as agents of social redemption.

In the United Kingdom the Barlow Report and Patrick Abercrombie's 1944 Plan for London provided the rationale for the development of new towns that were to be sited around London and a few other large cities in order to facilitate the decentralization and diversification of industry and the reorganization of congested urban areas. They were conceived in direct continuity of planning thought from the utopian visions of Ebenezer Howard and the garden city movement. In Germany, the former GDR also drew on Howard's garden city principles in building four new towns: Stalinstadt (later renamed Eisenhüttenstadt), Hoyerswerda, Halle-Neustadt, and Schwedt. In Scandinavia and The Netherlands, new town development was inspired more by the Modernism of the Athens Charter than by the garden city movement. In France, the new town programme did not get under way until the mid-1960s, when it was part of a strategic planning response to the super-dominance of the Paris metropolitan region.

Scharnhauser Park has inherited a great deal from these mid-twentieth-century developments, though it is also somewhat distinctive for its mode of delivery – public-private partnership rather than purely public funding – and for its emphasis on 'green' building. Previously a royal stud farm amid fields of linseed and lavender, the land here was bought by the Luftwaffe in the 1930s and became a military airbase that was taken over by U.S. forces in 1945. The U.S. military's withdrawal from the site of the Nellingen Barracks southeast of Stuttgart in 1972 provided an opportunity to develop a considerable amount of housing; the U.S. army had housed more than 7,000 personnel on the site. The land was acquired by the local municipality, Ostfildern, in conjunction with the federal government under the auspices of a national programme of demonstration projects on former military sites (*Konversion – Städtebauliche Möglichkeiten durch Umwidmung militärischer Einrichtungen*). The project was conceived as a family-friendly and ecologically exemplary district that would help meet housing demand in Ostfilden, a peripheral metropolitan municipality with limited opportunities for physical growth; its loose framework of nucleated settlements (Nellingen, Ruit, Kemnat, and Scharnhausen) were hemmed in by the rich agricultural lands of the Fildern plateau between the Neckar and Körsch rivers.

The construction of the district was contracted to a private developer, with strict planning guidelines on density, energy consumption, stormwater management, and recycling. More than 80 per cent of the waste materials of the former barracks were recycled and reused for landscaping and the construction of the district's basic infrastructure of roads, paths, and playgrounds. The site was laid out with careful attention to stormwater run-off, with drainage swales and detention spaces designed to double as recreational spaces and green corridors.

In contrast to many of Europe's earlier new town developments, investment in the district's infrastructure was largely complete before any residents moved in. Stuttgart's light rail system was extended to Nellingen, with a stop at Scharnhauser Park at a very early stage of the development. The transit stop then became the

Apartment buildings along the landscape stairs have been designed squarely in the tradition of Modernist European New Towns.

Scharnhauser Park town hall. Designed by Jürgen Mayer H., the building contains municipal administrative offices, a public library, an art gallery, classrooms for music lessons and night school classes, a wedding room, sports facilities, and a multipurpose hall.

site of the district centre with a market square, a commercial centre with a supermarket, several small shops and office spaces, a town hall with a municipal library and art gallery, a sport centre, a kindergarten, and a primary school and a secondary school. The other principal feature of the district is a kilometre-long spine of open space, 40 m wide, descending the south-facing slope in a series of shallow steps from the centre to the periphery of the district toward the scarp of the Swabian highlands. At the summit of the slope in the northern part of the district is an east-west grid of trees that accommodates a children's playground and gives character to the commercial centre.

The 'landscape stairs' serve as a district park and connect the district's residential sections with each other and with the surrounding landscape. The housing itself was designed to accommodate a total of 8,000 residents with a variety of household types and has been built in an assortment of forms, mostly apartment buildings, townhouses, and maisonettes but with some semi-detached houses and terraced houses, and a few luxury apartments in a small cluster of high-rise apartment blocks. Most of the dwellings are for owner-occupiers and are sold at market rate, though state programmes provide housing subsidies for lower-income households.

In order to achieve relatively high densities and to make public transport viable, private parking was restricted to one parking space per unit. The terraced houses are accessed via the smallest roads, accessible only for delivery and emergency vehicles. Residential roads in the denser areas are provided with a continuous shared surface, with parking spaces allocated on one side.

All of the district's residential buildings, and public buildings are built to the national low-energy standard (50 kWh/m²/a) or better. Additional heating and hot water are provided by a district heating system fuelled by wood chips. Other 'green' features such as geothermal energy systems and photovoltaics have

Clockwise, from top left: **Mid-rise apartment blocks** along Reinachweg; **low-rise apartment blocks** at the top of the 'landscape stairs' (photo by Apdency, used under a creative commons Attribution-Share Alike License at Wikimedia Commons); **low-rise apartment blocks** along Niemöllerstraße; **biomass co generation power plant**, providing 80 per cent renewable energy for the district.

been implemented in various projects, partly funded by various statewide programmes and initiatives.

Barely completed, the district nevertheless has a rather dated feel, echoing the placelessness and sterility of mid-twentieth-century new towns. The wide-open space of the landscape stairs gives the district a rather exposed and windswept character, and the absence of terminal landmarks to the vista along the landscape stairs lends an air of incompleteness, adding to the sense of the district as an end-of-the-line exurb.

Further reading on Scharnhauser Park

Jessen, Johann, 'Regional Governance and Urban Regeneration: The Case of the Stuttgart Region, Germany', Tetsudo Kidokoro, et al., eds., *Sustainable City Regions*, Berlin: Springer, 2008, 227–45. *A review of planning and policy in the Stuttgart region that features the Scharnhauser Park development and places it in a regional context.*

Pascaline, Gaborit, *European New Towns*, Bern: Peter Lang, 2010. *This book examines the capacity of New Towns, in a time of demographic stagnation and economic crisis, to manage a transition to maturity: to be viewed as liveable towns, rather than 'dormitory towns'.*

Schöneberg Berlin

Schöneberg, an inner-tier, lower-middle-class suburb of five-storey apartment buildings, has long been famous as a gay district. Nollendorf Platz, at the northern end of the district, is where the first gay bars were opened and the neighbourhood has become the gay cultural centre of Berlin. The notoriety of the district stems from the famously louche and hedonistic Berlin scene of the late 1920s and early 1930s. Repressed by the Nazis, the district's gay community eventually reestablished itself as part of a neobohemian social ecology that has become increasingly gentrified and diverse.

Novelist Christopher Isherwood, who spent four years (1929–1933) living on Nollendorf Straße, wrote about it in *Goodbye to Berlin* (1939), which provided the basis for the prize-winning stage musical and 1970s movie *Cabaret*. Isherwood famously described the tenement buildings of the district as:

> *… crammed with the tarnished valuables and second-hand furniture of a bankrupt middle class.*
>
> *Goodbye to Berlin*, London: The Hogarth Press, 1939, p. 1

It was distinctive, though, for its gay nightlife in pubs, cafés, ballrooms, and clubs. Needless to say, when Hitler rose to power homosexuals were systematically persecuted by the Nazis, and Schöneberg's identity as a gay district was sharply attenuated.

After World War II Berlin returned to its liberal ideals and in the 1950s Schöneberg developed something of a reputation as a red-light district until an intensive urban renewal programme and the introduction of strict regulations on bars combined to eradicate – or at least diminish – prostitution. Nevertheless, the district remained unattractive, its apartment buildings run-down and the 'bankrupt middle class' replaced by immigrants and low-income households during the 1960s and 1970s. Emblematic of the period was the construction of the Sozialpalast, a prefabricated high-rise apartment block that was built by the West Berlin government for families on welfare and the homeless. Out of scale with the surrounding buildings, its ugliness contributed at once to the downgrading of the area. Today it houses some 1,500 people in 500 apartments, with a fifty-fifty split between Germans and immigrants.

Meanwhile, during the 1970s and 1980s West Berlin developed a lively and politically rebellious subculture in several inner-city districts, and Schöneberg was prominent among them. It developed a social ecology that encompassed a variety of new social movements, squatters, community organizations, and student milieux, as well as a steadily reemerging gay scene. Schöneberg also developed a distinctive music scene that was culturally located somewhere between punk rock and *Neue Deutsche Welle* (the German equivalent of New Wave music). This innovative music scene, together with West Germany's liberal licensing laws and late night opening, led to an intense clubbing scene in Schöneberg, mainly around Winterfeldtplatz. Some of the clubs were men-only, catering to 'nightlife tourism' as well as to the local gay

Figure-ground diagram of part of Schöneberg.

An example of the district's 'top-heavy balconied facades' described by Isherwood.

The Metropol, one of the district's landmark buildings, originally a theatre and concert hall, now a dance club.

The district's gay scene attracts mainly gay males, with many premises being 'men only'. Nevertheless, there are plenty of mixed bars and clubs that attract people of all sexual orientations and genders.

Sozialpalast, Pallasstraße, an unwanted landmark, out of scale and out of place. Originally designed by the West German government to house welfare-dependent families and homeless individuals, the Sozialpalast became notorious as the locus of antisocial behaviour. After reunification it was refurbished and rededicated to low-income households, many of whom are immigrant workers. With its distinctive array of satellite television dishes, it remains an unavoidable and unwanted landmark. Photo: FocusEurope/Alamy.

population. Meanwhile, the district's daytime economy also began to be oriented increasingly to gay men, with cafés as well as bookshops and stores specializing in fetish accessories.

With reunification in 1989 and an increasing societal acceptance of gay and lesbian lifestyles, Schöneberg began to mature into a more relaxed residential setting. The district's central location within the city and its solid yet affordable apartment buildings with their leafy streets and courtyards led inevitably to renovation and gentrification. Today Schöneberg is little different in appearance from the district that Isherwood described in the 1930s. The foliage of the linden trees is more luxuriant, providing summer shade for the sidewalk cafés that have proliferated throughout the district; the facades of the buildings along many of the streets have been restored and painted in the pale pastel palette favoured by property developers. Winterfeldtplatz remains the locus of the gay nightlife, though it is now best known for its weekend farmers' market.

Nollendorf Platz is still dominated by the Streamline Moderne Art Deco-style *Metropol*, originally opened in 1906 as a theatre and concert hall complex. The concert hall soon became a cinema and, when that finally closed in the 1970s, it was used by an evangelical church before being opened as a discothèque, catering to both gay and straight clubbers. After an expensive refit in 2005 it had a brief spell as an up-market nightclub before reverting to a dance club. European techno music had its roots in Schöneberg's hedonistic gay scene, but techno music has been eclipsed by a mixture of house music, soul, R&B and hip hop that appeals to the broader audience of the district's clubs.

The physical and social landscape of the district certainly includes all the hallmarks of a gay district. There are plenty of people wearing the latest gay fashions and more than a few who conform to the more extreme gay fashion stereotypes. There are street posters advertising gay meetings and events; there are gay bookstores, shops spruced up with rainbow flags and selling condoms, leatherwear, and DVD porn; there are fetish bars, gay cafés, saunas, and clubs; and there is a gay community centre, the Mann-O-Meter, at Nollendorf Platz. But the dominant affect of the district is relaxed and cosmopolitan. Gentrification has diversified the social mix of the district, albeit at the expense of displaced lower-income households.

Clockwise, from top left: **Café,** Maaßenstraße; **farmers' market**, Winterfeldplatz; **shoppers,** Winterfeldstraße; **gentrified apartment buildings**, Schwerinstraße. (photo by Assenmacher, used under a creative commons Attribution-Share Alike License at Wikimedia Commons); **Boyz 'R' Us** store, Maaßenstraße.

Further reading on Schöneberg

Bader, Ingo, and Scharenberg, Albert, 'The Sound of Berlin: Subculture and the Global Music Industry', *International Journal of Urban and Regional Research* 34.1 (2010), 76–91. *Examines the connections between local social ecologies, including Schöneberg, and the development of the city's creative economy.*

Shaw Washington, D.C.

Shaw is best known as one of America's most important African American neighbourhoods, a place where black cultural and educational institutions developed alongside the first black middle and élite classes. The early development of the district was as a streetcar suburb, and initially it was predominantly white and middle-class in character. Then, for the first half of the twentieth century, it flourished as the heart of Washington's black business and cultural community, centred along the U Street corridor. Ironically, the civil rights movement prompted the decline of the district, with middle-class households moving out to newer suburbs where racially restrictive real estate covenants were no longer legal. Two decades of impoverishment and decay in Shaw were halted by municipal investment in the district's infrastructure, prompting a revitalization that is now associated with a multiracial community.

Afro Colombian mural, 'Currulao y Desplazamiento', by Joel Bergner, on U Street, NW.

The district originally stood on the northern edge of the new federal city designed by Pierre L'Enfant in 1791. Until the Civil War (1861–1865), when the Union Army set up military camps and a hospital there, it had only a few farm buildings scattered among the woods and fields. After the war the district developed rapidly. The Washington and Georgetown Railroad Company had laid tracks for horsedrawn streetcars along 14th and 7th Streets in 1862, making the district very attractive for middle-class suburban development just as demand for housing increased in response to the expansion of the federal government.

In the early 1870s a massive city-wide public improvement project, led by Alexander Shepherd, head of the District of Columbia Board of Public Works from 1871 to 1873 and governor of the district from 1873 to 1874, paved the streets, planted trees, and laid water and sewer lines. Shaw's layout and physical fabric dates from this period: a coherent group of brick row houses constructed predominantly by speculative builders and real estate developers between 1862 and 1910, along streets established by the L'Enfant Plan. The 1890s saw the development of electrified cable cars and streetcars serving the district, and by 1900 the transportation corridors along 14th and 7th Streets had developed as neighbourhood-based commercial strips.

Meanwhile, many of the district's white middle classes decided to move to new streetcar suburbs to the north. At the same time, large numbers of African Americans were arriving in Washington. The black intelligentsia of the nation had begun to congregate in Washington immediately after the Civil War, and by the turn of the century many more black migrants were

U Street, the district's principal commercial street. Many of the three- and four-storey brick buildings and storefronts along U Street were shuttered and derelict for decades after the riots that followed the assassination of Dr. Martin Luther King, Jr. in 1968, but some of the district's landmark buildings and businesses have survived.

being drawn in by the opportunities for modest but secure job opportunities in the federal government and by the city's excellent black public schools. Blocked from the city's new streetcar suburbs because of racially restrictive real estate covenants, many of the aspiring incomers settled in Shaw, just to the west of Howard University, which had been established by Congress in the 1860s for the education of black students.

As Washington became increasingly segregated, Shaw emerged as a self-reliant district. The U Street corridor became the city's most important concentration of businesses, entertainment facilities, and fraternal and religious institutions owned and operated by African Americans. Between 1895 and 1920 the number of black-owned businesses in Shaw grew from 15 to 300. Black entrepreneurs financed and built key community institutions such as the Twelfth Street YMCA, True Reformers Hall, Whitelaw Hotel, and the Industrial Savings Bank, while some of the city's prominent black churches, including the Metropolitan Baptist Church and Vermont Baptist Church, originated in Shaw. U Street became known as the Black Broadway, with first-run cinemas, drinking clubs, theatres featuring vaudeville and burlesque, and nightclubs that featured stars such as Duke Ellington, Pearl Bailey, and Billy Eckstine. As Kathryn Smith points out (p. 34):

U Street was also where African Americans visited the doctor, dentist, barber, or beauty shop, where they played pool and hung out with friends. It was the setting for Elks parades, Easter Sunday promenades, and Halloween revelry.

Row housing on 13th Street, NW. The construction of a nearby Metro stop in 1991 and the rise of real estate prices in Washington brought new interest in the district, resulting in the renovation of much district's housing stock.

True Reformer Building, U Street, NW. A testament to black economic achievement, the building was completed in 1903 for the Grand United Order of True Reformers, a benevolent society that provided insurance and banking services for the African American community. They hired John Lankford, believed to be the first black registered architect in the city, when he was 28 years old. The mural, by Byron Peck, honours Duke Ellington, who was born in the district and whose first performance was in the True Reformer Building.

Crucial to the success of the district as a whole was its mixture of social classes and occupations that provided support and opportunities for individual and group development. Social clubs, fraternal organizations, churches, and schools organized meetings, dramatic and musical productions, sporting events, and other activities that helped to knit the district together. In this setting, people felt secure, valued, and comfortable.

But while the district remained an important commercial and cultural centre for the black community through the 1960s, it began to change in character after racially restrictive real estate covenants were declared unconstitutional by the U.S. Supreme Court (*Shelley v. Kraemer*, 1948). Significant numbers of Shaw's élite and black middle classes moved out to emerging black suburbs in Maryland's Prince

Revitalized U Street has been colonized by bistros, stores, and galleries catering both to the district's new residents and to visitors from elsewhere in the city, drawn by the newly vibrant ambiance of frontier gentrification.

George's County, and Shaw lost the social mix that had been one of its great strengths. A downward spiral of disinvestment and decay prompted federal redevelopment authorities to designate Shaw as an Urban Renewal Area in 1966, but just two years later extensive tracts of the district were devastated by riots following the assassination of Martin Luther King, Jr. More households departed, buildings fell into disuse and disrepair, and many remaining residents struggled with problems associated with poverty and unemployment. By the late 1960s the once-vibrant district had come to be known as Shameless Shaw, with some of the highest concentrations of poverty and crime in a city that itself had become notorious for drugs, crime, and violence.

For a long time regeneration efforts were unsuccessful, partly because of the district's

Lincoln Theatre, U Street, NW. Built in 1922, the Lincoln Theatre first featured silent film and vaudeville but soon became the centre of Washington's 'Black Broadway', featuring artists like Duke Ellington, Pearl Bailey, Ella Fitzgerald, Billie Holliday, Nat King Cole, Cab Calloway, Louis Armstrong, and Sarah Vaughn. The theatre closed after the 1968 riots but was restored and reopened in 1994.

Remnant stretches of pregentrified Shaw, as in the 2200 block of 14th Street, NW, feature boarded-up, spray-painted storefronts, liquor stores with bulletproof cashier's windows, and struggling businesses.

large number of absentee landlords. In the 1980s and 1990s the city as a whole experienced an economic and real estate boom as business associations, educational services, legal services, investment trusts, mortgage banking, professional associations, and services to buildings and real estate leasing all expanded rapidly. The consequent recentralization of employment made Shaw very attractive to pioneer gentrifiers and small service-sector enterprises. In Shaw itself the construction of the Frank D. Reeves Municipal Center at 14th and U Streets in 1986 and the opening of the U Street Metro station in 1991 were decisive in prompting revitalization. Immigrant Ethiopian entrepreneurs opened restaurants and retail businesses along the largely abandoned retail corridor along 9th Street between U and T Streets, bringing a degree of vitality to the district that in turn helped to

Gentrified terrace, 12th Place, NW. Note the barred windows at street level.

Property redevelopment is reshaping parts of the district. The owners of the Vegas Lounge, an R&B club on the 1400 block of P Street, NW, on the southern edge of the district, clearly decided not to sell up. New-build gentrification is taking place throughout much of the district, often taking advantage of lots that had become vacant after arson or damage during the 1968 riots.

attract people to reopened jazz clubs and restaurants. Important U Street buildings such as the Lincoln Theater, Bohemian Caverns, and Industrial Bank were renovated and reopened.

Black middle-class households were once again attracted to the district, but they were outnumbered by Hispanic and white middle-income households. Much of the early white in-migration consisted of gay men who rehabilitated many of the Victorian-style homes and row houses in the Logan Circle section of the district. Shaw's reputation now rivals the Dupont Circle neighbourhood as the centre of gay life in the District of Columbia, with many gay-oriented clubs, restaurants, and stores. With a significant fraction of very low-income households along with more affluent newcomers, the district now has a distinctly neobohemian and cosmopolitan feel. On the other hand, the cultural coherence and political consensus of the district has been replaced by multiple identities and contested politics. The Ethiopian business community, for example, has lobbied for its small 9th Street corridor to be given official designation as Little Ethiopia, provoking strong opposition from the African American community.

Meanwhile, the African American heritage of the district has been recognized by the listing of the Greater U Street Historic District in the National Register of Historic Places in 1998. Among the 1,500 buildings in the designated district are a number of individually notable buildings, including the Evans-Tibbs House (the home of Lillian Evans Tibbs, the first internationally acclaimed African American opera star), designed by R. E. Crump and built in 1894; the

Left: **Shaw's landmark restaurant**, Ben's Chili Bowl, now a feature of the Greater U Street Historic District. The restaurant was opened in 1958 by a Trinidadian immigrant. During the 1968 riots it was famously allowed to stay open past curfew in order to serve policemen, firemen, and community activists.

Busboys and Poets, a bookstore, cafe, and performance space, captures the gentrified neobohemian element that has emerged in Shaw. Photo by Jim Stroup, Virginia Tech.

True Reformer Building, the first major commission of John A. Lankford, the prominent African American architect, built in 1903 for the United Order of True Reformers; the Howard Theater, the city's first legitimate theatre for African American audiences and entertainers, built in 1910 and designed by J. Edward Storck; and the Whitelaw Hotel, designed by Isaiah T. Hatton, a locally trained African American architect, built in 1919 and subsequently a unique meeting place for prominent African Americans during the era of legalized segregation.

Further reading on Shaw

Nieves, Angel David, 'Revaluing Places: Hidden Histories from the Margins', *Places* 20.1 (2008), 21–5. *Describes the tensions associated with the movement of Ethiopian immigrants to part of the district.*

Ruble, Blair A., *Washington's U Street. A Biography*, Washington, D.C.: Woodrow Wilson Center Press, 2010. *Traces the history of the U Street corridor from its Civil War-era origins to its recent revitalization.*

Smith, Kathryn S., 'Remembering U Street', *Washington History* 9.2 (1997), 29–39. *A summary of community history based on public art sponsored by the Historical Society of Washington, D.C.*

South Beach Miami

In less than 100 years the South Beach district of Miami Beach has gone from a speculative development of modest single-family residences to a booming resort and retirement district; to a run-down district infiltrated by crime and vice; to a renovated district on the National Register of Historic Places; and, now, to an exclusive residential enclave, an international destination district and celebrity haunt. In the process it has changed from a segregated Anglo American community to a predominantly Jewish community, and now to a multiethnic, cosmopolitan population, the setting for an unabashedly vulgar hedonism.

Construction of the initial development, a small oceanfront residential district on part of a former coconut plantation, began in 1913. A year later Carl G. Fisher, a successful entrepreneur who made millions selling his business to Union Carbide, began to invest in property development and infrastructure improvements (including a vital road bridge to the mainland), and by 1915 Miami Beach had become established as an independent township. The southern part of Miami Beach – South Beach – steadily filled up in the 1920s during a real estate boom that was supercharged by the palatial homes built by several prominent millionaires. The boom coincided with the blossoming of stylish Modern architecture inspired by the Paris Exhibition of 1925. The new styles reflected a fascination with the streamline design and comfort features of mass transportation of the era, especially transatlantic ocean liners, luxury automobiles, and passenger trains.

Property development and redevelopment continued even during the Great Depression of the 1930s, creating a distinctive district of hotels and residences – about 800 buildings in 1.6 km^2 – in what later became known as Art Deco styles. Characteristic elements include massing with a strong central element and symmetrical elements either side (the 'Rule of Three'); building form based on geometric shapes, with sharp angles and/or curved corners; 'eyebrows' above windows; jutting towers, ziggurat rooflines, glass-block windows, porthole windows, deck railings, racing stripes, and chevron decorations; the use of modern materials like chrome, plastic, and aluminium; distinctive signage and lettering with exaggerated or multilineal stroke details; and neon lighting. There is, however, no single definitive Art Deco style. Rather, there are variations that reflect the cultural preoccupations of the era: Nautical Deco, Chinese Deco, Mayan Deco, Egyptian Deco, and so on. Developers also favoured Streamline Moderne and Mediterranean Revival and, later, Fifties Deco, referred to by design historians as Miami Modern.

After World War II South Beach became a seasonal haven for wealthy northerners. Morris Lapidus, who had designed the flamboyant Fontainebleu Hotel just to the north, also designed one of the first outdoor pedestrian malls in the United States, Lincoln Road,

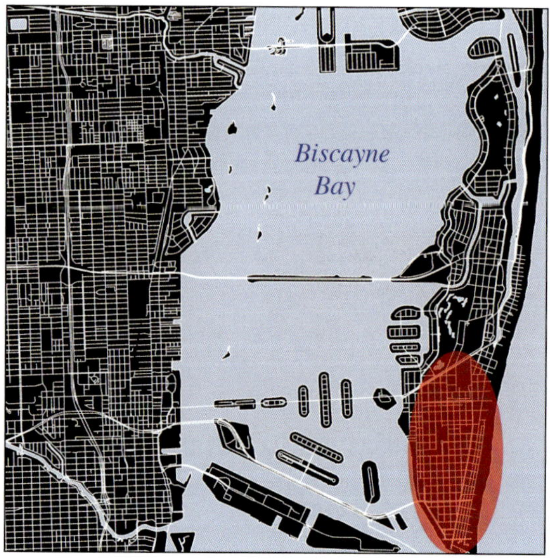

South Beach is located at the southern tip of a 15 km-long barrier island, part of the municipality of Miami Beach.

converted from a heavy traffic artery and promoted as the Fifth Avenue of the South.

The arrival of retirees from the Northeast and Midwest brought a new dimension of ethnic diversity to the city. Jewish retirees in particular were drawn to Miami Beach but had to contend with segregation ordinances that restricted them to the area south of Fifth Street, the southern tip of South Beach. Civil rights activism, combined with the sheer weight of increasing numbers, overcame segregation by the 1960s and within a few years Jews had come to dominate the entire city of Miami Beach. In South Beach (i.e., south of 23rd Street), synagogues, Yiddish theatres, and kosher restaurants and delicatessens proliferated. While there were some upscale hotels and residences, the district came to be dominated by modest, deteriorating low-rise buildings populated by retirees on small, fixed incomes. For a while, South Beach acquired the cruel nickname of God's Waiting Room.

Before long, however, as metropolitan Miami absorbed increasing numbers of immigrants from Cuba and Latin America, South Beach was infiltrated by drug dealers and the associated crime and vice. Further investment in the district was largely limited to the installation of security bars on ground-floor windows. Lincoln Road lost its glamour and upscale retailing moved north to Bel Harbor. Wealthy households also moved out, leaving behind less-affluent households, mostly retirees on fixed incomes.

By the mid-1970s South Beach was down-at-heel, no longer attracting many new retirees, and on the cusp of irretrievable deterioration. It was saved by the activism of conservationists,

Ocean Drive, facing the sea, is the district's principal tourist haunt, with its beach access, restaurants and Art Deco hotels.

led by Barbara Capitman and Leonard Horowitz. By 1979 the Miami Design Preservation League, which they helped found, had secured a 1.5-km^2 portion of South Beach as the Miami Beach Art Deco District on the National Register of Historic Places. The district can be divided into three functional areas: the seasonal hotel area along Ocean Drive and Collins Avenue; the commercial area along Washington Avenue and Lincoln Road; and the residential area, low-rise Art Deco apartment buildings concentrated in the eighty square blocks surrounding Flamingo Park.

Horowitz promoted the idea of renovating the buildings with a palette of pastel hues – flamingo and bubblegum pink, peach, periwinkle, purple, aqua, and lavender blue – on what had originally been whitewashed surfaces. Hotels and restaurants began to pay attention to one another when selecting their shades of colour, so as to heighten the effects of juxtaposition, and to invest in classic Art Deco neon lighting that provides an exotic nightscape. The makeover was enough to attract new investment, new visitors, and new residents. The scenographic combination of distinctive architecture and wide stretches of soft, almost-white sandy beaches, together with the subtropical light, made South Beach an attractive location for photo shoots. In 1989 Irene Marie purchased the Sun Ray Apartments and opened a full-service modelling agency. Many of the large New York-based agencies soon followed, bringing an influx

Art Deco design, in various forms, provides the distinctive element of the district's built environment.

Opposite: **classic Art Deco hotel** on Ocean Drive.

The beach: a wide stretch of soft, nearly-white sand. The lifeguard huts, mostly in pastel colours and in a variety of designs, many of which echo Art Deco styling, have become emblematic of the district. Photo courtesy of Lynne Knox.

COLONY
COLONY
HOTEL

Top: **Art Deco hotel**, Ocean Drive; middle: **mixed-use development** at the northern end of Ocean Drive; bottom: **luxury condominium towers** at South Pointe, the southern tip of the district.

of fashion industry professionals. Sidewalk cafés, boutiques, nightclubs, and chic restaurants followed, along with models, celebrities, and international tourists.

South Beach became a hedonistic setting, a 24-hour playground dominated by the young and affluent. Restored Art Deco and Mediterranean Revival buildings were joined by new contemporary architecture and ultraluxurious condominiums. The southern tip of the district, now branded as 'SoFi', has been redeveloped with exclusive, resort-like condominium towers that generate a significant fraction of the residential tax base of the whole of Miami Beach. The run-down, low-rise apartment buildings in the Collins Park area in the north of the district have been gentrified, orchestrated by real estate developers who have converted the apartment buildings into condominiums.

Inevitably, the district's demography changed again. Jewish households had represented almost two-thirds of the total population of Miami Beach in 1980. By 2010 the figure was less than 15 per cent. Similarly, whereas elderly households had long dominated South Beach, less than 15 per cent of its population was aged 50 or more in 2010; the majority were aged between 20 and 40. The traditional flow of Jewish retirees on modest incomes had been priced out of the district, while the more affluent gravitated to Broward and Palm Beach counties as greater Miami became increasingly Hispanic in demographic composition.

South Beach itself has developed a unique cultural mix, in many ways more temperamentally like the European Mediterranean coast or parts of Latin America. Spanish is the first language of more than half of the population, while English is the first language of about a third and the numbers are rounded out by a cosmopolitan mix of Italians, French-Canadians, Russians, Germans, and Brazilians.

This cosmopolitanism is reflected in entertainment and cuisine: Colombian discos, European club scenes, traditional American bars, Cuban cafés, and restaurants specializing in Eurasian, New World, and Nuevo Latino cuisine have displaced the kosher delis and seafood shacks. Bikini shows and wet T-shirt contests have replaced the mah-jong and canasta of retirees seated quietly on hotel porches. 1950s lounge music has been displaced by Europop, samba from Brazil, salsa from Colombia, tango from Argentina, reggae from the English-speaking Caribbean, flamenco from Spain, and merengue and bachata from the Dominican Republic. The influence of sun, sea, and the warm weather has fostered a distinctive body-consciousness and standard of public exposure that would be censured in other American cities.

Meanwhile the new affluence of residents and visitors is reflected in a retail framework that includes high-end designer-label stores as well as exclusive independent boutiques and galleries along pedestrianised boulevards. Increased tax revenues have paid for lavish urban design improvements, including new terraces and landscaping with plenty of space for local restaurants to set up large outdoor seating areas, and extended and improved boardwalks, parks, and pedestrian areas that allow people to see and be seen, drawn to the colourful mixture of beautiful people and – not necessarily mutually exclusive – various categories of exhibitionists, rollerbladers, joggers, cyclists, skateboarders, Segway riders, bodybuilders, flâneurs, clubbers, and tourists.

Delano Hotel, Collins Avenue, one of the district's luxury resort hotels. It was built in 1947 and completely refurbished in 1995. In 2007, it was ranked among the top 50 buildings in the American Institute of Architects' survey of 'America's Favorite Architecture'.

Further reading on South Beach

Capitman, Barbara, *Deco Delights: Preserving Miami Beach Architecture*, Miami: Studio, 1988. *The author, a leader in the campaign to establish the Art Deco historic district, describes the struggle between the pressure for development and the necessity for preservation.*

Chase, Iris G., and Russell, Susan, *South Beach Deco: Step by Step*, New York: Schiffer, 2004. *An illustrated guide to the Art Deco architecture of the district.*

Stofik, M. Barron, *Saving South Beach*, Gainesville: University Press of Florida, 2005. An account of the fight to preserve the decaying neighbourhood, only to see it transform into one of the world's most glamorous hotspots.

SouthPark Charlotte

SouthPark is emblematic of the way that America's metropolitan areas have been thoroughly remade in the image of consumer society. Charlotte itself is a vast, sprawling region of 'metroburbia' – a fragmented and multinodal mixture of employment (mostly retail and office employment) and residential settings, shaped more by consumption and the exclusionary impulses of affluence than by the logic and imperatives of production. Within this matrix, SouthPark has developed from a regional shopping mall into an embryonic edge city as a result of its situation amid one of the most affluent suburban regions on the East Coast of the United States.

Charlotte, North Carolina, is classic example of sunbelt suburbanization. Formerly a typical Southern city, sharply segregated along race lines and dependent on low-cost female and African American labour for its mills and factories, it changed dramatically from the late 1970s, registering double-digit annual growth rates as migrants and immigrants were drawn to the city, first by manufacturing jobs relocated from the deindustrializing Northeast and then – and in much greater numbers – by the growth of 'new economy' jobs in banking, advanced business services, digital technologies, and biotechnology. As elsewhere in the country, a big gap suddenly opened up between middle-middle- and upper-middle-income households. The new higher-income earners had emerged in occupations that had only a weakly established social status. As a result, they tended to assert themselves through relentless lifestyles of competitive consumption and attention-getting extravagance. Instructed by glossy lifestyle magazines, America's upper-middle classes developed chronic cases of 'luxury fever' and 'affluenza'. As a result, cities like Charlotte have seen the 'secession of the successful' into upscale, gated, and packaged apartment complexes and master-planned subdivisions. In Charlotte the southern suburbs were the preferred location for affluent white households.

SouthPark sits amid the consequent 'vulgaria' of ostentatious residential neighbourhoods. Located 10 km south of Charlotte city centre, the district was once part of a 1,200-hectare farm owned by former North Carolina Governor Cameron Morrison. The farm's main house – the Morrocroft Mansion, built in Tudor Revival style in the 1920s – still stands on its original site and is listed in the National Register of Historic Places. Apart from the mansion, SouthPark is almost entirely a product of the recent past. It is anchored by, and named after, SouthPark Mall. The mall emerged as the principal 'cathedral of consumption' for the affluent southern realm of metropolitan Charlotte, the place where the affluent can depend on finding the requisite gear to maintain lifestyles of positional consumption, and with some of the appropriate settings, such as upscale restaurants, in which to display them.

The mall itself is owned and administered by an international corporation, Simon Property Group, Inc. the largest public U.S. real estate company with ownership interest in more than 380 other properties, comprising more than

Figure-ground diagram of SouthPark, dominated by the shopping mall and adjacent 'lifestyle centre'.

24 million m^2 of gross leasable space in North America, Europe, and Asia. Originally developed in 1970, SouthPark Mall is now one of the largest shopping malls in the region, with 116,000 m^2 of retail space anchored by Nordstrom, Belk, Dillard's, Macy's and Neiman Marcus department stores, and with luxury fashion stores such as bebe, Burberry, Coach, Hermès, Tiffany, and Louis Vuitton. For the people who can afford it, consumption plays a key role in the construction of distinct and fashionable identities, and so the mall, its stores, and its immediate environs have been designed with a particular sensory experience in mind: an affect of casual luxury and taken-for-granted privilege.

Meanwhile, the district around the mall has become an embryonic edge city, an important node of office and retail employment in Charlotte's polycentric metroburban sprawl. Attendant to the mall are several hotels and a new complex, The Village (also a Simon Property Group holding), which comprises 4,500 m^2 of specialty retail, along with upscale dining, fitness clubs, and one-, two- and three-bedroom condominium apartments. Altogether, SouthPark is the second-largest business district in the city, with an estimated 4,000 workers.

Just a few hundred metres away is Phillips Place, an example of one of the newest forms of real estate investment: a 'lifestyle centre'. Based on the booming luxury goods market, lifestyle centres mimic old-fashioned Main Street settings, with tree-lined sidewalks and lampposts, manicured shrubbery, made-up street names, and plenty of free parking. Phillips Place stretches 300 m, an ideal distance for a window-shopping stroll but not too long a walk. Besides containing upscale retail stores, the development also offers a boutique cinema, upscale restaurants, outdoor cafés, a hotel, and condominium apartments.

As with any other district, SouthPark's built landscape can be construed as a 'moral geography'. Our daily surroundings are powerful

Phillips Place, a 'lifestyle centre' – basically an outdoor mall anchoring a mixed-use development in neotraditional style, with upscale shops and restaurants.

SouthPark's standing in the social geography of the city is anchored by old-money homes such as this.

'The Village' at SouthPark, a mixed-use development of condominiums and shops on the edge of SouthPark Mall.

but stealthy backdrops that can naturalize and reinforce dominant political and economic structures as if they were simply given and inevitable. Laden with layers of symbolic meaning, everyday landscapes – including the people who inhabit them, their comportment, their clothes, their accessories – amount to moral landscapes that both echo and tend to reproduce a society's core values. The taken-for-granted familiarity of contemporary suburban landscapes constitutes a stealthy, almost hallucinogenic normality but, as sociologist Pierre Bourdieu has observed, 'The most successful ideological effects are those that have no words, and ask no more than complicitous silence' (1977, p. 188). In a society dominated by divisions between success and failure, winners and losers, the most powerful moral landscapes of all are arguably those like SouthPark, home and habitat to the success-oriented, affluent 'winners' of American society.

Further reading on SouthPark

Anon., *City by Design: Charlotte: An Architectural Perspective of Charlotte*, Charlotte, NC: Panache Partners, 2009. *An illustrated treatment of contemporary architecture in the metropolitan area.*

Bourdieu, Pierre, *Outline of a Theory of Practice*, Cambridge: Cambridge University Press, 1977. *A major theoretical text on the foundations of anthropology and sociology.*

Knox, Paul, *Metroburbia USA*, New Brunswick, NJ: Rutgers University Press, 2008. *Provides broad coverage of the economic, social and cultural imperatives that have shaped U.S. metropolitan areas.*

Clockwise, from top left: **Luxury condominiums**, in faux French Chateau style; **gated community** entrance; **Phillips Place** shops and penthouse apartments; **SouthPark Mall**, one of the largest in the region; the **Rotunda Building**, upscale office space; new-money **McMansion**.

Spitalfields London

Spitalfields is one of the oldest districts of London, a traditionally working-class area on the fringe of London's business and financial district. In many ways it has always been a transitional district, home to successive waves of migrants and immigrants who found work in London's docks and transport services and in the workshops, breweries, and factories of Spitalfields itself. The building on the corner of Fournier Street and Brick Lane, in the heart of Spitalfields, is emblematic of the district's experience of the classic process of sequent occupance. It was built in 1743 by French-speaking Protestant Huguenot refugees as La Neuve Eglise (the 'New Church'). A Methodist church from 1819, it became an orthodox Jewish synagogue in 1898. In 1976 it became the community mosque for the Bangladeshi population that had come to constitute three-quarters of the district's population.

As the financial district of the City of London expanded in the booms of the 1980s and 1990s, the pace and nature of transition changed. Designated by planners as 'City fringe', Spitalfields is now deep in the process of being reconstructed, both physically and socially. Developers, aided by government agencies, have made major investments in commercial real estate along the western edge of the district that is adjacent to the Broadgate office complex in the City, home to many of the world's leading financial and advanced business services firms. Residential and industrial gentrification has seen affluent households move into Spitalfields's townhomes and row houses and design-, media-, and fashion-related firms move into its old industrial spaces. Meanwhile, Spitalfields's proximity to City offices and tourist destinations has prompted entrepreneurs, community groups and local government agencies to exploit the district's gritty character, its street markets, and its curry shops, simultaneously exoticizing the district and making it accessible, safe, and visually appealing to visitors through a combination of urban design interventions, branding, and invented traditions as backdrops and context for entertainment and consumption.

Spitalfields takes its name from a contraction of 'hospital fields', the area surrounding a priory and its hospital – 'The New Hospital of St Mary without Bishopgate' – that was founded in 1197 on the site of a former Roman cemetery. The district as a whole did not really get built up until after the Great Fire of London in 1666. Located beyond the city boundaries, Spitalfields was a natural location for dirty trades such as leather working and brick manufacture: Brick Lane was the route along which carts carried bricks from the kilns in Spitalfields to Whitechapel, Shoreditch, and beyond. Spitalfields Market, founded in 1638 by Charles I, was for trade of 'flesh, fowl, and roots'. Brewing was another early industry, drawing on water from deep wells. Later in the seventeenth century the silk industry was brought to Spitalfields by French Protestant refugees – Huguenots – after they

Spitalfields is situated just to the north of the City, London's financial centre.

were driven out of France by the Catholic king Louis XIV in the 1680s. Huguenot master weavers built some of London's first brick townhouses, while more humble weavers' dwellings were clustered around the Tenter Ground, the place where woven cloth was washed and then stretched on frames called tenters to dry. This, incidentally, is the origin of the expression, 'to be on tenter hooks'. In the early eighteenth century a decline in the Irish linen industry led to the arrival in Spitalfields of Irish weavers to take up work in the silk trade.

Sustained by a continuous supply of semi- and unskilled immigrant labour, Spitalfields became an important centre for weaving, tailoring, and the clothing industry. But in 1860 a treaty was established between Britain and France, allowing the import of cheaper French silks and plunging many Spitalfields weavers into ruin. Nineteenth-century Spitalfields was the archetype of Victorian urban poverty, mapped and catalogued by Charles Booth and described by Charles Dickens. It was the scene of several Jack the Ripper murders and the port of entry for destitute Yiddish-speaking Jews escaping from the pogroms that followed the assassination of the Tsar of Russia in 1881. Brick Lane became the heart of the shtetl, with a local economy distinctive for its bagel shops and tailors' workshops.

The mid-twentieth century saw the arrival of immigrants from South Asia, and in particular from the Sylhet region of what was to become Bangladesh. Chain migration, with families from Sylhet moving into Spitalfields by word-of-mouth contact with friends and relatives already settled there, gradually displaced the Jewish population. By the 1970s Brick Lane had become notorious as the front line of defence of the diasporic Bangladeshi community against racist violence orchestrated by the National Front and the British National Party. Leveraging the lobbying power of community groups and their sheer weight of numbers in local elections, the Bangladeshi community was able to secure public funding for mosques, madrassas, and

Brushfield Street. The Bishops Square development, on the site of what had been part of Spitalfields Market, is to the left; the church at the end of the street is Christ Church, built between 1714 and 1729 to a design by Nicholas Hawksmoor.

Islamic community organizations in the 1980s and 1990s, while secularist members of the community remained involved in local administrative affairs, building alliances with state and private funding organizations. Among their successes was funding for a new 'invented tradition' – the Bengali New Year Festival (*Baishakhi Mela*).

The consolidation of the Bangladeshi community in Spitalfields coincided with the 'entrepreneurial turn' of urban policy of the late 1980s. In central London, this translated into the Cityside strategy: extending the financial district of the City onto cheaper land, promoting the construction of office and retail facilities through subsidies, providing regulatory relief to property development firms, and encouraging diversification of the local economy, especially leisure and tourism. In Spitalfields the prime site for this strategy was Spitalfields Market, at the western end of the district and close to the Liverpool Street railway station and the City's Broadgate complex. The market was relocated to Leyton, 6.5 km to the northeast, in 1991, leaving the site available for redevelopment.

The eventual solution, by Foster + Partners, involved the demolition of two-thirds of the historic market buildings along with other adjacent structures to make room for several high-rise office buildings and a landscaped civic space, Bishops Square, with an outdoor performance area and water feature. The regeneration project also involved a general tidying-up of the facades and remaining interior spaces of the old market to accommodate boutiques, cafés, and upscale chain restaurants, as well as new market space, Crispin Place, covered by a glazed canopy that connects the new office buildings to the remaining portion of the old Spitalfields Market.

Another initiative of the Cityside strategy was aimed at Brick Lane. Coordinated by the City Fringe Partnership, Brick Lane was identified as a Developing Cultural Quarter. Branded as Banglatown, it was promoted to tourists as well as City employees and business visitors.

Spitalfields Market. The remaining structures from the redevelopment of 1887, designed by George Sherrin; now Grade-II listed buildings.

Above: **Brune Street**, on the old Tenter Ground.

Above: **Bishops Square** office buildings.

Below: **Fashion Street** graffitti.

Below: **Brick Lane**: one of the two remaining bagel shops.

Clockwise, from top left: **'Banglatown'**, a few of the dozens of curry restaurants along Brick Lane; **Jamme Masjid**, Brick Lane, originally a Protestant chapel founded by the district's Huguenot community; the **London Hebrew Soup Kitchen**, Brune Street, founded in 1854; **design services** on Fashion Street; **traditional-style food emporium**, Brushfield Street; **Market Street**, connecting Bishops Square with Crispin Place, all part of the redeveloped Spitalfields Market site.

Brick Lane gentrification. A corner pub, transformed into a fair trade coffee shop.

Chinatown-style ornamental gateway arches were introduced, along with new signage and new, brighter street lamps, custom-designed to incorporate Asian motifs. Curry restaurants were the principal tourist draw; they grew in number along Brick Lane itself, from just eight in 1989 to forty-one in 2002. Guidebook and media coverage, together with notoriety stemming from the popularity of Monica Ali's 2004 novel, *Brick Lane*, and its movie adaptation, brought international tourists into the heart of what had hitherto been a vibrant but relatively unknown area.

Meanwhile, the area was also discovered by design-, media-, and fashion-related firms. For example, the Milanese fashion school Instituto Marangoni took advantage not only of inexpensive real estate but also of the opportunity to exploit a unique address, moving into old factory space on Fashion Street. Developers took over the Old Truman Brewery on Brick Lane that had closed in 1988, refurbishing the buildings and converting them to design studios, bars, nightclubs, cafés, galleries, speciality shops, and a large exhibition centre and event space. Exoticized and edgy-but-safe, the transitional dynamism of Spitalfields is increasingly driven by a lunch-time and night-time experience economy catering to students and young white-collar workers. Meanwhile, the existence of extensive tracts of un- and underdeveloped real estate in the district has left it poised for a further phase of transition, as developers envisage additional series of high-rise, mixed-use regeneration schemes and community groups and established gentrifiers campaign to 'Save Spitalfields'.

Further reading on Spitalfields

City of London Corporation, *Revitalising the City Fringe: Inner City Action with a World City Focus*, London: City Corporation, 1996. *The official strategy for the district.*

Hebbert, Michael, *London*, Chichester: Wiley, 1998. *Provides the overall context for understanding the changing geography of London.*

Lichtenstein, Rachel, *On Brick Lane*, London: Hamish Hamilton, 2007. *A history of the Brick Lane area and its successive waves of migrants.*

Shaw, Stephen, et al., 'Ethnoscapes as Spectacle: Reimaging Multicultural Districts as New Destinations for Leisure and Tourism Consumption', *Urban Studies* 4.10 (2004), 1983–2000. *A critical analysis of the emergence of the Brick Lane area as 'Banglatown'.*

Temple Bar Dublin

Temple Bar has a long, layered history. The site of a Norse settlement on the southern bank of the River Liffey, it was an important strategic site that was occupied by Anglo Normans in the twelfth century and that subsequently developed as an important wharfside district as Dublin grew in importance. Much of the current fabric of Dublin's inner districts dates from the city's Golden Age in the eighteenth century. Increasingly obsolescent and neglected during the twentieth century, Temple Bar became one of the first tentative examples of culturally led urban regeneration. As a branded cultural quarter, it has become an important component of Dublin's 'experience economy' and a precursor of the night-time economy of clubs, discos, bars, pubs, restaurants, and theatres that has become characteristic of many cities in northern Europe.

Temple Bar takes its name from William Temple, a provost of Trinity College who built his home in the district early in the seventeenth century. A 'bar' at the time was the name for a pathway by the river. The area, along the River Liffey between present-day Trinity College to the east and Dublin Castle to the west, was first settled some 800 years before by Norsemen. By Temple's time it had become a busy wharfside district, embedded at the centre of the slowly growing city. Its busy commercial character accelerated in the eighteenth century as the affluence of Georgian Dublin generated a building boom. Partly because of its tight medieval streets and partly because of its mix of trades, Temple Bar acquired only a few of the classic Georgian structures that characterise much of inner Dublin. Some speculative builders did follow the classical rules of proportion of Georgian townhouses, building in small groups of two to five houses, each of three or four storeys high above basements, the light-wells for which were fronted by cast-iron railings.

Much of the rest of the built fabric of the district dates from the Georgian era, but was built for the district's commercial and industrial firms. Wharves lined the quay, while the surrounding streets carried a mixture of shipping companies, merchants, instrument makers, printers, publishers, bookbinders, stockbrokers, and brothels. With the building of a new Custom House in

Figure-ground diagram of Temple Bar, a district with a compact morphology built around narrow streets and alleys.

Opposite page: **Temple Bar** at night.

THE
TEMPLE
BAR
FINE SMOKING
TOBACCO
Always in Stock
Traditional
Irish Music

National Photographic Archive, Meeting House Square, houses the photographic collections of the National Library of Ireland.

Essex Street, one of the most popular among tourists, with its mixture of pubs, clubs, and cultural institutions.

the nineteenth century, the quay at Temple Bar fell into disuse and the district began a slow and steady slide into something of a backwater, despite its situation at the very centre of the city. The decline became all too apparent in the 1950s as the district's manufacturing firms closed or moved away. By the 1960s Temple Bar was blighted by decay and neglect. Eventually the strategic value of the site was recognized by the state-owned transport company, Córas Iompair Éireann (CIE), which began to buy up property in the area with an eye toward redeveloping a new transportation centre, linking bus and rail services. While this was in the planning stages, some properties were demolished by CIE while others were let out at low rents.

Paradoxically, this triggered a process of revitalization. Activities which could afford only low rents on short leases moved into the district. These included artists' studios, galleries, recording and rehearsal studios, pubs and cafés, second-hand clothes shops, small boutiques, bookshops and record stores, as well as a number of voluntary organizations. Together with the district's architectural character, the youth culture attracted by the district's new commercial tenants brought a neobohemian atmosphere to Temple Bar, and its proximity to the river and to the city centre suddenly made it attractive to pioneer gentrifiers.

Meanwhile, opposition to CIE's plans was mobilized by An Taisce (the National Trust for Ireland). A report issued in 1985 condemned CIE's proposals as a threat to the district's historic streets and buildings, and emphasized the potential of the district as an historic cultural quarter that could improve the city's image and thereby attract tourists as well as local residents. This was very much in line with attitudes toward urban policy at the time. The European Union had begun to sponsor the promotion of culture and design in the early 1980s as a way of promoting both regional development and the notion of a common European cultural heritage. Its Capitals of Culture programme was conceived in 1983 by Melina Mercouri, then Greek Minister for Culture. (Athens was duly appointed the first European Capital of Culture in 1985.)

In 1988 a self-organized group of local traders, community organizations, and conservationists formed the Temple Bar Development Council as an advocacy group for the district. The following year they produced a report calling for the creation of Temple Bar as a cultural enterprise centre. The overall aim was to revitalize the district as a focus of cultural activity, initially as a flagship for Dublin's anticipated designation as the EU Cultural Capital of Europe for 1991, but subsequently as a permanent cultural district. The idea was favourably received by Dublin's press, and in 1990 the Irish government formally stopped the CIE's proposals to clear Temple Bar for a new transport interchange. At the same time the city published its Temple Bar Action Plan, which included proposals for tax incentives, physical improvements such as access, lighting, and public art, and a new pedestrian route through the district.

Pubs and restaurants of Temple Bar. There are more than twenty pubs in the district, along with more than sixty restaurants. Most of the restaurants sell alcohol, and most of the pubs sell food. Top: The Oliver St John Gogarty; middle: Farrington's; bottom: The Quays.

Merchants Arch, Temple Bar. Photo © Superbass / CC-BY-SA-3.0 (via Wikimedia Commons).

Temple Lane, in the heart of the district, where warehouses and workshops have been converted to apartment buildings, shops, and recording studios.

Temple Bar Renewal Limited was established as a policy-making body to oversee renewal plans, approve development proposals, and administer the financial incentives. In addition, Temple Bar Properties Limited, a property development company with the Irish Government as sole shareholder, was established to implement regeneration proposals.

A powerful combination of property and investment powers, planning control, and tax incentives was set in place. Temple Bar Properties set about acquiring properties, renewing them, and undertaking development schemes of its own or as joint ventures with private owners and developers. The overall strategy aimed at a mix of cultural, residential, and retail uses, as well as environmental improvements. The cross-subsidy of unprofitable uses by profit-making uses was encouraged in order to maintain some of the lower-profit uses that had prompted the district's original attraction.

Over the past twenty years the city has invested in the district's infrastructure, re-laying granite setts and calming traffic. As a result of the city's renewal policies, Temple Bar has attracted several cultural institutions, including the Irish Photography Centre, the Ark Children's Cultural Centre, the Irish Film Institute, Temple Bar Music Centre, the Arthouse Multimedia Centre, Temple Bar Gallery and Studio, the Project Arts Centre, and the Gaiety School of Acting. Together, they have made Temple Bar into an incipient cultural quarter.

Lunchtime crowds along Temple Bar. Always busy, the street is the centre of the district's night-time economy.

Meanwhile, the district's rejuvenated pubs, restaurants, and small businesses have formed the basis of an experience economy. For a significant fraction of consumers – relatively young and relatively affluent – the principal component of the experience economy revolves around the urban night-time economy of clubs, discos, bars, pubs, restaurants, and theatres rather than the daytime attractions of cultural institutions. Temple Bar provided a particularly attractive setting for this, and by the late 1990s it had become a destination district for 'stag parties' and 'hen nights' as well as for a regular clientele of young singles. As a result, Temple Bar acquired a reputation for noise and anti-social behaviour fuelled by excessive alcohol consumption, tarnishing its image as a cultural quarter. Meanwhile, the district has been discovered by international tourists – a success in terms of the original policy aims but a qualified success insofar as it has changed the character of the district, eroding the neobohemian atmosphere that had underpinned the district's initial success.

Further reading on Temple Bar

McCarthy, John, 'Dublin's Temple Bar – A Case Study of Culture-Led Regeneration', *European Planning Studies* 6.3 (1998), 271–81. *A critical appraisal of the strategy of culture-led regeneration in the district.*

Montgomery, John, 'The Story of Temple Bar: Creating Dublin's Cultural Quarter', *Planning Practice and Research* 10.2 (1995), 135–72. *Provides a detailed account of the development of policies and politics that have shaped the development of the district.*

Temple Bar Old City, a newly rebuilt, pedestrianised and branded area of the cultural quarter.

Temple Bar Gallery and Studios, one of the first artist-led initiatives in Ireland, designed by architects McCullough/Mulvin.

Theatreland London

London's Theatreland consists of more than fifty theatres, ten cinemas, the Royal Opera House, and dozens of hotels, restaurants, pubs, and cafés that cater to their clientele, all interlaced within a busy district that also has a broad spectrum of shops, offices, and residential spaces. By day, the district is merely part of London's extensive West End, but in the evenings it takes on a coherence and distinctiveness that derives from its theatres, cinemas, and crowds of theatregoers.

London's theatre district, now a branded international tourist district with a capital T, has its origins in the 1660s, when two theatres were allowed to open after the Puritan regime had been replaced by the monarchy of Charles II. The Puritans had banned all theatre, seeing it at best as a frivolous pastime and at worst as seditious. With the restoration of the monarchy, King Charles promptly granted Letters Patent to two companies, giving them a shared monopoly of what became known as 'legitimate theatre' in London. One opened a theatre on Drury Lane in 1663 on the site of what is now the Theatre Royal Drury Lane. The other opened on Bow Street on the fringe of Covent Garden, a newly prestigious area that had been redeveloped in the 1630s with an arcaded piazza and church designed by the famous English Renaissance architect Inigo Jones.

But the Patent Acts that granted legitimacy to these two theatres applied only to spoken drama and not to other forms of entertainment. Melodrama, for example, did not break the Patent Act because it was accompanied by music. It did not take long before unlicensed, 'illegitimate' theatres opened, catering not only to melodrama but also to burlesques, extravaganzas, circuses, farces, pantomimes, quadruped dramas, and performing dog shows. They tended to cluster, along with taverns, coffee houses, cockfight pits, and brothels, around the western edge of the City, sandwiched between the commercial districts of the City and the bourgeois respectability of Westminster and St James's. Over time the theatre district took on a distinctive character – a space of plebeian immorality and political radicalism – that lasted well into the nineteenth century.

In the latter part of the nineteenth century the theatre district changed altogether in character. The Industrial Revolution prompted the modernization of the city, while the associated social and cultural shifts were reflected in new spaces of consumption as well as a new social geography. The theatrical monopoly bestowed by Charles II had been abolished in 1843,

Theatreland is located in London's West End, which contains many of the city's major tourist attractions and cultural institutions as well as threatres.

Shaftesbury Avenue is widely regarded as the heart of Theatreland. In addition to the Gielgud and Queen's theatres, shown here, the short avenue also has four others – the Apollo, the Lyric, the Palace, and the Shaftesbury – and two cinemas.

Apollo Theatre, Shaftesbury Avenue, a Grade II listed building, designed in 1900 by architect Lewin Sharp. Inside there is a three-tiered auditorium with elaborate plasterwork.

Prince of Wales Theatre, Coventry Street. The present Art Deco structure, built in 1937 and designed by C. J. Phipps, replaced the original 1884 structure.

recognizing not only the irrelevance of the old Patent Act but also the increasing fashionability of theatregoing among the newly expanded middle and upper-middle classes. The physical framework of the theatre district was reorganized in the 1870s and 1880s as the Metropolitan Board of Works took advantage of slum clearance legislation and modernized the road system. Shaftesbury Avenue was built between 1877 and 1886 to provide a north-south traffic artery through the crowded districts of Soho, and it provided the ideal setting for new theatres. By 1907 there were six of them: the Apollo, the Lyric, the Hicks (now the Gielgud), the Royal English Opera House (now the Palace), the Queen's, and the Shaftesbury. The theatre boom that continued until the outbreak of World War I in 1914 also saw the opening nearby of the Aldwych, the Ambassadors (now the New Ambassadors), the Coliseum, the Duke of York's, Her Majesty's, the London Palladium, the New Theatre (now the Noel Coward), the Peacock, the Savoy, the Waldorf (now the Novello), and Wyndhams. Three architects dominated the design of theatres during this great building boom: W. G. R. Sprague, Thomas Verity, and Bertie Crewe. Their preferred styles were ornate, mixtures of the Italian Renaissance, the Baroque, and French classicism.

Another theatre boom, sparked by the cultural energies of the Roaring Twenties, added still more theatres, including the Arts Theatre, the Apollo Victoria, the Cambridge, the Duchess, the Phoenix, the Piccadilly, and the Prince Edward. The Windmill Theatre opened in a converted cinema on Great Windmill Street and became notorious for staging nude *tableaux vivants*. It famously never closed during World War II, despite the Luftwaffe's bombing raids. But after the war live theatre – including live revues and vaudeville – was dead on its feet. Theatres that had not been destroyed by bombing during the Blitz seemed obsolete and anachronistic. The tube station at Covent Garden was closed on Sundays because so few people wanted to go there. The film industry and television seemed to be the way of the future. Leicester Square, just 100 m south of Shaftesbury Avenue, was colonized by large cinemas, while Wardour Street, less than a block away, became the centre of the British film industry, with the headquarters of the big production and distribution companies. The professional ecology of the theatre district also lent itself to the popular music industry. Denmark Street – London's equivalent of Tin Pan Alley in New York – filled with specialist music shops and recording studios. In between were the bars, jazz clubs, and rock music clubs of London's Swinging Sixties. Theatres, meanwhile, began to be demolished to make way for the grand schemes of the postwar property boom.

Ironically, it was one of these schemes – a massive redevelopment of the Covent Garden area – that preserved the theatre district. The proposed scheme met with strong and sustained opposition, and the impasse between would-be developers and the local community was resolved only when the government added scores of buildings in the area, including several theatres, to the list of those with protected status. The old fruit and vegetable market decamped from Inigo Jones's Market Hall in 1975, allowing the hall and surrounding piazza to be restored and redeveloped by the Greater London Council as one of the first-ever 'festival

Garrick Theatre, Charing Cross Road. Named after David Garrick, an actor, manager, and impresario who dominated West End and London theatre throughout the eighteenth century. The theatre opened in 1889, having been financed by playwright W. S. Gilbert, coauthor of the Gilbert and Sullivan comic operas. Photo courtesy of Anne-Lise Velez.

Left: **St Martin's Theatre**, West Street, was designed by architect W. G. R. Sprague as one of a pair of theatres with the adjacent Ambassador's Theatre. The world's longest-running play, *The Mousetrap*, opened in the Ambassador's in 1952 and transferred next door to the St Martin's in 1974. Photo: Anne-Lise Velez

Below: **Palace Theatre**, Cambridge Circus and Shaftesbury Avenue. Designed by Thomas Collcutt in 1891, it was intended it to be the home of English grand opera. Its 1,400-seat capacity has made it a profitable venue for the blockbuster musicals for which Theatreland has become famous. Photo: Anne-Lise Velez

Street entertainment in Covent Garden. The refurbished market area attracts more than 30 million tourists each year and is an important part of the 'experience economy' of Theatreland.

The Ivy, opened on West Street in 1917 to cater to theatregoers, has become one of London's most exclusive restaurants, especially popular with celebrities.

market' settings, with tourist-oriented shops, cafés, restaurants, and street performers. The new tourist draw opened in 1980, just ahead of the growth of the 'experience economy' and the wave of economic and cultural globalization that London has helped to facilitate and which, in turn, has shaped character of contemporary London.

The visiting business professionals and tourists drawn by London's status as a preeminent global city have provided Theatreland with an affluent and expanding market. The renovation of Covent Garden market prompted a renaissance of the daytime and weekend economy of the district, with Monmouth Street, Neal Street, and Floral Street, in particular, flourishing with specialist shops and boutiques, while lunchtime crowds are drawn to the neobohemian atmosphere of Neal's Yard and Seven Dials. The alleyway of antiquarian bookshops in Cecil Court includes Drummond's, specializing in books about actors and the theatre, along with posters, postcards, manuscripts, and theatre memorabilia. Other important elements in the ecology of Theatreland include the various professional and institutional elements that contribute to the agglomerative forces that bind the district. The Society of London Theatre, the trade association that represents the producers, theatre owners, and managers of the major commercial and grant-aided theatres in central London, is located in Rose Street, a little alley between Floral Street and Garrick Street in Covent Garden. The headquarters of Equity, the actors' union, is located in St Martin's Lane, while *The Stage*, the newspaper for the performing arts industry, is published from the Bedford Street location of the Club for Acts and Actors.

Clockwise, from top left: **Antiquarian bookshops** in Cecil Court. With nearly twenty antiquarian and second-hand independent bookshops, including specialists in modern first editions, collectible children's books, rare maps and atlases, antique prints, and theatrical ephemera, it is known colloquially as Booksellers' Row; **Prince Charles Cinema**, Leicester Square; **Goodwin's Court**, an alley just off St Martin's Lane that features a row of former Georgian bow-fronted shops; **pre-performance theatregoers** and tourists on Catherine Street.

The Garrick, just off Leicester Square, is a private members' club oriented to Theatreland, with an important theatrical library that includes many manuscripts and documents and a comprehensive collection of theatrical paintings and drawings. In Leicester Square itself is Dewynters, a theatrical marketing and public relations company that also produces programmes and souvenir brochures.

In the 1990s the Royal Opera House, which had occupied the northwest corner of Covent Garden piazza since 1732, was given a major overhaul, and Paul Hamlyn Hall, historically part of the old flower market, was absorbed into the complex as the atrium and main public area of the opera house, with a champagne bar, restaurant, and other hospitality services. In contrast, most of the other forty or so theatres in the district are rather cramped and lacking in amenities, the result of confined sites and, in many cases, the protected status of the buildings. Their shortcomings, however, have not hindered the popularity of spectacular big-production musicals like *Cats, Chicago, Les Misérables, The Lion King, Mama Mia!*, and *The Phantom of the Opera*.

The box-office success of these shows is a vivid manifestation of the experience economy and is closely tied to the increasing importance of London as a tourist destination. Yet while

Leicester Square. Initially developed in the 1670s as a fashionable residential square, it had become a setting for hotels and theatres by the nineteenth century. The small park in the centre of the Square contains a nineteenth-century statue of William Shakespeare. Today the Square is dominated by cinemas, nightclubs, and souvenir stores.

blockbuster musicals have become emblematic of Theatreland's brand image, the night-time economy of the district still relies heavily on 'legitimate' theatre, on the dozen or so cinemas that between them have about 6,500 seats, and on the dense array of bars, pubs, supper clubs, and restaurants that cater not only to the pre- and postperformance crowds but also to visitors who are drawn to the buzz of the district and who come to eat, drink, and stroll. Altogether, theatregoers spend more than £1 billion annually on tickets restaurants, hotels, transport, and merchandise. As a net currency earner for the UK, West End theatre is of a comparable size to the entire UK advertising, accountancy, and management consultancy industries and is considerably bigger than the UK film and television industry.

Further reading on Theatreland

Hughes, Howard, 'Theatre in London and the Inter-Relationship with Tourism', *Tourism Management* 19.5 (1998), 445–52. *Explores the influence of tourism on the programming of the theatre district.*

Ibell, Paul, *Theatreland: A Journey through the Heart of London's Theatre*, London: Continuum, 2009. *Combines historical narrative of the district with a unique exploration of the social and cultural ecology of London theatre.*

Trastevere
Roma

With a history of settlement lasting more than 2,500 years, the Trastevere is a richly detailed palimpsest of urban change. Etruscan villages gave way to Roman villas and townhouses, and they in turn were mostly overwritten by medieval infilling. The construction of several imposing Renaissance villas prompted a further recasting of the district's physical fabric and social geography before large tracts of the district were replaced or filled in as a result of the building boom prompted by Rome's new status as the capital of the newly minted national state in the late nineteenth century. Overlooked by the city's modernization schemes, the district settled into a predominantly working-class residential role, with a neobohemian flavour that derived from the combination of ancient, picturesque buildings and the low rents that attracted a youthful, cosmopolitan, but low-income population. The resulting character of the district has subsequently attracted gentrification, provided the setting for an important night-time economy, and established the Trastevere as a tourist landmark.

Before the establishment of the Roman Republic in 509 B.C.E., the area across the River Tevere (Tiber) from Rome belonged to the hostile Etruscans. As Rome grew, the area was gradually settled by sailors and fishermen making a living from the river, along with immigrants from the Eastern Mediterranean, mainly Jews and Syrians. By the time of Augustus (63 B.C.E.–14 C.E.), the Trastevere was recognized as part of the city, one of its more cosmopolitan districts, inhabited by a combination of Romans, Greeks, and Jews. The affluence of the Imperial Age (14–180 C.E.) saw the completion of Trajan's aqueduct, which culminated in a fountain on the Gianicolo hill at the western boundary of the Trastevere. The plentiful supplies of fresh water, brought from Lake Bracciano, 40 km to the north, prompted several important figures (including Clodia and Julius Caesar) to build villas and gardens on the hill, their opulence contrasting sharply with the typical fabric of the Roman era, the modest *domus*: a town house

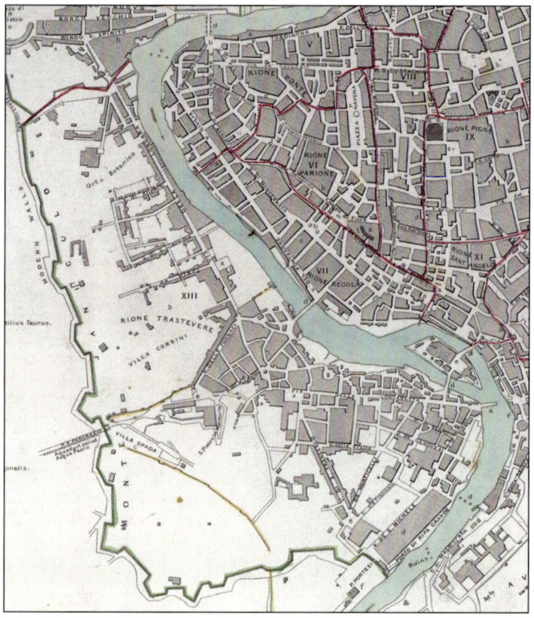

Trastevere in 1830. The district, on the western side of the river, did not expamd much beyond its medieval core until later in the nineteenth century. Map extract courtesy of David Rumsey Map Collection <www.davidrumsey.com>.

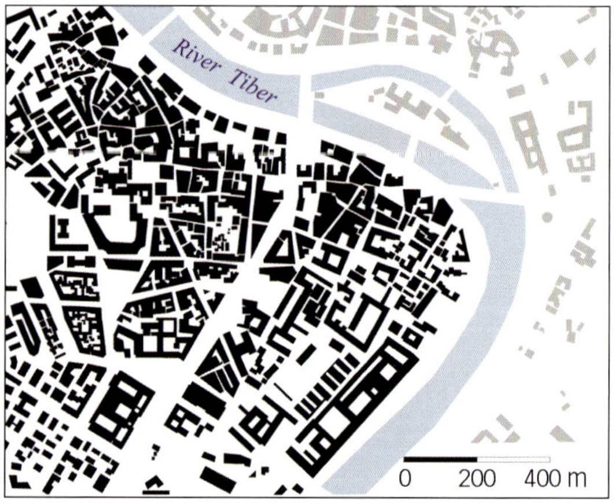

Figure-ground diagram of part of Trastevere. Note the contrast between the morphology of the older core of the district and that of the newer elements to the south and west.

consisting of an enclosed plot of land with a house on one part of it.

In order to have a stronghold on the right bank of the river and to control the Gianicolo hill, Trastevere was incorporated within the Aurelian walls (271–275 C.E.). This consolidated the district's ties with the city, but when Vandals cut the aqueduct (455 C.E.) the district lost its fashionability. Over the next thousand years the Trastevere developed its medieval fabric of narrow, winding streets and alleys and haphazardly arranged buildings. The district's distinctive cobblestones (*sampietrini*) of black porphyry were not laid until the mid-sixteenth century. Over the next 300 years most of the Roman fabric of the district was overwritten or reshaped. Accommodation for the growing population of the district was provided by converting one-family houses into multifamily dwellings, either by dividing the house into apartments or by restructuring and amalgamating adjoining houses, rather than by building new houses. The *domus* plots were subdivided, resulting in a pseudo row house format, resulting in *insulae*, or street blocks with a main street in front and narrow side streets. Shops and workshops were located on the ground floor, with living and sleeping quarters on the first and second floors. The hillside of the Gianicolo became popular once again among some of the city's more affluent and powerful families. Among the imposing residences were the Villa Giraud-Ruspoli (now the residence of the Spanish ambassador), the Villa Sciarra (built on

Piazza Trilussa, at the edge of the medieval core of the district. The small piazza was carved out of the early medieval fabric of the district. The buildings along the Via del Moro (to the right) are a mixture of modified medieval turret-houses and Baroque and Renaissance palazzi.

Clockwise, from top left: **Piazza di Santa Maria in Trastevere**: the fountain is considered to be the oldest monumental fountain in the city; the present version is the work of Bramante, with additions by Carlo Fontana and Bernini; **Instituto san Michele** and the nineteenth-century embankments (photo by Lalupa, used under a creative commons Attribution-Share Alike License at Wikimedia Commons); **decaying palazzo**, Via della Lungaretta; **nineteenth-century apartment buildings**, Via Luigi Santini.

the site of Caesar's gardens and now the home of the Instituto Italiano di Studi Germanici), and the Villa Farnese-Aurelia (which now houses the American Academy).

The Trastevere was significantly reshaped once again in the nineteenth century. The unification of Italy in 1870 and the adoption of Rome as its capital created a building boom and an enthusiasm for modernization, emphasizing the restructuring of the city to accommodate large new national ministries and to create new roadways or widen older ones to cope with dramatically increased volumes of traffic. The Viale di Trastevere was straightened and widened, creating an axial thoroughfare linking Rome's new southern suburbs with the city centre, across the Ponte Garibaldi. Either side of it, preservationists fought an unequal and losing battle with developers. All of the remaining vacant sites were filled in and much of the older urban fabric was torn down to make way for large five- to eight-storey apartment buildings, laid out in a loose grid pattern that had hitherto been alien to the district. In keeping with the fashion of the time, the apartment buildings were given neoclassical facades with a typical rhythm created by the regular spacing of windows.

Equally striking in its impact on the character of the district was the embankment of the river. Although the Tevere had always been central to the city's trade and commerce, it flowed at street level, frequently bursting its banks and occasionally flooding with disastrous results. In 1598 the Tevere rose 19 m and in 1870 it rose 17 m. The river was eventually walled in between 1883 and 1892, finally affording protection from flooding but effectively cutting off the Trastevere from the river and its former commerce. The district was spared, however, from further modernization schemes, including those of the Mussolini era. As a result, the post-World War II character of the district was distinctly down-at-heel. It started to change in the 1970s, when gentrifiers discovered its low rents and tourists discovered its authenticity and rough charm.

Since then, Trastevere has been filling up with tour buses, and the medieval core of the district has been colonized by sidewalk vendors, bars, cafés, and countless little trattorias and osterias with menus printed in English. Trastevere has become a destination district, with guidebooks extolling the picturesque authenticity of the district's maze of narrow cobblestone-paved streets, its laundry hanging from marble windowsills set in crumbling ochre-plastered walls, and its inhabitants seemingly cast from a Roberto Rossellini movie.

By day, Trastevere is a pale version of the guidebook eulogies. The core of the medieval section retains a certain amount of character: the buildings are certainly picturesque and there are a few remaining hole-in-the-wall shops selling domestic goods, along with scooter repair shops and local bars that lend an air of quaint authenticity. But the overlying affect is one of careless neglect. Clumsy attempts to stabilize the cobblestones by filling the joints with tar have resulted in ugly smears across the streets; every convenient surface is tagged with graffiti; the alleys smell of cats and dogs; and the district's honeycomb of spaces attract a seemingly disproportionate share of the city's beggars, buskers, and street people.

These shortcomings, though, are obscured with the setting of the sun. Night obscures the graffiti, dirt, and dereliction, while any whiff of cat pee is obscured by the aroma of cooking. Tourists, along with crowds of young Romans, are drawn to Trastevere's thriving night-time economy of bars and restaurants. In summer, especially, the heart of the district around the Piazza di Santa Maria is transformed with outdoor seating and the streets are filled with strollers enjoying the atmosphere.

Trastevere at night. The district's narrow streets, with their bars, trattoria, and gelateria, are popular with both tourists and locals. Photo: Susan Wright/Alamy.

Further reading on Trastevere

Corsini, Maria Grazi, 'Residential Building Types in Italy before 1930: The Significance of Local Typological Processes', *Urban Morphology* 1 (1997), 34–48. *Compares the morphological evolution of the Trastevere to that of older districts in Milan and Genoa.*

Costa, Frank, 'Urban Planning in Rome from 1870 to the First World War', *GeoJournal* 24.3 (1991), 269–76. *Reviews the city's approach to planning in the context of changing politics after the unification of Italy.*

Tysons Corner Virginia

A classic product of twentieth-century automobile-oriented urbanization, Tysons Corner is a major node of office and retail development, notorious for its network of traffic-clogged streets, the absence of pedestrian walkways, and its lack of green space and civic amenities. In haphazard fashion it has grown from an office park occupied largely by defence contractors to a massive concentration of high-tech and Internet-related employment and an enormous upscale shopping complex, currently reimagined – much too late – by local planners as a transit-oriented, walkable district.

Located at the intersection of country roads that would become Virginia Routes 7 and 123, Tysons Corner was chosen in 1742 as the site of the first courthouse in Fairfax County. A decade later the courthouse was moved to Alexandria, and for the next 200 years Tysons Corner remained a rural crossroads. As recently as the 1960s it was entirely unremarkable, a location with a few dairy farms, truck farms, and a gravel pit, a service station, a restaurant, a general store, a feed store, a motor repair shop, and a few small residential subdivisions edging out along the main roads toward Washington, D.C., 18 km away. By the 1990s the district had become the archetype of a new metropolitan phenomenon: an 'edge city' – a large peripheral node of office employment and retailing that had sprung up to take advantage of relatively cheap land, relatively loose zoning laws, and easy accessibility from interstate highways.

Tysons Corner has no postal code of its own, no political boundary, no subway or railway station, no library, post office, or public school, no park, or town square. After Manhattan, New York, it has the highest concentration of high-end retail on the east coast of the United States; and after Silicon Valley, California, it has the heaviest concentration of high-salary, high-technology, knowledge-based employment. Overall, it is the twelfth-largest employment centre in the entire country. It has 2.3 million m^2 of office space, 14 hotels with nearly 3,900 rooms, and it has nearly 170,000 parking spaces but only 17,000 residents.

Speculative developers, encouraged by the progrowth policies of Fairfax County in the 1960s and 1970s, saw the potential of the Tysons Corner site as soon as the route of the circumferential Washington Capital Beltway had been announced. Federal engineers, minimizing right-of-way acquisition costs, routed the Interstate Beltway through open fields to the east of Tysons Corner, while almost simultaneously the federally funded road to the newly opened Dulles International Airport was built to the north, so that the district was flanked on two sides by interstate highways. Meanwhile, the Fairfax County Board of Supervisors approved a Tysons Corner Shopping Center of 36 hectares, planned as one of the first super-regional malls in the country and expected to draw customers from an extensive catchment area thanks to the Beltway, the proximity of Interstate 66 (just to the south), and the booming off-ramp suburbs of Arlington, Fairfax County, and Montgomery

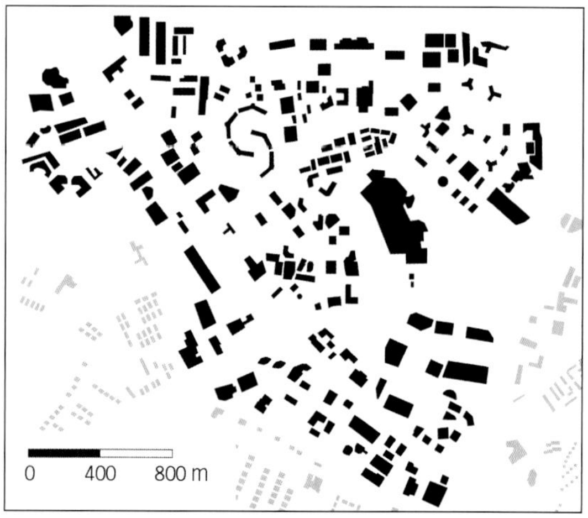

Figure-ground diagram of Tysons Corner: widely scattered buildings, separated by broad swathes of asphalt.

County (Maryland). After its beginnings in the late 1960s, Tysons Corner grew steadily. As Paul Ceruzzi observes:

For the next twenty years, then, Tysons Corner, almost exactly halfway between the airport and the White House, was not only the first but also the last practical place for commercial activities between Dulles and the District.

2008, p. 55

All this took place at the height of the Cold War, which brought increasing numbers of specialized, defence-related firms to the Washington area in order to take advantage of proximity to the Pentagon and defence-related federal agencies. Melpar, a company that specialized in electronic warfare and other, mostly top-secret work for the Pentagon, had built a facility along Route 50 in the early 1950s, near where the Beltway would come a decade later. When speculatively built office developments opened around Tysons Corner, many of the buildings were leased to the CIA, the Department of Defense, and their private contractors. As developers continued to add buildings, the district developed an agglomeration of companies performing weapons-related systems integration contract services for the Pentagon. These included BDM (a firm that specialized in mathematical analyses of missile trajectories, tracking, telemetry, reentry heating, guidance and control, and targeting), Planning Systems, Inc. (which specialized in undersea warfare work), and SRA International (whose work was mostly with intelligence agencies and highly classified). It was an agglomeration that, in turn, attracted other high-tech and communications companies, including SAIC, Honeywell, Gannett Corporation, Boeing, Verizon, MCI, Planning Research Corporation (PRC), and Gannett Corporation.

In the 1990s, after the Cold war had ended, the district's pool of engineering and programming talent proved attractive to venture capitalists investing in dot-com industries. Within a few years the corridor between Tysons Corner and Reston, adjacent to the Dulles Airport Access Road, became known as Internet Alley,

Galleria at Tysons II. Extensive parking lots and parking decks have been an inevitable consequence of piecemeal speculative development.

Clockwise from top left: **Speculative office building**, Towers Crescent Drive; next three: **office buildings** on International Drive. In many of the district's office buildings, the floorplates have elaborate security measures, including brick walls immediately behind windows, because of the nature of the work undertaken inside – top-secret defence-related contracting and commercially sensitive information technology work. Left-middle: **Galleria at Tysons**.

with the offices of companies that provide the infrastructure of the Internet (including PSINet, UUNet, Network Solutions, and CNRI), as well as some, like America Online, that provide its content.

The high-tech, dot-com wealth, along with the increasing prosperity of suburban Virginia and Maryland, supercharged the retail setting that had developed at the core of the district. The original mall, Tysons Corner Center, opened in 1968, prompting the construction of hotels, office buildings, and apartment complexes. In 1988 a second super-regional mall, Tysons Galleria, opened, anchored by Macy's, Saks Fifth Avenue, and Neiman Marcus and with a distinctively upscale cast of luxury boutiques such as Bally, Bottega Veneta, Chanel, Gucci, Ermenegildo Zegna, Juicy Couture, Hugo Boss, Max Mara, and Versace. Sales per square metre at these stores are reputed to be as great as any on the East Coast, including their flagship stores in midtown Manhattan. Altogether, Tysons Corner has more than 230 stores, with an aggregate 7,500 m^2 of retail space.

The district is effectively the downtown for Fairfax County, one of the most affluent counties in the entire country. A tangle of sleek-looking mid-rise and high-rise offices, high-rise mid-range hotels, shed-like retail buildings, ugly parking garages, and vast parking lots, it is riven

Tyson Towers I, completed in 1985 and one of the district's early landmark buildings, in postmodern style and remarkable for its grotesque seven-storey columns. It is known locally as 'The Shopping Bag Building' because of its distinctive shape.

by busy highways and rendered incomprehensible by the haphazard patterns of development. Public transport is perfunctory and sidewalks are rare. Walking anywhere within the district, apart from inside the malls, is difficult and dangerous. In short, it has become the epitome of all that has been wrong with unplanned and loosely regulated automobile-oriented development.

Recognizing the problems of sprawling congestion that threaten to deter further development, Fairfax County officials have approved a $5.25 billion proposal to transform the district from a car-dependent office park and mall complex into a walkable and transit-oriented neighbourhood. The Metrorail extension to Washington Dulles International Airport (scheduled to open in 2016) will include four stations within the district, around which 95 per cent of future development will be focused, at high densities, with an increase in the number and proportion of residences (including affordable housing), walking and bike paths, manicured courtyards, sidewalk cafés, a new internal grid of streets, and designer street furniture. Realistically, though, it seems unlikely that this vision of a more liveable Tysons Corner will ever be achieved, given the combination of weak planning legislation and strong progrowth development interests that exist in Fairfax County.

Further reading on Tysons Corner

Ceruzzi, Paul, *Internet Alley: High Technology in Tysons Corner, 1945–2005*, Cambridge, MA: MIT Press, 2008. *An account of the agglomerative ecology of defence- and Internet-related employment cluster in the district.*

Garreau, Joel, *Edge City. Life on the New Frontier*, New York: Doubleday, 1991. *The book that first drew attention to the 'edge city' phenomenon, with a focus on developers' perspectives in Washington-area edge cities.*

Mastran, Shelley, 'Tysons Corner, Virginia: Planning for the Urban Retrofitting of a Suburban Edge City', *Real Estate Review* 39.1 (2010), 63–81. *A detailed account of the real estate deals and planning decisions behind Tysons Corner, together with details of the planned retrofitting of the district.*

Quartier Vauban Freiburg im Breisgau

The Quartier Vauban has become internationally famous for its innovative approaches to sustainable development. Built on the site of a former French barracks on the southern edge of Freiburg im Breisgau, in southwestern Germany, Vauban is a compact district of some 5,000 people. There is a long-standing tradition of sustainable urban development in the region, and when the barracks were vacated in 1994 the site was purchased by the city with the goal of converting it into a flagship environmental and social project.

Freiburg im Breisgau is a significant destination for lifestyle migration because of the region's sunny climate, its natural scenery, its local cuisine and wines, and the city's progressive reputation in terms of 'green' planning. The University of Freiburg, meanwhile, has 'green' research institutes of international stature, including the Fraunhofer-Institut (focused on renewable energy), the International Solar Energy Society, ICLEI (an umbrella organisation for sustainability policy in local communities), and the Öko-Institut (a nonprofit environmental research centre). The city had pioneered a local energy efficiency code for buildings in its innovative planned extension of Rieselfeld in the early 1990s; in this context Vauban was a logical extension of progressive 'green' planning in practice.

Vauban's development has been achieved through an extended framework of citizen participation. While the City of Freiburg has well-established legal requirements for citizen participation in planning, a new citizen's association, Forum Vauban, emerged at the outset and was promptly recognized by the city council as the legal entity responsible for coordinating the participation process in the district. Forum Vauban's goal from the start was to go significantly beyond the ecological standards laid down in the city's development plan. The Forum has been of critical importance in encouraging developers to adopt an ecological approach and has organized information exchanges and events to help inform self-builders, along with practical DIY seminars and information on energy-saving techniques for homeowners. Together with the city council, the Forum established an ambitious set of progressive objectives. These included an emphasis on car-free living, the division of land into small lots with preferential allocation to private builders and cooperative building projects, the prohibition of detached houses and of buildings exceeding four storeys, the extensive use of ecological building materials and solar energy, a diversity of building shapes, and strict standards on domestic energy consumption.

The first stage of Vauban's development took place in converted barracks buildings and included a student village and an alternative cohousing group, *Selbstorganisierte Unabhängige Siedlungs-Initiative* (SUSI). Subsequent development was new, laid out either side of a broad central east-west spine – Vauban Allee – that carries the tram line that connects the district with Freiburg's Altstadt, 3 km away. The development encompasses a remarkable diversity of housing and open space in a fine-grained mix of lot sizes, building types, and individually designed facades, from single-family terrace

Figure-ground diagram of Vauban.

Vauban Allee, the central spine of the district. Members of the district's car-sharing organization receive a free pass for all public transportation within the city. Photo courtesy of Heike Mayer.

houses to four-storey, twenty-unit apartment buildings. This diversity is a result of the strategy of selling building lots to small cooperatives of owner-occupiers (*Baugruppen*), each comprising between three and twenty-one households. These co-housing groups are responsible for the detailed building design of their property, accommodating each household's specific needs and aspirations within a common plan. In addition, they frequently establish additional environmental and social objectives. There is dedicated accommodation, for example, for guests who come to visit Vauban residents, designed to avoid building large apartments with rarely used spare bedrooms.

At the eastern end of the district is another 'green' development, Solarsiedlung Freiburg am Schlierberg, featuring solar energy. It incorporates 58 'energy plus' homes whose solar energy is fed back into the public grid and generates a profit for homeowners. Nine of the homes are perched on the flat roof of an office block, the Sonnenschiff, which acts as a noise barrier to the nearby main road. The rest of the housing is arranged in two- and three-storey terraces of different widths. In accordance with classic solar building principles, the living/dining rooms and bedrooms are to the south, access is in the centre, and the service zones on the northern side include kitchens, bathrooms, and building services.

The domestic energy standard in the rest of Quartier Vauban is a maximum consumption of 65 kWh per m^2 per year, though forty-two units were built to more exacting 'passive house' (*Passivhaus* in German) standards (15 kWh per m^2 per year) and ten were built to 'energy plus' standards. Many of the units have solar collectors, and the entire district is connected to a heating grid with a co-generation plant that runs on wood chips. Most buildings have rainwater collection facilities that supply toilets and garden watering. A small number of projects have incorporated innovations such as vacuum converters for sewage and organic waste, producing reusable biogas.

Solarsiedlung Freiburg: a terrace that is part of the solar village. Photo courtesy of Rolf Disch SolarArchitecture, Germany.

More radical than the district's energy policies are its policies on car-free living. Although cars are allowed in the Quartier Vauban, their use and ownership are sharply restricted. The speed limit along Vauban Allee is 30 km/h, but elsewhere it is walking speed (5 km/h). There is a ban on parking on private property: cars may enter the residential streets but only for pick-up and delivery. Residents with cars are required to purchase or lease a parking space in one of the perimeter multistorey community parking garages. Visitors, too, are expected to park their cars in a parking garage and pay for the privilege as they would in a downtown car park.

Approximately 40 per cent of all households in Quartier Vauban have decided not to own a car. They have to sign a declaration of car-free living and become a member of the Club for Car-Free Living. They are able to join a car-sharing organization (whose vehicles are also parked in the peripheral garages), whose members also

Sonnenschiff ('sun ship'), the first positive-energy commercial building in the world, built in 2004 and designed by Rolf Disch. Photo by Sromuald, used under a creative commons Attribution-Share Alike License at Wikimedia Commons.

Clockwise, from top left: A **bicycle street** (Kurt Tucholsky Straße) (photo courtesy of Heike Mayer); **apartment buildings**, Kurt Tucholsky Straße; **car-free zone** (Heinrich Mann Straße) (photo courtesy of Heike Mayer); **townhomes** (Adinda Flemmich Straße); **car-share vehicle** on Vauban Allee; **first-generation passive house** (Walter Gropius Straße) (photo courtesy of Heike Mayer); **apartment buildings**, creekside development (photo courtesy of Heike Mayer).

Apartment building and town homes, Gerda Weiler Straße. Bicycles and shrubbery figure prominently in the district's townscape.

receive a free pass for all public transportation within Freiburg and a 50 per cent reduction on rail tickets. If members of the Club decide to purchase a car, they are required to make a one-time payment of 15,350 euros to the Club for the construction of a parking space as well as monthly rental fees and property taxes for the parking space.

Every street in the Quartier Vauban, except for Vauban Allee, is a play street, or *Spielstraße*. The concept derives from the Dutch *Woonerf* principle, whereby streets are designed as a shared space for all users. In the Quartier Vauban this means street widths of just 3 to 5 m with 1-m-wide pervious kerbs that allow for the occasional large vehicle to access the neighbourhood while providing for stormwater infiltration. These streets often function as extended front porches and are frequently used as places for neighbours to socialise. Some streets are designated as bicycle streets, allowing one-way access for slowly driven vehicles and two-way access for bicycles; in addition, there is a well-developed network of pedestrian-only paths.

The overall result is something quite unusual in contemporary residential districts: a sense of vitality that comes from the happy sounds of young children running around at play. The street names also give the district an additional dimension of distinctive identity. Named after the leading figures in Germany's political, artistic, and scientific developments of the past 200 years, from Rosa Luxemburg to Walter Gropius, the effect is to emphasize the progressiveness and intellectual commitment of the community. The main spine of the district, Vauban Allee, is less successful. It is about 35 m wide, with a streetcar track and stations situated in the median. It is lined with three- and four-storey apartment buildings with shops

Play zones. Almost 20 per cent of the inhabitants of Vauban are children under 10 years old, and more than 40 per cent are under 18.

and office space on the street level. The width of the street, together with the public open spaces around some of the institutional buildings, makes for a rather sterile and uninviting space. By way of compensation, the district's green spaces, collectively designed through Forum Vauban and the *Baugruppen*, are intimate and attractive. Green corridors providing space for social activities (playgrounds, sunbathing areas, barbecue areas, seating areas) have been created between building plots, while the bordering creek and its sixty-year-old trees provide an attractive natural ecology.

Further reading on Vauban

Beatley, Timothy, 'Green Urbanism in European Cities', *The Humane Metropolis: People and Nature in the 21st Century City*, Rutherford Platt, ed., Minneapolis: University of Minnesota Press, 2006, 297–314. *A summary of the key themes from case studies of 'green urbanism', including Vauban.*

Gauzin-Müller, Dominique, and Favet, Nicholas, *Nachhaltigkeit in Architektur und Städtebau: Konzepte, Technologien, Beispiele*, Basel: Birkhäuser Verlag, 2002. *A comparative review of urban sustainability projects, including Vauban and the broader strategies deployed in Freiburg im Breisgau (in German).*

Scheurer, Jan, and Newman, Peter, 'Vauban: A European Model Bridging the Green and Brown Agendas'. Case study prepared for *Revisiting Urban Planning: Global Report on Human Settlements* (2009).

Schroepfer, Thomas, and Hee, Limin, 'Emerging Forms of Sustainable Urbanism: Case Studies of Vauban Freiburg and SolarCity Linz', *Journal of Green Building* 3.2 (2008), 65–76. *Discusses complex relationships among design, dwelling, community in space, building technologies, environmental strategies, as well as models of affordability.*

Zähringerstadt
Bern

Bern was established in the twelfth century as a bastide, a fortified town planned and built by the ruling power and intended to serve as a defensive post and population centre in a sparsely inhabited district. Destroyed by fire in the fifteenth century, the town was rebuilt in grand style befitting one of Europe's most powerful city-states. In 1848 Bern became the capital of Switzerland, by which time the city had spread well beyond the *Altstadt* ('old town' in German). Insulated from two world wars by Swiss neutrality and spared automobile-related redevelopment because of its inaccessible site, the *Altstadt's* preindustrial character has been preserved and it is now listed by UNESCO as a World Heritage site.

In the twelfth century much of today's Switzerland was considered part of southern Burgundy. The dukes of Zähringen were responsible for exercising imperial power south of the Rhine and, in order to establish their hold over the region, they founded or expanded numerous settlements, one of which was Bern, an early example of the medieval bastide town. In addition to serving as defensive posts and centres of population for sparsely inhabited districts, bastides formed a source of revenue and power for their founders, who for their part conceded liberal charters to the new towns and sometimes subsidized people to settle there.

Other examples of bastide towns include Aigues-Mortes, Carcassonne, Cazeres, Monpazier, Montauban, and Villefranche du Périgord in southwestern France, all built in the thirteenth and fourteenth centuries in an effort to colonize territory that was constantly in dispute between English and French kings. As planned settlements, they were typically built with a grid layout of intersecting streets, with wide thoroughfares that divided the town plan into insulae, or blocks, each of which were subdivided into equal-sized 'homesteads': easy to lay out and convenient for calculating the taxes due from property owners, homestead by homestead.

It was Duke Berchtold V of Zähringen who founded Bern in 1191, and the city's medieval core, or *Altstadt*, takes its name from him. Situated 40 m above a sharp meander of the Aare River, the kernel of the bastide was a citadel, built on a site that had previously been used by Celts, Helvetians, and Romans because of its strategic location and the natural fortification of the steep banks on three sides of the long peninsula.

Zähringen followed the topography of the long narrow peninsula and laid the town out around three generously spaced long streets running east-west. The central spine

Zähringerstadt and the River Aare. Photo by de:Benutzer: Amstutzmarco <http://commons.wikimedia.org/wiki/File:Bern_luftaufnahme.png>.

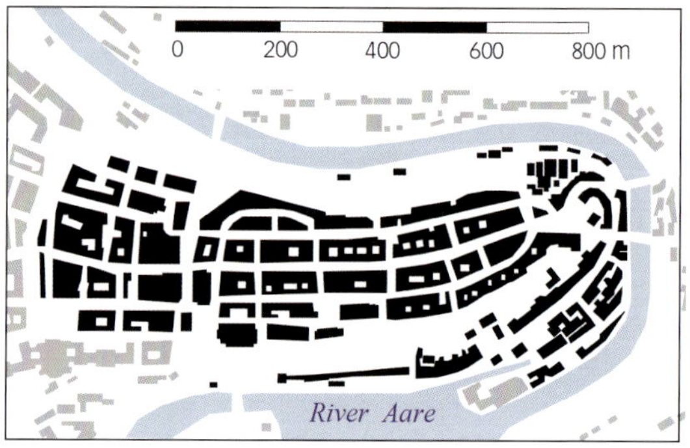

Figure-ground diagram of Zähringerstadt.

of Kramgasse and Gerechtigkeitsgasse was designed to be broad enough to accommodate markets (eliminating the need for a market square) and was lined with merchants' shops, stalls, inns, and guild halls. Zähringen laid out the rest of the town with an orthogonal grid of streets, dividing the land into equal-sized homesteads of 18 by 30 m and separating the citadel and the principal institutional buildings from the main axis of the town. The town hall and public buildings were situated around the Kreuzgasse, while ecclesiastical buildings were located at the Münstergasse and Herrengasse.

Under the protection of the Zähringens the master-planned town grew into a prosperous medieval city-state. The city expanded by lengthening Kramgasse down the central axis of the peninsula. As it did so, some of the existing fortifications were removed, leaving wide-open squares that stretched the whole width of the expanding city.

Almost entirely destroyed by fire in 1405, the *Altstadt* was quickly rebuilt around the original framework; but this time using local sandstone instead of timber. The reconstruction of the city coincided with a period of pronounced prosperity: by the late fifteenth century three decisive victories over the Duke of Burgundy had made Bern the most powerful city-state north of the Alps, with a territorial reach that extended southwest to Geneva and municipal coffers full of gold and silver. Zähringen's layout, together with one of the world's first formal building codes, lent a striking overall coherence and uniformity to the town's morphology. In detail, the buildings were constructed in high Gothic style, with gables, corner turrets, and oriel windows, reflecting the town's wealth and self-image.

Bern's townscape, restored and rebuilt, echoes its appearance during its heyday as a late medieval city-state.

Kramgasse. The arcades of Zähringerstadt's principal streets are the signature feature of the city. They were added during the fifteenth century as houses expanded their upper stories out into the street. Photo courtesy of Heike Mayer.

Nydegg Church, on the left, stands on the site of the original Zähringen fortress. The old stone bridge, the Untertorbrücke, was completed in 1487 and was the only crossing point of the river in Bern until the mid-nineteenth century. Photo by Daniel Schwen, used under a creative commons Attribution-Share Alike License at Wikimedia Commons.

The most significant change was the addition of sturdy arcades along the principal streets, an innovation that has provided one of the most distinctive features of the townscape. The arcades were independent of the street level and reached by stairways of varying height, depending on the topography of the peninsula, leaving building cellars directly accessible from the street. The arcades remained the property of the municipality and their form was prescribed by building codes that allowed the facades to change in style in accordance with

Zytglogge tower, originally the gate tower of Bern's western fortifications. Photo by Doug Pearson © Jon Arnold Images Ltd/Alamy.

Münsterplatz and Münstergasse, with the Zytglogge tower on the skyline.

the popular style of the day, so long as the proportions remained the same.

Over time, many of the old stone buildings were remodelled but their stone facades and arcades – some 6 km of them altogether – were mostly untouched. Although there are only a few remaining examples of the original stone buildings, the layout, dimensions, and form of the original medieval city are still clear today. The legacy of the basic fabric of Zähringerstadt is complemented by the surviving twelfth-century Zytglogge Tower (clock tower), the fifteenth-century cathedral, the fifteenth-century town hall, and elaborate sixteenth-century public fountains. From across the river the topography of the peninsula makes for a spectacular ensemble, the tile roofs cascading down to the tree-lined embankments of the Aare. Inside Zähringerstadt the continuing prosperity of the city is underscored by the colonization of its arcades by specialized luxury shops, fancy florists, boutiques, and cafés.

Further reading on Zähringerstadt

Lüthi, C., and Meier, B. *Bern - Eine Stadt Bricht auf: Schauplätze und Geschichten der Berner Stadtentwicklung Zwischen 1798 und 1998*, Bern: Paul Haupt, 1998. *An edited volume on the history and urban development of the town (in German).*

Schnell, D., von Fischer, H., Fröhlich, M., Locher, M., Telley, T., and Welti, E., *Rettet die Altstadt! Bern - vom Sanierungsfall zum Weltkulturerbe*, Bern: Berner Heimatschutzverein, 2005. *An account of the district's historic preservation and eventual status as a World Heritage site (in German).*

Zona Tortona Milano

Zona Tortona, an inner-city locality that was initially developed as a working-class factory and warehouse district, has become the world's definitive design district. Following a classic process of deindustrialization in the 1960s and 1970s, it has become gentrified and branded, its transition led by an agglomeration of design services, creative industries, and their ancillaries.

The district takes its name from via Tortona, a long, narrow street that parallels the nearby Naviglio canal and the railway lines that lead to the Porta Genova railway terminus. It was the railway that brought industry to the area in the last quarter of the nineteenth century. Around the industrial sites and workshops of the area there developed a typical Milanese workers' district with close-knit city blocks – *Case di Ringhiera* – apartment buildings with inner courtyards, shared washrooms, and outside staircases (*ringhiera*).

After World War II, when Milan boomed as Italy's leading industrial centre, big engineering firms like Ansaldo, General Electric, Osram, and Riva Calzoni clustered around Porta Genova's goods yards, along with food and drink manufacturers like Bisleri and Nestlé and scores of smaller workshops.

Elsewhere in the city hundreds of thousands of jobs were generated by the growth of steel works, chemical refineries, car factories, engineering and works. Milan produced Alfa Romeo cars, Pirelli tyres, Bianchi bicycles, Gaggia espresso machines, and Lambretta scooters. But Milan's heavy industrial boom was brief and the city, like many others, soon began to feel the effects of deindustrialization as big firms shifted production to locations with cheaper and more pliable labour, and smaller firms wilted in the face of overseas competition. One of the first districts in Milan to experience plant closings and job losses was Zona Tortona.

Fortunately, deindustrialization had set in before large-scale industrialization had completely obliterated the skilled workforce and the specialized workshops of the small furniture, furnishings, and lighting enterprises of the city that were to become the foundation of Milan's postindustrial standing as an international centre of design. Beginning in the 1960s Milan developed a strong international reputation for industrial design, thanks to a combination of a new generation of exceptional designers, including Ferdinando Innocenti, Giò Ponti, Sergio Pininfarina, Aldo Rossi, and Ettore Sottsass, and innovative entrepreneurs, including Cesare Cassina, Carlo Alessi, Piero Businelli (of B&B Italia), Giulio and Anna Castelli (of Kartell), and Gino Colombini and Joe Colombo (of Artemide).

In the 1970s the meteoric rise of Milanese fashion designers – Elio Fiorucci, Giorgio Armani, Gianni Versace, Miuccia Prada, Gianfranco Ferré, Stefano Dolce, and Domenico Gabbana – and their prêt-à-porter brands meant that the city became a magnet for photographers, models, magazine editors, critics, buyers, manufacturers, commercial traders, and journalists. A key

Zona Tortona is situated on the southwestern edge of the premodern core of Milan.

development here was the strategic alliance in the 1980s between the fashion industry and the city's socialist administration (Partito Socialista Italiano, or PSI). Political scientist John Foot notes that by the 1990s,

Milan and its surrounding territory constituted a design system. This system was made up of private and public institutions, industries, magazines, designers and studios and a series of services linked to production and advertising of design goods and ideas. The centre of this system was the annual Salone del Mobile, but design events took place in the city throughout the year, attracting international interest.
2001, p. 124

Zona Tortona's Design Week has become the most prominent of these events. Carefully curated and branded by DesignPartners, a consortium of eight companies specializing in marketing and communication for the design industry, the event involves about 100 different venues in the district. Together, they attract more than 100,000 visitors – designers, entrepreneurs, buyers, journalists from the leading trade magazines, students, and educators – two-thirds of whom come from abroad.

Zona Tortona's transformation began in the mid-1980s when *Italian Vogue* art director Flavio Lucchini and the photographer Fabrizio Ferri set up Superstudio, using a former bicycle factory and part of the former locomotive depot of Porta Genova as a fashion photography studio. Other photographic studios soon appeared: Carlo Orsi and Giovanni Gastel both opened studios in Via Tortona. Seeded by the cachet of these studios, the district soon attracted young artists, architects, and design consultants. Galleries, bookshops, trendy restaurants, bars, and cafés followed. In 1990 the City of Milan purchased the former Ansaldo engineering complex for the Teatro alla Scala's wardrobe

The former Ansaldo engineering complex on Via Tortona has been used as storage and rehearsal space by Teatro alla Scala and is now being redeveloped as a cultural centre, designed by British Architect David Chipperfield.

Models travelling to and from photo shoots provide an incongruous element in the district's industrial landscape.

and prop storage, rehearsal stage, laboratory, and workshop. Subsequently, the city commissioned the British architect David Chipperfield to transform part of the complex into a Centre for Advanced Studies of Visual Art, a photography museum, a Centre for Non-European Cultures, an auditorium, a restaurant, and a bookshop.

As the fashionability and buzz of the district became apparent, gentrifying households began to move in, and developer Alessandro Cajrati Crivelli saw an opportunity to redevelop some of the district's larger industrial sites. Crivelli's 37 Tortona project on the old General Electric site, for example, is a mixed-use complex laid out with a courtyard planted with trees. Each six-storey building has flexible interior spaces that contain showrooms, laboratories, professional studios, shops, and offices as well as apartments.

Other large-scale interventions include the former Nestlé factory, remodelled by Japanese architect Tadao Ando for the corporate headquarters of Giorgio Armani, and a former Riva Calzoni factory, redeveloped as a headquarters and showroom for Ermenegildo Zegna and for offices and showrooms for the Sportswear Company and Tod's. Flavio Lucchini, cofounder of Superstudio, saw the need for event space in the district and converted 8,000 m^2 of former General Electric engineering works into Superstudio Più, a multifunctional complex suitable for events, exhibitions, conventions, fairs, fashion shows, and performances, together with office space for fashion, media, and design firms (La Perla, Erreuno, Dsquared2, Videogang, FashionTV, Areart, D di Repubblica, Hi Communication).

What was happening in Zona Tortona was a classic case of agglomeration based on external economies. As Alfred Marshall famously noted in 1890:

> *So great are the advantages which people following the same skilled trade get from near neighbourhood to one another. The mysteries of the trade become no mystery: but are, as it were, 'in the air'.*
>
> *Principles of Economics*, New York: Macmillan, 1890, IV.X.6, § 3

Superstudio, Armani, Zegna, and the rest were joined by Diesel, Esprit, and Hugo Boss; editorial offices (*Sportswear, Nonsolomoda*); fashion and design schools (Domus Academy, Image Investment, Fashion Image, Image University, Italian Photography Institute); a superchic designer hotel (Nhow); an overstock discount designer women's wear store (DMagazine); and exhibition space for sculpture (the Fondazione Arnaldo Pomodoro). Co-located in localized clusters, design professionals can review one

Ermenegildo Zegna headquarters and showrooms on Via Savona, designed by Antonio Citterio and Partners in collaboration with Studio Beretta. Photo courtesy of leotorri.it.

Traditional working-class ***ringhiera*** apartments like this, once commonplace, have become a rarity as the district has been redeveloped.

The Naviglio Grande borders the district and provides a congenial setting for bars and restaurants catering to Zona Tortona's growing 'creative class' of design professionals. The canal was dug in the thirteenth century and was in use for commerce as recently as the 1970s.

The gentrification of the district is most readily apparent in the many bars that have been refurbished; exteriors rarely receive investment.

another's products, get to know clients face-to-face, understand their priorities and needs, and to keep abreast of the internal politics of their firms. Localized within a few city blocks, the commingling of artists, artisans, designers, photographers, actors, students, educators, and writers in cafés, restaurants, clubs, gallery openings, and fashion after-parties contributes to a blurring of the social worlds of work and lifestyle that is so important to the social production of knowledge and diffusion of innovation in design and design-related professions. Zona Tortona now represents one of the world's most vibrant communities of design practice, a distinctive district with a sociality that extends to models, photographers, art directors, film directors, stylists, craftsmen, industry workers, and small shopkeepers as well as designers of all kinds.

Further reading on Zona Tortona

Bovone, Laura, 'Fashionable Quarters in the Postindustrial City: The Ticinese of Milan', *City & Community* 4.4 (2005), 359–80. *Analyses the economic and sociocultural processes that have produced the 'fashionable quarter' that is Zona Tortona.*

Foot, John, *Milan Since the Miracle*, London: Berg, 2001. *An excellent account of Milan's changing political economy, with detailed commentary and analysis on the interdependence of the city's industrial base and its design industries.*

Index

A

B

C

D

E

F

G

H

I

J

K

L

M

N

O

P

Q

R

Y

Z

A CIP catalogue record for this book is available from the Library of Congress, Washington D.C., USA.

Bibliographic information published by the German National Library
The German National Library lists this publication in the Deutsche Nationalbibliografie; detailed bibliographic data are available on the Internet at http://dnb.d-nb.de.

P.O. Box, 4002 Basel, Switzerland
Part of ActarBirkhäuser

Copy Editing: Anda Divine, Boones Mill, Virginia, USA
Typography and layout: Paul L. Knox

Printed on acid-free paper produced from chlorine-free pulp. TCF ∞

Printed in Spain
ISBN 978-3-0346-0809-1

9 8 7 6 5 4 3 2 1

Distribution:
ActarBirkhäuserD
Barcelona - Basel - New York
www.actarbirkhauser-d.com